LONDON UNDERGROUND

London Underground

A Cultural Geography

David Ashford

LIVERPOOL UNIVERSITY PRESS

First published 2013 by
Liverpool University Press
4 Cambridge Street
Liverpool
L69 7ZU

This paperback edition published 2025

Copyright © 2025 David Ashford

The right of David Ashford to be identified as the author of this book has been asserted by him in accordance with the Copyright, Designs and Patents Act 1988.

All rights reserved. No part of this book may be reproduced, stored in a retrieval system, or transmitted, in any form or by any means, electronic, mechanical, photocopying, recording, or otherwise, without the prior written permission of the publisher.

British Library Cataloguing-in-Publication data
A British Library CIP record is available

ISBN 978-1-84631-859-7 (hardback)
ISBN 978-1-83624-391-5 (paperback)

Typeset in Warnock and P22 Underground by Carnegie Book Production, Lancaster

Socrates: Behold! human beings living in a underground space which has a mouth open towards the light; here they have been from their childhood, and have their legs and necks chained so that they cannot move, and can only see into the cave, being prevented by the chains from turning round their heads. Above and behind them a fire is blazing at a distance, and between the fire and the prisoners a raised way, and a low wall is built along the way, like the screen over which marionette players show their puppets. Behind the wall there are men, who raise up into the fire-light various works of art, and among them images of men and animals, stone and wood.

Glaucon: You have shown me a strange vision; and they are strange prisoners.

Socrates: They are ourselves, I replied; and they see only the shadows of the images that the fire throws onto the wall of the cave.... To them the truth is literally nothing but the shadow of an image.

(Plato, *The Republic*, Book VII)

CONTENTS

Acknowledgements	ix
Notes on Convention	xi
List of Illustrations	xii

The Book of the Machine   1
A User's Guide

1 **Psychopathology of Modern Space**   11
The Underground Railways of the Inner Circle in the Victorian Imagination

2 **The Lord of the Dynamos**   45
The American Invasion of the Tube-Network in Theodore Dreiser's *The Stoic* (1947)

3 **Blueprints for Babylon**   63
Modernist Mapping of the London Underground

4 **Making a Home in Modernity**   93
The Conceptual History of Metroland

5	**Christmas in Hell**	115
	Tube-Shelter Children in Images by Bill Brandt and Henry Moore	
6	**Insurrection in Alphabet-City**	135
	Counterculture in the London Underground	
7	**The Ghost in the Machine**	167
	Psychogeography in the London Underground	
	Select Bibliography	185
	Index	207

ACKNOWLEDGEMENTS

On resurfacing I found that I had at some point acquired the nickname "Underground Man". In fact, my isolation was not nearly as complete as this title might suggest, and I now take the greatest pleasure in acknowledging the constant help and support that made this book possible. My thanks to Sarah Rowe, James Riley, Catherine Brown, Liz Pender, Marco Wan, Heather Tilley, Hannah Haines, Tony Paraskeva, Daniel Cook and Simon Goldman in particular; and to my parents for their faith, their love and their encouragement.

My special thanks to Rod Mengham of Jesus College, Cambridge – for his expert guidance and for his friendship over the past seven years. My thanks too – to Prof. Lawrence Rainey, at the University of York, for that initial push, and also to Prof. David Trotter of Gonville and Caius College, Cambridge and Prof. David L. Pike at Columbia University NY, for ideas that have made for a much stronger book.

I would like to thank the librarians at the various archives I have consulted while writing this book – particularly those working at the Henry Moore Foundation, the Imperial War Museum, the Museum of London, the Royal Institute of British Architects and the Mass-Observation archive at the University of Sussex.

I also wish to express my thanks and admiration for the work undertaken by Liverpool University Press – in particular my editor Anthony Cond, for believing in the book and for his editorial expertise, the readers, for their detailed and encouraging feedback, and the designers and typesetters, for producing a beautiful book. Any mistakes that remain in the text are entirely my responsibility.

Earlier versions of certain chapters in this book have appeared in *Symbiosis* (October 2007), *The Cambridge Quarterly* (December 2007), *Literary London* (September 2008), and *Modernism/Modernity* (November 2010). My thanks both to the editors for their permission to reproduce this material; and to the reviewers for their suggestions on how those first, tentative drafts were to be improved.

Finally, I wish to thank Selwyn College, Cambridge, for providing me with a warm and supportive environment while this book was in preparation and the Arts and Humanities Research Board for the generous financial support that made this book possible. In what is a difficult time for the university sector, I would like to stress again the importance of the AHRC's work, both for young academics and for what remains an unusually vibrant and innovative research culture.

NOTES ON CONVENTION

In conventional usage the term *Tube* can refer to any part of the London Underground. This is how the term is used in much of this book, but in the first and second chapters I have maintained the historic distinction between sections that are *deep-level Tube-railways* and those that are *subsurface railways*, created by digging up a road, installing the railway and restoring the surface. The term *Underground* refers to any part of the system at any point in its history, and the term *Underground Group* is reserved for that combine of underground railways that achieved total control of the rail-network in the early 1930s.

Full citations are given at the start of each chapter, with author's name used as shorthand subsequently. Where the author has more than one work cited I also provide abbreviated titles. Emphases are in the original text unless otherwise stated.

LIST OF ILLUSTRATIONS

Between pages 92-93

Figure 1.   Harry Beck's Tube Map (1933).
            © TfL from the London Transport Museum collection.

Figure 2.   Poster art by E. McKnight Kauffer: *Winter Sales Are Best Reached by Underground* (1924).
            © TfL from the London Transport Museum collection.

Figure 3.   Jacob Epstein's sculpture on 55 Broadway, *Day* (1929).
            © TfL from the London Transport Museum collection.

Figure 4.   Charles Holden's Tube-station at Arnos Grove (1932).
            © TfL from the London Transport Museum collection.

Figure 5.   Bill Brandt's photograph of a family sheltering in the Liverpool Street extension (1940).
            From the Imperial War Museum Photography Archive, negative number D1578.

Figure 6.   M. McNeill's photograph of children sheltering in the Tube during the Blitz published anonymously in the *Evening Standard* in 1940.
            Hulton Archive, ref. 149606564. © Getty Images.

Figure 7.   Henry Moore, *Women and Children in the Tube*, 1940 (HMF 1726).
            Reproduced by permission of the Henry Moore Foundation.

Figure 8.   Henry Moore, *Group of Draped Figures in a Shelter*, 1941 (HMF 1807).
            Reproduced by permission of The Henry Moore Foundation.

THE BOOK OF THE MACHINE
A User's Guide

Imagine, if you can, a small room, hexagonal in shape, like the cell of a bee. It is lighted neither by window nor by lamp, yet it is filled with a soft radiance. There are no apertures for ventilation, yet the air is fresh. There are no musical instruments, and yet, at the moment that my meditation opens, this room is throbbing with melodious sounds. An armchair is in the centre, by its side a reading-desk – that is all the furniture. And in the armchair there sits a swaddled lump of flesh – a woman, about five foot high, with a face as white as a fungus. It is to her that the little room belongs.

(E.M. Forster, 'The Machine Stops', 1909)[1]

Her name is Vashti and she lives in the Machine, a subsurface residential complex that has evolved over time from the London Underground. But in Forster's 'The Machine Stops', the rail-network stretches from Somerset to Sumatra, and the tubes containing railways have been supplemented with speaking-tubes, food-tubes, medicine-tubes and music-tubes to form a colossal automated service-provider capable of supplying its users with every commodity they could ever desire, at the mere touch of a button: 'There was the cold-bath button. There was the button that produced literature. And there of course the buttons by which she communicated with her friends. The room, though it contained nothing, was in touch with all that she cared for in the world.'[2] The comprehensive nature of the Tube-network in the story reflects the huge expansion of the system taking place at the time that Forster was writing. London's was the first underground network in the world; the earliest line was opened in 1863, but for the first thirty years expansion was slow, and trains, for the most part, ran through open cuttings. The completion of the first ever deep-level Tube-railway in 1890 ushered in a new era. Soon an enormous subterranean transit network extended beneath the metropolis, and though it was never in fact to offer the full range of services listed in the fable, Forster was right to suggest that the London Underground represents the earliest phase in the development of that new category of space embodied in his story by the Machine. In so saying, I am not referring to the pivotal position each space has been shown to possess in the cultural history of subterranean space by Rosalind Williams and David L. Pike, but to the fact that, in being cut off from surface topography, the fictional space presented in Forster's story follows the precedent established by the spatial network that inspired it, mediating itself to its users. The Tube-network was perhaps the first example of what French ethnologist Marc Augé has termed *non-lieu*: spaces such as the motorway, supermarket and airport lounge that are compelled to interpret their relation to the invisible landscapes they traverse through the media of signs, maps and verbal messages.[3] Like these similarly mediated spaces, the London Underground is a Plato's cave (see epigraph, p. v) in which the shadow of every product or landmark in the world might appear in the space of a six-foot poster glued to the wall. The Underground is a transitional form, linking the alienated space of production created by the Industrial Revolution to the fully virtual spaces of late capitalism that emerged following the Cold War. In fact, Forster's tale is as insightful as it is eerily prescient. The writer had perceived that the Tube-network foreshadowed the sterile, international *non-places* of our increasingly virtual world.

> Rapid intercourse, from which the previous civilisation had hoped so much, had ended by defeating itself. What was the good of going to Peking when it was just like Shrewsbury? Why return to Shrewsbury when it would all be like Peking? Men seldom moved their bodies: all unrest was concentrated in the soul.[4]

The significance of the cultural history of the Tube-network is largely overlooked. In the course of surveying the literature featuring the Underground produced in the first eighty or so years, David Welsh, *Underground Writing: The London Tube from George Gissing to Virginia Woolf* (2010) suggests representation of the system has two main themes: firstly, the *infernal*, in which the subterranean railway was perceived as a form of hell, abyss or underworld into which London and its inhabitants were being drawn, and, secondly, the *utopian*, in which the underground helps to integrate the modern metropolis by offering new freedoms.⁵ This stark binary imposes a strict limit on what can be said in relation to the material. As David L. Pike has warned, 'For all its resemblance to conditions in the modernizing city, not even during the nineteenth century could the vertical framework account for the contradictions of actual experience without severe distortion'.⁶

In his own examination of buried obsessions and anxieties within nineteenth-century London and Paris, Pike therefore supplements the historical concept of the vertical city with the theoretical framework for the consideration of social space established by French philosopher Henri Lefebvre in *The Production of Space* (1974): the spatial triad of 'perceived', 'conceived' and 'lived'.⁷ The first category is, first and foremost, a product of the individual body, resulting in those *spatial practices* that ensure continuity and cohesion. The second category is the conceptual space of the scientist, town-planner, engineer and a certain type of artist: those *representations of space* which are produced by those who identify what is lived and perceived with what is conceived, and which rise from the order imposed by social relations, ideal and abstract, erasing the historical. The third category is space as directly lived through images and symbols by its users and inhabitants, the passively dominated spaces which the imagination seeks to change and appropriate: *representational spaces* that are 'linked to the clandestine or underground side of social life, as also to art'.⁸

In Lefebvre's study, the history of conceived space is inextricably intertwined with the rise of global capitalism; and it is surely to this element in the spatial triad that Pike is referring when he suggests that 'The technological boom of the nineteenth century introduced a novel category of space that has continued to expand in scope while its challenge to the traditionally vertical conception has remained unremarked'.⁹ The London Underground is the most salient example of this new space and, though Pike is chiefly interested in tracing 'the consequences of the continued recourse to those past obsessions to make sense of a contemporary experience of urban space that, in fact, has little in common with the cities in which they first appeared', he recognises that it is important to integrate his account of the network into the conceptual history of modern space provided by Henri Lefebvre.¹⁰ He therefore situates the famous schematised Tube map, perhaps the most prominent indication that the system is an ideal and abstract space, within the history of modernist reordering of urban space on the continent.

In so doing, Pike builds on pioneering research by Michael T. Saler, who established in his book *The Avant-Garde in Interwar England* (1999) that, in the inter-war period, the network constituted a *Modernist Gesamptwerk*.

Read together, Pike and Saler hold out the tantalising possibility that the cultural history of the London Underground occupies an integral position, hitherto unrecognised, in the formulation of modern space. This has excited speculation. Andrew Thacker registers the potential significance of the Tube-network in the course of a chapter on representations of public transport by London-based Imagist poets, in his book on modernist geography *Moving Through Modernity* (2003), and Ana Parejo Vadillo touches on the subject in a book on the relationship between mass-transit systems and the women poets of the *fin de siècle*, *Women Poets and Urban Aestheticism* (2005). However, there is no single work devoted to charting the emergence of abstract space in the London Underground, or to exploring how this *conceived* space is turned into *lived* space by its users, as forecast by Lefebvre, or to recounting the clandestine means through which Londoners have attempted to rewrite the functional cartography imposed upon the capital.

This book is the first full account of this spatial history of London's Underground. The project reflects the 'spatial turn' that has taken place in cultural studies, highlighted by Peter Brooker and Andrew Thacker in the introduction to *Geographies of Modernism* (2005), and ought to provide a fresh angle on the four conceptual problems that bedevil the field of 'critical literary geography', identified by Thacker.[11]

The first is that the emphasis on metaphorical spaces in literary and cultural studies prevents an engagement with the material spaces of, for example, the city. In examining the representations of an urban space that is heavily mediated, this project should assist the effort to understand that metaphorical and material spaces are 'mutually implicated', to view space not as a neutral canvas but as a 'social space', as geographer Neil Smith has suggested.[12] It will be shown that the metaphorical treatment of the Underground in modernist literature and art, for instance, was rapidly incorporated into the fabric of that space. In this history there are no hard and fast boundaries between the physical and metaphorical; and this book might therefore prove useful in an increasingly virtual world.

The second is that insufficient attention is paid in cultural texts to that distinction between *representation of space* and *representational spaces* set out in the spatial triad. But in the following cultural history these categories are politically polarised, presenting us with a forceful illustration of how certain representations impose on space a *plan* that is *ideal and abstract*, while others set out to transform the resulting *non-place* into a *habitat*. The material invites the use of the striking military terminology employed by theorist Michel de Certeau, who noted that the space of consumer capitalism is shaped by *strategies*, while the users of that space use *tactics* to inhabit it.

The third problem considers the impact of physical space on the form of the material. As Thacker observes, 'Discussion[s] of how the formal features of literature are influenced by social or historical circumstances are always fraught with difficulty'.[13] The cultural critic is often too quick to infer a causal relationship between technological innovation and superficially similar changes in the form of an art. I believe the chances of making such a mistake can be considerably reduced if the critic is equipped with a sufficiently large and varied dataset. In setting out to survey the influence a single space has had over a period of almost 150 years on material ranging from poetry, music-hall, literature, journalism, painting, poster art, sculpture, architecture, photography, pop music, mosaic, graffiti art and the internet novel, it is hoped that this book can avoid this pitfall, in order to cast light on how spaces of one particular network have moulded *metaphors*.

Finally, there is the risk that a focus on geography might result in the neglect of those historical coordinates within which social space and literary space ought to be examined. In part, this seems to have been a result of the fact that the 'spatial turn' took its first impetus from a specific response to postmodernist theory. Frederic Jameson speculated in his *Postmodernism* (1991) that 'our daily life, our psychic experience, our cultural languages, are today dominated by categories of space rather than by categories of time, as in the preceding period of high modernism'.[14] By contrast, this project's starting point can be found in two texts central to the cultural historicist tradition – Walter Benjamin's *Arcades Project* (1927–40) and Wolfgang Schivelbusch's *The Railway Journey* (1977). These writers demonstrated that the industrial spaces of the nineteenth century possess signifying structures that have become obscured through the passage of time, but that these might be recovered by assembling surviving representations of those spaces into an image of their lost psychological landscape, a mirror world. This project is committed to the same historicist method. Each chapter sets out a precise historical framework for the material.

Chapter 1 situates the conceptual origins of the Underground in those industrial spaces of the nineteenth-century railway and shopping arcade examined by Schivelbusch and Benjamin. Like these earlier spaces, the metropolitan railways were physical manifestations of that paradigm of circulation that obsessed the Victorian mind. Running for much of its length through tunnels and open cuttings, the Underground came close to realising the ideal of a vast and abstract circulatory network that expressed the economic might of an imperial capital. But the completion of the Metropolitan and the District Railways is revealed to have had unforeseen and terrifying consequences. The freedom of movement they permitted was believed to possess an alarming potential to eliminate those social structures that impeded open circulation, no matter how vital these might be to the establishment. Resulting fears of invasion were borne out at the turn of the century when rapacious and corrupt millionaires from the United States fought it out for total control of the capital's infrastructure. This traumatic violation of a transit network with such enormous national resonance has ensured that the London Underground has served as an arena for covert trans-national conflict in British spy fiction ever since. (In Chapter 2 it is shown that, when novelist Theodore Dreiser wished to stage his own metaphorical invasion of the United Kingdom in the Second World War, it was to this fraught spatial history that he returned.)

Furthermore, in realising the metaphor of circulation, the Underground completed that alienation from natural topography initiated by the railways and shopping arcades. Passengers were baffled by an environment that seemed tied to the urban landscape only by spoken messages and insufficiently distinct station signs. The Victorian Underground is the *non-place* of consumer capitalism in embryo. It is where the psychopathology of the nineteenth-century railway carriage blurs into that heightened state of silence and isolation that remains such a notable characteristic of Tube-travel in the twenty-first century. In each instance, the user is caught in an industrial process that mimics an environment for social interaction: and without the panoramic vision offered by the mainline railways, there is no obvious excuse to avoid the eyes of the passenger seated opposite. Instead, early passengers were forced to escape into those virtual spaces provided by advertising and the literature on sale at the station stalls. The latter sometimes presented fantasies in which the railway carriage is put to non-functional uses by passengers who, for one reason or other, are better able to resist the psychopathology of the Machine. Perceiving that the Underground was therefore capable of transporting passengers into the internal landscapes of their own private stories, certain women poets of the *fin de siècle* forged an aesthetic that might facilitate this process. Their attempt to transform urban transit into a metaphor – a vehicle for significant transport – was taken up by the Vorticists. This avant-garde group realised that introducing their art into the posters that constituted such an important element in this heavily mediated environment might effect a radical change in the nature of life in the capital. Chapter 3 reveals how the Tube-network underwent a reordering in the inter-war period intended to refine the pleasurable reverie of individual passengers, examining poster art by E. McKnight Kauffer, controversial sculpture by Jacob Epstein and station architecture by Charles Holden. Contrary to what the Vorticists had hoped for, the result was the formulation of what Lefebvre termed *abstract space*, the rationalising rather than the cultural revolution of the modern world. In response to this unexpected outcome, Wyndham Lewis, the ringleader of the Great English Vortex, called for a new approach, anticipating post-war theorists Certeau and Lefebvre in calling for *tactics* rather than *strategy*, for the messiness of the individual rather than the order of a caliph, for the desecration of the Vorticist's newly realised blueprints for Babylon.

This approach already characterised the psychic landscape embodied by 'Metroland'. Chapter 4 begins with a radical revisionist reading of H.G. Wells's *The Time Machine* that establishes that the first version of the tale was a response, not to class segregation in the vertical city, but to the spatial fragmentation of the intelligentsia in the 1890s (into the decadent and the scientifically minded) resulting from the centrifugal force exerted upon the capital by the railways. The fable is an attack on the ideal of the underground garden suburb, on that conceptual space that would later be embodied by Metroland, the archetypal suburban landscape north-west of London, created in the inter-war period by the Metropolitan Railway. Like H.G. Wells before, the avant-garde vituperated this environment for its messy escapism and its individualism. But in the wake of the Second World War the space underwent a re-evaluation which recognised that, with the scope it provided for the expression of personal taste, its formal indeterminacy ought to be valued in a machine age operating on a superhuman scale. J.M. Richards, John Betjeman and Julian Barnes praised Metroland for remaining loyal to the significance of the individual, and noted that in this space fantasy was functional.

But the struggle to make a home in the machine-age metropolis was to find its most powerful expression in the pictures of children sleeping in the Underground produced by Bill Brandt and Henry Moore in the Blitz. Chapter 5 investigates how writers and artists made sense of the seemingly impossible spectacle unfolding under the capital. The pictures are shown to exploit religious imagery, transforming the sleeping children who embodied national unease at the threatened erasure of the individual into a metaphor that possessed the power to transmute even the space of non-place into the cradle for a redemptive and radical future.

In the post-war period, the Tube-network retained this metaphorical potential. Chapter 6 reveals that the absolute beginners of Britain's pop culture started out busking in the Tube-network, inspired by the playful misappropriation of the space by those migrants from the Caribbean celebrated by Sam Selvon, for whom the capital had always been a virtual place, known only through the imagination, and therefore susceptible to a subversive rewriting that might transform a functional transit network into their playground. The rewriting of a space constituted by signs was literalised from the 1960s through the medium of graffiti. Persons inspired by the

Situationist International are shown to have introduced the first political graffiti into the Tube-network, and to have imported the highly sophisticated style that emerged in New York, believing that the 'faith of graffiti' (the circulation of the artist's personal brand through the system) can produce social space within non-place. Initially supported by the Greater London Council, the radical potential of this art seems to have remained dormant until Prime Minister Thatcher began to install her programme for the regeneration of the capital. In the late 1908s, the mediated spaces of the Tube-network became the battlefield for an unprecedented form of semiotic warfare, which inspired writers such as Hanif Kureishi, Alan Moore, Barbara Vine, John Healy and Salman Rushdie to situate fictional resistance to various totalitarian blueprints for the capital in the London Underground.

Chapter 7 surveys the spate of millennial fiction set on the London Underground. It is suggested that these works express a new interest in recovering the material history of place that is a marked feature of psychogeography. Privileging urban sites that are not reducible to economics, this material represents a last-ditch attempt to resist the programme of urban renewal initiated in the Thatcher era. The ghost stations within the system and the homeless people who sleep in such spaces emerge as recurring tropes in this fiction. This is shown to be part of a resurgence of interest in the potential of the *Unheimlich* that reflects similar preoccupations in contemporary philosophy. Nicholas Royle and Conrad Williams engage with Derrida's work on the *revenant*, while Geoff Ryman and Christopher Ross are shown to explore the category of the *viral* in work by Jean Baudrillard. The material speaks to our sense that we *haunt* rather than *inhabit* the spaces of the metropolis, presenting a stark vision of a society threatened on the one hand by the sterility of the Machine and on the other by the catastrophe that this elimination of the human must eventually bring about.

In this respect, this material rather resembles the conclusion to Forster's meditation 'The Machine Stops'. Having failed to escape into pastoral fantasy, or to misappropriate the platform for illicit play, or to recover the city's material history in the abandoned railway tunnels in the topmost storey, Forster's hero Kuno, son of Vashti, reasons that, having processed out of existence the humanity that is its reason for being, the Machine must at last become riddled with the viral and stop: 'The Machine is stopping, I know it, I know the signs'.[15] In this he is proven right. The music in Vashti's room is interrupted by a gasping sigh like that of someone in pain. Her friend suffers from a slight jarring noise that might be inside her head or inside the wall and is not fixed. The artificial fruit is mouldy. The bath water begins to stink. And the human tissues are so subservient that they readily adapt to every caprice of the Machine. 'But there came a day when, without the slightest warning, without any previous hint of feebleness, the entire communication-system broke down, all over the world, and the world, as they understood it, ended.'[16]

Terrified, Vashti presses on button after button and kisses the Book of the Machine: 'In it were instructions against every possible contingency. If she was hot or cold or dyspeptic or at a loss for a word, she went to the book, and it told her which button to press.'[17] But this apparently functional user's manual has nothing to say to the ghost in the machine that is the very life blood of the virtual.

> Man, the flower of all flesh, the noblest of all creatures visible, man who had once made god in his image, and had mirrored his strength on the constellations, beautiful naked man was dying, strangled in the garments that he had woven. Century after century he had toiled, and here was his reward. Truly the garment had seemed heavenly at first, shot with colours of culture, sewn with the threads of self-denial. And heavenly it had been so long as it was a garment and no more, so long as man could shed it at will and live by the essence that is his soul.[18]

In revealing how humanity has haunted the London Underground over nearly 150 years, it is hoped that this present Book of the Machine may prove rather more helpful than its counterpart in Forster's fable. In their final moment it is the thought of the Homeless, those restless spirits the Machine could not comprehend and cast out, that comforts Kuno and Vashti: 'I have seen them, spoken to them, loved them. They are hiding in the mist and the ferns until our civilisation stops.'[19] The various stories discussed in these pages reaffirm the power of the dispossessed to possess the imagination – and this has truly startling implications in a material reality that is increasingly shaped by the virtual. This project indicates that the means of production in one such mediated environment has been seized by everyone from radical artists to teenage vandals, from a communist novelist to the Blitz babies sleeping through Hell. This cultural geography of the London Underground indicates that we really do possess the potential to rewrite our material reality, to make a metaphor of each and every Nowhere Machine.

NOTES

1. E.M. Forster, 'The Machine Stops' (1909), *The New Collected Short Stories*, ed. P.N. Furbank (London: Sidgwick and Jackson, 1985), p. 108.
2. *Ibid.*, p. 111.
3. Marc Augé, *Non-Places: Introduction to an Anthropology of Supermodernity*, trans. John Howe (London and New York: Verso, 1995).
4. Forster, p. 115.
5. See David Welsh, Underground Writing: *The London Tube from George Gissing to Virginia Woolf* (Liverpool: Liverpool University Press, 2010).
6. David L. Pike, *Subterranean Cities: The World Beneath Paris and London, 1800–1945* (New York: Cornell University Press, 2005), p. 14.
7. The following lines paraphrase Henri Lefebvre's 'Plan of the Present Work', in *The Production of Space* (1974), trans. Donald Nicholson-Smith (Oxford: Blackwell, 1991), pp. 1–67.
8. Pike, p. 15.
9. *Ibid.*, p. 2.
10. *Ibid.*, p. 3.
11. Andrew Thacker, *Moving Through Modernity: Space and Geography in Modernism* (Manchester: Manchester University Press, 2003), p. 3.
12. Neil Smith, 'Homeless/Global: Scaling Places', in *Mapping the Future: Local Cultures, Global Change*, ed. Jon Bird, Barry Curtis, Tim Putnam, George Robertson and Lisa Tuckner (London: Routledge, 1993), pp. 87–120.
13. Thacker, p. 4.
14. Frederic Jameson, *Postmodernism, or the Cultural Logic of Late Capitalism* (London: Verso, 1991), p. 16.
15. Forster, p. 134.
16. *Ibid.*, p. 137.
17. *Ibid.*, p. 112.
18. *Ibid.*, p. 13
19. *Ibid.*, p. 140.

PSYCHOPATHOLOGY OF MODERN SPACE

The Underground Railways of the Inner Circle in the Victorian Imagination

A spoiler follows: the woman was murdered by her husband, who pushed a ring containing prussic acid onto her finger as they travelled together in a compartment on London's steam-powered Victorian Underground. The resolution to Baroness Orczy's 'The Mysterious Death on the Underground Railway' (1901) might suggest a malevolent inversion of the Orpheus myth, the transposition of that primeval narrative of descent into an Industrial Underworld.[1] It is therefore baffling to find no reference to the infernal properties of this smoky, subterranean space in Orczy's story. The reader is presented with a first-class carriage merely, like that on any conventional railway, save that there is nothing to see through the window. Yet setting is certainly central to the plot. The premise of Orczy's murder mystery is that the average Englishman might get away with murder on the Underground, because he can count on the fact that the other passengers will resolutely refuse to pay any attention whatsoever to anyone else in their compartment.[2] The first witness, Mr Joseph Campbell, can recall that a man in a tweed suit seated himself next to Mrs Hazeldene and that the man alighted at Farringdon Street, but took no notice of them because he was very much engrossed in some calculations, buried in the Stock Exchange quotations of his evening paper.³ The second witness, Mr James Verney, can recollect that there was a lady sitting in the corner opposite to him, apparently asleep, but he paid no special attention to her: 'He was like nearly all business men when they are travelling – engrossed in his paper'.⁴ The phenomenon explored in 'The Mysterious Death' is not the nineteenth-century Industrial Underworld but the peculiar behaviour generated by modern urban spaces like the Underground railway. 'The great secret of successful crime is to study human nature,' observes Orczy's sinister sleuth, the Man in the Corner: '[and] Edward Hazeldene knew it well'.⁵

Orczy's curious failure to engage with the popular trope of the Industrial Underworld reflects the limitations of the vertical framework employed in the only full-length critical survey of the nineteenth-century Underground railways, David Welsh, *Underground Writing: The London Tube from George Gissing to Virginia Woolf* (2010). As David L. Pike notes in *Subterranean Cities* (2005), 'For all its resemblance to conditions in the modernizing city, not even during the nineteenth century could the vertical framework account for the contradictions of actual experience without severe distortion'.⁶ The steam-powered Underground may have been noisy and suffocating but in nineteenth-century London it was often perceived as considerably less infernal than the city above. In Robert Barr's short story 'The Doom of London' (1893), for example, a smog wipes out every living creature in London, with the exception of the narrator, who is equipped with a machine that produces oxygen, and people in the tunnels of the Underground, where 'a current through the tunnel brought from the outlying districts a supply of comparatively pure air that, for some minutes after the general disaster, maintained human life'.⁷ In fact, far from thinking of the Underground as Industrial Underworld, the Victorians seem to have felt that it was rather too close to the surface for comfort. As Welsh admits, while trying to conflate the early subsurface railways with the Industrial Underworld represented in the novels of George Gissing: 'Like most other seasoned commuters on the Underground, Gissing found nothing odd in the notion of travelling in an artificial environment beneath the streets, only complaining bitterly when nature invaded or disrupted this environment'.⁸ For much of their length, London's so-called 'underground' railways passed through open cuttings between stations, and elsewhere shafts or spacious glass canopies let in air and daylight. According to Pike, it was the very proximity of the Underground to the surface that caused the most anxiety: 'After all, the construction of the Metropolitan line, which, being a shallow tunnel, followed the line of existing streets and was run through by "cut-and-cover" – digging up an entire street and covering it over again – was itself a blatant staging of the interrelationship between the two spaces, gaping wounds opened up in the middle of public thoroughfares.'[9] Although the subsurface railways clearly facilitated the segregation of the metropolis into rich and poor, above and below, west and east, their construction also threatened to open up a new space in which the polarities of the vertical framework would blur: 'The image galvanized by the technological development of the London Underground Railway in the 1860s invoked the mingling of classes and the fear of contamination; it reflects a city replete, or afraid of being replete, with easy thresholds both material and metaphorical between above and below ground, wealth and poverty, morality and immorality.'[10] The result was an increasingly homogenous environment in which it became progressively more difficult to maintain that there was anything but a superficial difference between workers on their way to the dockyard and clerks on their way to the city: 'The numbingly inclusive postwar phrases of middle-class monotony, "Métro boulot metro dodo" and "Tube work tube bed," were already present many decades earlier in all but name'.[11] In short, the construction of the subsurface railways marked a radical break with previous conceptions of subterranean space and the emergence of an unprecedented form of modern urban space. To situate the London Underground within the cultural history of the subterranean world alone must therefore obscure much that is essential to the representation of this environment. This chapter provides a fresh perspective on the literature of the Victorian Underground. It will indicate that the conceptual history of this remarkable transport system is rooted not in the myth of the Underworld, but in the nineteenth-century reaction to the railways – as characterised by Wolfgang Schivelbusch in *The Railway Journey* (1977).

THE SPACE OF ALIENATED CONSUMPTION

In this new context it becomes obvious that 'The Mysterious Death on the Underground Railway' is, in fact, a variation on the nightmarish vision of the railway compartment as a provocation to murder that had so 'captivated the nineteenth-century imagination'.[12] According to Schivelbusch, the face-to-face arrangement taken from the stagecoach that had once institutionalised a need for conversation became unbearable as soon as the speed of the railway made such interaction obsolete: 'The seating in the railroad compartment forced the travelers into a relationship based on no living need but an embarrassment'.[13] The total optical and acoustical isolation of the compartment from the rest of the train worked to transform such embarrassment to the fear of potential threat, 'a crime that could take place unheard and unseen by the travelers in adjoining compartments'.[14] That only two murders – four years apart and in different countries – were able to trigger expressions of anxiety across Europe indicates the extent to which the dysfunctional nature of the compartment troubled the nineteenth-century psyche.[15] But on the conventional railways passengers were at least afforded some sort of relief in the panoramic vision provided by the view from the train window: 'it turned the travelers' eyes outward and offered them the opulent nourishment of ever changing images that were the only possible thing that could be experienced during the journey'.[16] In a compartment on the subsurface railways, there would have been no excuse to avoid the stare of the person across the aisle. As Pike points out:

> Until the inclusion of advertising and subway maps, there was nothing else to look at in the Underground except the other passengers. The first electric tube train, the Central & South London Railway, which opened in 1890, did not even include a pretence of windows; hence the coaches' nickname of 'padded cells'. The underground continued to be defined as what one could see, but instead of the hidden spaces of the metropolis, it was the hidden interiors of the apparently blank and empty faces around one that either frightened, intrigued, or went wholly unnoticed.[17]

The extent to which the psychopathology of the compartment had been exacerbated by the perpetual tunnels and cuttings on the early subsurface railways can be gauged from the astonishing reaction to the serial publication of 'A Murder of the Underground' by mysterious freelance correspondent John Oxenham (William Dunkerley) in *To-Day* magazine in 1897. Every Tuesday, a former employee of the District Railway would butcher randomly selected passengers in their compartments with a 'spidery implement, with a curved horse-shoe clutch and the pronged lever [or with] the deadly death-tube'.[18] Written in the clipped style of the popular press, Oxenham's story was so convincing that passenger numbers dropped dramatically on Tuesday nights, provoking a formal letter of complaint from the railway's managers to the magazine's editor, the humorist Jerome K. Jerome.[19] In later instalments, Oxenham even incorporated the resulting mass hysteria into the tale itself, mournfully observing that 'travel on the Underground is less attractive than of yore and the homely bus is rising in public estimation [because] a cold-blooded murderer is at large in our midst, and travellers on that all-times depressing Line [the District Railway] are completely at his mercy'.[20] Jerome K. Jerome relished the unease and gossip the gruesome tale had generated and reprinted a cartoon, purportedly from *Punch*, in which a city gentlemen was seen to boast that he had travelled in a District Line compartment alone: the ladies swoon at his story 'while the season's lions scowl at him from a distance and twirl their moustaches and growl in their neglected corners'.[21]

Given these conditions, it comes as no surprise that passengers like Mr Campbell and Mr Verney should have figuratively put out their eyes, should have chosen to block out the compartment with the aid of a broadsheet, like Soames Forsyte in John Galsworthy's *The Man of Property* (1906): 'he opened *The Times* with the rich crackle that drowns all lesser sounds, and, barricaded behind it, set himself, set himself steadily to con the news'.[22] Orczy's 'The Mysterious Death' cleverly plays on the fact that such remedial action can only exacerbate the isolation of passengers, separating people within the same compartment, making even murders possible in public. This form of self-induced isolation remains to this day a notorious feature of travel on the London Underground. There are a number of entertaining photographs in Mecca Ibrahim's guide to travelling on the Tube, *One Stop Short of Barking* (2004), which capture perfectly that sorrowful, somnambulant, fixed expression worn by passengers as they con the *Evening Standard*. One photograph merits particular attention: former Prime Minister Tony Blair is pictured travelling on the new Jubilee Line, hoping to burnish his man-of-the-people image, but is clearly rather ill at ease, standing in a near-empty compartment, having tried and failed to elicit a glimmer of recognition from the stony-eyed woman in the foreground. In spite of the media circus about her, in spite of the fact that she has no paper to hand, the lone woman has successfully maintained her state of withdrawal from the physical space. It is an astonishing feat. Although the compartment has long since been replaced by the open-plan carriage, it seems that contemporary Tube-passengers are still suffering from the psychopathology that afflicted their forebears on the Victorian Underground: 'like any reasonable commuter, the woman had decided to blank this animated fellow, knowing that only utter psychos smile at you on the Tube'.[23]

In part this may be because, though the compartment has long since been abolished, the antiquated face-to-face seating arrangement that rendered it problematic has survived intact. According to Schivelbusch, the seating arrangement of the stagecoach had been adopted in order to reassure railway travellers that they were moving along in much the same way as before, only at less expense and at greater speed. Unfortunately, its effect proved to be the exact opposite of the one desired: 'Precisely because the compartment was so closely linked to traditional pre-industrial travel – imbued with its spirit as it were – the new industrial mode of transportation was experienced as even more traumatic'.[24] Bourgeois first-class passengers complained that they no longer felt like travellers, but like mere parcels: their subjective experience of their well upholstered compartment was just as industrial as the objective experience of the lower classes seated in their open wagons.[25] As Karl Marx observes in *Das Kapital*, the utility of transportation can be consumed only in the process of the production of that transportation: while the industrial origin of other manufactured products is obscured by the spatial and temporal distance between production and consumption, railway travel is necessarily an industrial experience.[26] In fact, the railway journey could be interpreted as the earliest example of *alienated consumption*. In order to consume rail travel, bourgeois passengers had to subsume themselves within an industrial complex that confronted their insignificant, individual movements with the total process of the Machine. Their plight was thus much like that of the labourer examined by Marx: 'The science which compels the inanimate limbs of the machinery, by their construction, to act purposefully, as an automaton, does not exist in the worker's consciousness, but rather acts upon him through the machine as an alien power, as the power of the machine itself'.[27] Schivelbusch goes so far as to suggest that 'the railroad, the industrial process in transportation, did become an actual industrial experience for the bourgeois, who saw and felt his own body being transformed into an object of production'.[28] Like the labourer, the businessman was compelled to make his individual consumption a mere incident of the production process: 'In such a case, he supplies himself with necessaries in order to maintain his labour-power, just as coal and water are supplied to the steam engine and oil to the wheel'.[29] And, like any product shipped to market, both labourer and businessman had become the object of an industrial process that transformed him into an economic unit: 'This locational moment – the bringing of the product to market, which is a necessary condition of its circulation, except when the point of production is itself a market – could more precisely be regarded as the transformation of the product *into a commodity*'.[30]

The industrial nature of the Underground was a salient fact for early passengers. Throughout the 1860s, the excavation of the Metropolitan and District Underground Railways confronted Londoners with visual spectacles of industrial modernity that were without precedent in the history of the capital. As Lynda Nead has said, 'The tunnelling itself summoned images of the sublime, with excavations on an apparently limitless scale and tiny figures dwarfed by massive building works'.[31] Unlike the conventional railways, the Underground tore right through the heart of the city. The nineteenth-century journalist John Hollingshead laconically remarked that Londoners could now see how tunnels were made without leaving the warm shelter of their drawing rooms: 'A father of a family looks out of his window one morning after shaving, and finds a large breezy clearance among his neighbours' houses to the right or left, which ventilates the neighbourhood, but fills his mind with doubts about the stability of his dwelling'.[32] As Nead has indicated, in the course of a fascinating review of the images of sublime ruin that proliferated at this time in the pages of the *Illustrated London News*, this insane, illegible landscape was to spur the development of a new urban aesthetic, built around the form of the tunnel, the trench, the vault and scaffolding.[33] On 7 April 1860, the first feature on the railway's construction to appear in this popular periodical is accompanied by a picture in which burly workmen shift debris at the head of a complex of gargantuan timbers and gently curving brick walls abruptly truncated, a foreman pointing at the bank behind its retaining wall at what will become the Underground.[34] On 2 February 1861, a full page shows a great pit in the centre of a waste stretching from one side of the picture to the other; covered over with massive planks, the pit terminates in a chunky archway of brick under the road before the mainline station. Navvies clamber over the planks, or peck at the waste with pickaxes, or heave bricks into a chute; they are few in number and appear miniscule in the desolation, about which small coffee-houses, shops and hotels appear incongruous.[35] On 15 February 1862, battered buildings, sheared of their sides, loom tall upon an impossible terrain, a gloom planked over and propped, that sweeps about the isolated houses at the centre of the picture; minute navvies wheel barrows or sit perched on timbers above the abyss.[36] On 28 June 1862, the front page is given over entirely to an image of the devastation resulting from the collapse of the Fleet sewer, fatally undermined by the excavation of the Underground: 'the massive brick wall, eight feet six inches in thickness, thirty in height, and 100 yards long, rose bodily from its foundations as the water forced its way beneath, and, slowly breaking up into fragments, fell over with the scaffolding, roadway, lamps, pavement, and "plant" of every description into the road beneath'.[37] The picture depicts the terrific aftermath: 'the liberated sewer rushed in a black cascade; huge masses of brickwork lay strewn here and there; while on the opposite side of the railway, the water gradually creeping up its dark brown walls, stood the great burial vault containing the bodies from the old Clerkenwell pauper burial-ground, [one end of which] had been already partially burst open by the shock, and at every moment threatened altogether to fall and scatter its ghastly contents upon the stream'. Entranced by this spectacle, the writer concludes that 'The scene was, indeed, well worthy of a visit'.[38]

This fascination with the industrial space of the construction site reflects the fact that the Underground railways were themselves the most striking manifestation of a concept that had obsessed the nineteenth-century imagination: the metaphor of obstruction and flow that had first found favour with political economists like Adam Smith and Karl Marx – who wrote of the circulation of capital and commodities – and which had soon found a remarkable range of applications, permitting the Victorians to manage traffic flow and to institute circulating libraries, as David Trotter has demonstrated in his book on this subject.[39] 'The formula is as simple as can be', observes Schivelbusch: 'whatever was part of circulation was regarded as healthy, progressive, constructive; all that was detached from circulation, on the other hand, appeared diseased, medieval, subversive, threatening'.[40] This logic is particularly evident in the proposals for an urban transport network presented to the Parliamentary Select Committee on Metropolitan Communications in 1854–55. Sir Joseph Paxton, for instance, claimed that his Grand Girdle Railway would relieve the 'whole arterial communication throughout London', 'to the advantage of the trade of the empire'.[41] In Paxton's view, the capital city of a nation at the height of its imperial prestige required an ambitious circulatory infrastructure; and the extent of this ambition would be reflected in the colossal rubbish of the construction site, where the future resembled the sublime ruins of the classical past. As Nead explains, 'This is the representation of imminence, of that which is on the verge of becoming; in artistic terms, it is the archaeology of modernity'.[42] The images published in the *Illustrated London News* represent the spectacle of ruins in reverse – a monumental order in the earth meant to become Rome.

In spite of such efforts, the industrial transport infrastructure of the Underground railways would be represented in other media, not as a vindication of imperial ambitions, but as an overt threat. In a series of photographs produced by early professional portrait photographer Henry Flather to record progress on the District Line between 1866 and 1869, there are images that capture the monstrous spectacle of the pit as it passes through Parliament Square: as Nead has pointed out, the excavations had no respect for status or tradition and, in one photograph, 'Westminster Abbey itself seems threatened with destruction'.[43] Though this system of industrial circulation promised to transform social, economic and environmental conditions in London for the better, it also possessed an alarming capacity to eliminate those social structures that impeded its flow, no matter how vital these might be to the establishment. As journalist Henry Mayhew observed at the time, the ultimate object of this undertaking was to gird London round with an iron belt of rails – 'the metal ring that is to wed the wealthy and fashionable West to the poor and squalid East, and to unite the healthy North to the pestiferous South'.[44] The Underground reconfigured the socio-political spaces of the capital, opening up, for some, the terrifying possibility of invasion and contamination. In Anthony Trollope's *The Prime Minister* (1876), the Metropolitan Railway is the means by which the exotic and malevolent Ferdinand Lopez enters and departs the action of the novel.

Trading beyond his means while effortlessly penetrating the highest echelons of society, Lopez represents a new social and economic mobility hateful to Trollope, who spitefully turns him into a pantomime villain, before hounding him out of the novel altogether and into the path of an oncoming train.[45] Such fears of invasion and subversion were to be borne out at the turn of the century, when sharkish millionaires from the United States fought among themselves for total control over London's Underground. This traumatic experience found oblique expression in Sir Arthur Conan Doyle's classic short story 'The Adventure of the Bruce-Partington Plans' (1908). In this tale, Sherlock Holmes investigates the mysterious death of a naval clerk, who has been found on the tracks at Aldgate Station with the blueprints for a top-secret submarine in his pocket called the Bruce-Partington: an unusual moniker that fuses the name of a Gaelic warrior with the American nickname for Lord Hartington, who repeatedly sank the Parliamentary Bill for Irish Home Rule, and which serves to reflect the fact that submarines were invented by an Irish-American terrorist organisation, the Fenian Brotherhood, in order to destroy Britain's maritime empire. Holmes realises that the plans were stolen by a foreign agent called Oberstein and finds that the latter has made inventive use of the District Railway in order to circulate misinformation: the body was placed on the roof of a train from a house overlooking an open section of track and taken far from the scene of the crime (with the non-vital plans) in total secrecy. In this story, as in much subsequent spy fiction, such as John Buchan's *Mr Standfast* (1919), Geoffrey Household's *Rogue Male* (1939), Frederick Forsyth's *The Fourth Protocol* (1987) and the James Bond film *Die Another Day* (2002), the Underground is presented as peculiarly open to trans-national threat, and the space in which to reassert national resolution and independence. As Chapter 5 will show, this is a major theme in much of the visual material relating to families sheltering in the network in the Second World War. Throughout the twentieth century, the London Underground remained an important arena for what Dr Watson terms the 'secret history of a nation'.[46]

However, the most intriguing use of this perceived subversive potential occurs in Arnold Bennett's little-known novel *Riceyman Steps* (1923), which itself constitutes an important if belated contribution to the nineteenth-century discourse of flow and obstruction. The novel focuses on a miserly couple in Clerkenwell shortly after the First World War. Starving themselves to save money in case of revolution, Mr and Mrs Earlforward finally succumb to the lethal vitality of cancerous growth – seemingly brought about by the consumption of a wedding cake baked for them by their servant girl Elsie. '[Elsie] had noticed that [Earlforward] had never been the same since the orgy of her wedding-cake, and she had a terrible suspicion that immoderate wedding-cake caused cancer.'[47] In this Elsie is, in fact, not far from the truth: within the symbolic structure of the novel, the open-handed generosity embodied by her wedding cake must necessarily prove fatal to the Earlforwards, vampires whose ruling passion is the accumulation of capital. Throughout 'the seemingly careless profusion' of the wedding breakfast, Earlforward 'had been unable to dismiss the disturbing notion that England was decadent, and the structure of English society threatened by a canker similar to the canker which had destroyed Gibbon's Rome'.[48] This canker is revealed to be communism and Earlforward will later come to regard Elsie as its embodiment, 'connected by blood with communists and foreigners!'[49] In this intricate and resonant metaphorical pattern of accumulation and circulation, the puncture of the Fleet sewer by the Metropolitan in 1862 occupies an integral position. Early in the novel, Riceyman relates to his young nephew Earlforward the most marvellous outstanding event in the history of Clerkenwell – the construction of the Underground Railway from Farringdon Street to Euston Square.[50]

> The old man swore that exactly one thousand lawyers had signed a petition in favour of the line, and exactly one thousand butchers had signed another petition. All Clerkenwell was mad for the line. But when the construction began all Clerkenwell trembled. The earth opened in the most unexpected and undesirable places.... The thousand lawyers and the thousand butchers wished they had never humbly prayed for the accursed line. And all this was as nothing compared to the culminating catastrophe.... The pavements sank definitely. The earth quaked. The entire population fled to survey the scene of horror from safety. The terrific scaffolding and beams were flung like firewood into the air and fell with awful crashes. The populace screamed at the thought of the workmen entombed and massacred. A silence! Then the great brick piers, fifty feet in height, moved bodily. The whole bottom of the excavation moved in one mass. A dark and fetid liquid appeared, oozing, rolling, surging, smashing everything in its resistless track, and rushing into the mouth of the new tunnel. The crown of the arch of the mighty Fleet sewer had broken. Men wept at the enormity and completeness of the disaster.[51]

Bennett presents the technologically innovative railway and the perilously antiquated River Fleet as mighty opposites: the freedom of movement promised by the modern and the messy accumulation of human traces that constitutes the historical. The convergence of the twain is a foreshadowing of the plot of the novel, in which Elsie's single-minded devotion to the Earlforward marriage opens the locked up lives of the couple to lethal effect. The navvies are working on a fluid, rootless modernity that smashes the historic district of Clerkenwell, punctures the famed River Fleet and even brings an end to the old man telling the tale: having told his tale with fire and force, Riceyman suffers a sudden stroke and expires.⁵² In Bennett's *Riceyman Steps*, the construction of the earliest Underground railway is revealed to represent the very essence of the modern, as defined by Marshall Berman in *All That Is Solid Melts Into Air* (1982): 'To be modern is to find ourselves in an environment that promises us adventure, power, joy, growth, transformation of ourselves and the world – and, at the same time, that threatens to destroy everything that we have, everything that we know, everything we are'.⁵³

In fact, the modernity embodied by the Underground seemed to pose an existential threat to the individual, as well as the abolition of the establishment. Charles Pearson, for instance, the inventor of the Underground, found himself compelled by the logic of the circulatory paradigm at the heart of his plan to justify a philanthropic concern for the impoverished in Clerkenwell (his plan to commute them from a spot where they were crushed to a place where they might live with their families in comfort) with the hard language of commodity circulation: 'I believe nothing connected with this question is sound unless it can be proved to be commercially remunerative', Pearson announced to the Parliamentary Select Committee. 'I ask to carry a ton of human beings at a remunerative price, as much as the railway companies would carry the coals they burn, or the beef they eat, or the clothes they wear'.⁵⁴ The language of circulation eliminated the distinction between the circulation of passengers and the circulation of commodities. This is particularly evident in the speculative images that accompanied the various proposals for new urban mass-transport systems presented to the Select Committee in 1854–55. William Moseley's 'Crystal Way', Sir Joseph Paxton's 'Great Victorian Way or Grand Boulevard Under Glass' and Pearson's 'Arcade Railway' can all clearly be seen to evoke the architectural form of the shopping arcade.⁵⁵ The starting point for his monumental work of cultural history, *The Arcades Project*, Walter Benjamin described the glass and iron structures as shrines to the nineteenth-century preoccupation with commodity circulation.⁵⁶ According to Schivelbusch, the railway and shopping arcade shared much the same function: 'The city names on the station buildings are evidence of the same process that attaches price tags to the commodities'.⁵⁷ The projects examined by the Select Committee would have literalised this perception, incorporating metropolitan railways into gargantuan shopping malls.⁵⁸ Paxton's proposal, for instance, envisaged an urban railway running in a circle about the city through an enormous glass-roofed boulevard closely modelled upon the Crystal Palace: the Committee was told that 'the structure is in the same style as the Crystal Palace', 'is precisely the same breadth as the transept in the old Crystal Palace and about 16 feet broader than the nave in the present Crystal Palace'.[59] As its name would suggest, Pearson's Arcade Railway was itself a variation on the form of the glass-roofed boulevard: the railway was initially intended to run through the Fleet Valley in an envelope of glass that would make it 'as lofty, light and dry ... as the West End arcades'.[60] By the time Pearson presented his plan to the Select Committee, this format had been abandoned for the combination of tunnels and cuttings that provided the basis for every subsequent Underground railway constructed before 1890. But the architectural idiom of the shopping arcade continued to haunt stations like that at King's Cross, where trains would halt in an arcade of neo-classical pillars beneath a glass ceiling, a space that bore witness to the Metropolitan Railway's conceptual origin in a form that marked the emergence of commodity culture.

However, it was the tunnel linking stations that presented passengers with the most troubling reminder of their status as 'commodities' – plunging them into an environment in which their condition most closely resembled that of the metaphorical parcel mentioned by Schivelbusch. Henry Mayhew recalls smiling at the earnestness with which his friend Charles Pearson 'advocated his project for girding London round with one long, drain-like tunnel and sending the people like so many parcels in a pneumatic tube'.[61] It would seem that even committed supporters of the scheme like Mayhew could not help feeling that the Underground bore a resemblance to the Tube-railway operated by the Post Office, connecting Euston and Eversholt Street, that opened to widespread acclaim in 1864. Though not intended for passenger traffic, the brave or plain foolhardy sometimes ventured to travel on the network (Prince Jerome Napoleon was one such traveller) and their tales were featured in the popular press.

> The sensation at starting, and still more so upon arriving (say some of the passengers), was not agreeable. For about a quarter of a minute in each case there was a pressure upon the ears suggestive of diving-bell experience, a suction like that with which one is drawn under a wave, and a cold draught of wind upon the eyes, having almost the effect of falling water; but, once fairly within the tube, these sensations were got rid of, or left behind, and the motion had little more positive discomfort about it than would be attendant on riding on a 'lorry' on the worst ballasted line in England.[62]

The use of the same simile for Underground travel nearly sixty years later in a short story by Virginia Woolf (considered later in this chapter) indicates that these two transport networks remained long associated in the public mind.[63] The Underground Railway had made real what Schivelbusch declares was the worst fear of the nineteenth-century railway traveller – passengers really were being treated like parcels, hurtled through the dark, packed tight against faces blank as stamps, offloaded at stations that looked like nothing so much as a shopping arcade. The Underground presented passengers with the final stage in that process of alienation from landscape initiated by the mechanisation of motive power: 'As the natural irregularities of the terrain that were perceptible on the old roads were replaced by the sharp linearity of the railroad, the traveler felt that he lost contact with the landscape, and surely experienced this most directly when going through a tunnel'.[64] As Nead has observed, the Underground reconceptualised modern space: 'Now, instead of traversing space by following the logic of streets and other identifiable external features, people could travel below the ground, on routes that obeyed the logic of their own lines and expediency. They could descend at one point in the city and emerge at another, with little sense of the spaces between, or the meaning of the time taken to make the journey'.[65] The nineteenth-century passenger was confronted in the Underground with the metaphor of circulation made tangible, the template for an entirely new type of space that challenged conventional representation. 'Posterity may be shot, like a bullet through a tube, by atmospheric pressure from Winchester to Newcastle', reflects George Eliot in *Felix Holt* (1866); and though she agrees that this is a fine result to have among our hopes, she concludes that 'The tube-journey can never lend much to picture and narrative; it is as barren as an exclamatory O!'[66]

This estrangement from urban topography was to have peculiar consequences that soon attracted comment from contemporary observers. In 1868, a sketch published in *Punch* picked up on the fact that the passenger's sense of direction in this space must depend entirely on the (muffled) announcements and (obscured) station signs provided by the railway company:

> Unless you are so familiar with the line as to be able to recognise every station at a glance, you will scarcely ever know which is which. The porters still continue to shout 'Oosh! Oosh!' for Shepherd's Bush, and 'Nil! Nil!' (which of course is nothing) for Notting Hill; never articulating the name of any station. As you can seldom hear, so neither can you hardly ever see, on the Metropolitan line, the name of the station at which your train has stopped at. It is posted on a single board, so that the chances against your catching a sight of it are numerous.[67]

The inadequacy of these ties to the landscape above threatened to turn the Underground into a fearsome space of abstract and unrelenting circulation.

'As you will find no one on the platform who can or will give you any information', writes *Punch*, 'always get into the first train that arrives'. For, at intermediate stations, 'the train sometimes stops only a few seconds; and, if you don't jump in at once, will be off without you'. The bewildered traveller should then 'Hold the carriage door open until the Guard comes to shut it, and then shout out your destination. If you are right for it, he will most likely tell you; if you are not, you can get out again.'[68] These observations find confirmation in *Ricordi di Londra* (1874), a travel journal produced by the novelist Edmondo de Amicis, who, with no knowledge of English, was to experience the full horror of abstract transit without the mediation of the indistinct signifiers available to the writer in *Punch*.

> At one time, finding myself near a station, I thought I would take a trip in the Underground Railway. I go down two or three stairs and find myself suddenly thrown from daylight into obscurity, amid feeble lights, people, and noise, trains arriving and departing in the dark. Mine draws up and stops; people jump down and people jump into the carriages; while I am asking where the second class is, the train is gone. 'What does this mean?' I say to an employé. 'Never mind,' he answers; 'here is another.' The trains do not succeed, but pursue each other. The other train comes, I jump in, and away we go like an arrow. Then begins a new spectacle. We run through the unknown, among the foundations of the city. At first we are buried in thick darkness, then we see for an instant the dim light of day, and again plunge into obscurity, broken here and there by strange glowings; then between the thousand lights of a station, which appears and disappears in an instant, trains passing unseen; next an unexpected stop, the thousand faces of the waiting crowd, lit up as by the reflection of a fire, and then off again in the midst of a deafening din of slamming doors, ringing bells, and snorting steam; now more darkness, trains, and streaks of daylight, more lighted stations, more crowds passing, approaching, and vanishing, until we reach the last station; I jump down, the train disappears, I am shoved through a door, half carried up a stairway, and find myself in daylight. But where? What city is this?[69]

This aspect of the space impressed itself on passengers again with the misinformation provided to passengers by the Metropolitan and the Metropolitan–District Railways in that period of intensified commercial rivalry between the two companies that followed the completion of the Inner Circle: 'when relations between the two companies went through one of the regular bad patches in 1886, [for instance], both companies [started] issuing tickets for their own trains to hapless passengers irrespective of the fact that it might involve a journey of, say, twenty-two stops instead of five'.[70]

Frustration manifested itself in the music-hall song 'Timothy Tott or The Metropolitan Railway' (1883), in which an elderly gentleman takes a train at Moorgate Street and is never seen again. The protagonist searches for his relative throughout the network but comes to realise that 'poor Tim' cannot be found because, with the Inner Circle complete, 'the train's go round and round, / And never stop'.[71]

> It's my belief that Timothy ne'er left that fatal train;
> For all the pallid porters speak (I hope it isn't true)
> Of a ghostly voice that asks each night 'Oh! Where do I change for Kew?'

The cover art for the sheet music confirms the worst: a porter peers into a compartment in which a spectre sits still clutching his ticket to Kew. The song seems to have been a tremendous popular success: it was performed by Herbert Campbell, one of the most famous music-hall comedians of the period and the sheet music was sold alone, rather than as part of an anthology. The cunning incorporation of a station stall run by W.H. Smith into the artwork on the cover might even suggest that the sheet music would have been available to passengers waiting in the Underground. Attracted to this brilliantly illustrated popular hit, passengers may have purchased it on the way home, hoping to conjure something like the personal stereo's bubble of sound from the printed page.

In short, the subsurface railways were perceived as abstract spaces of circulation, tied ineffectually to the metropolis above with the inadequate spoken and written messages provided by the railway companies: and in this respect the space can be interpreted as a precursor to what French ethnologist Marc Augé has termed *non-places*, commercial spaces, such as the motorway or supermarket or airport lounge, that are largely defined by the words and texts they offer us:

> spaces in which individuals are supposed to interact only with texts, whose proponents are not individuals but 'moral entities' or institutions (airports, airlines, Ministry of Transport, commercial companies, traffic police, municipal councils); sometimes their presence is explicitly stated ('this road section financed by the General Council', 'the state is working to improve your living conditions'), sometimes it is only vaguely discernible behind the injunctions, advice, commentaries and 'messages' transmitted by the innumerable 'supports' (signboards, screens, posters) that form an integral part of the contemporary landscape.[72]

Augé explains that his distinction between places and non-places is loosely based on the opposition between place and space formulated by Michel de Certeau: 'If a place can be defined as relational, historical and concerned with identity, then a space which cannot be defined as relational, or historical, or concerned with identity will be a non-place'.[73] As opposed to place, which produces the organically social, the text-mediated environment of the non-place creates a contractual relation between each user and the powers that govern the space:

> The only face to be seen, the only voice to be heard, in the silent dialogue he holds with the landscape-text addressed to him along with others, are his own: the face and voice of a solitude made all the more baffling by the fact that it echoes millions of others. The passenger through non-places retrieves his identity only at Customs, at the tollbooth, at the check-out counter. Meanwhile, he obeys the same code as others, receives the same messages, responds to the same entreaties. The space of non-place creates neither singular identity nor relations; only solitude, and similitude.[74]

As we have seen, this 'gentle form of possession' – in which the person entering the space of non-place becomes no more than what he or she does or experiences in the role of passenger – remains the default mode of behaviour on the London Underground.[75] This presents us with the possibility that the alienation experienced in the non-place is in essence the psychopathology of the railway carriage. The London Underground might well represent a transitional form that links those nineteenth-century spaces of industrial circulation considered by Benjamin and Schivelbusch to the contemporary virtual spaces of consumer capitalism.

FANTASIES OF GUERRILLA CONSUMPTION

The managers of the railway companies themselves were extremely slow to comprehend the extent to which their rail network was a text-mediated environment. The first station interiors, for instance, to be colour-coded for the illiterate came forty years after the completion of the Metropolitan Line; the first concerted attempt to ensure station signs were prominent and standardised came in the First World War; and the first map to aim for clarity rather than verisimilitude was printed in 1933. (It was, in fact, the English modernists who first recognised and formulated the London Underground as an abstract space in the years following the First World War.) Britain's nascent advertising industry, on the other hand, grasped the peculiar potential of this space from the outset. In 1866 the advertising contractor J.

Willing paid £34,000 for the right to sell books and to post advertisements on the Metropolitan Railway.[76] And by the end of the nineteenth century, stations on the system resembled Plato's cave. Passengers found themselves in a mediated world – among the shadows of what Augé has termed the cosmology of consumption.[77] The following is a description of the station at King's Cross in George Gissing's novel *The Year of the Jubilee* (1894):

> High and low, on every available yard of wall, advertisements clamoured to the eye: theatres, journals, soaps, medicines, concerts, furniture, wines, prayer-meetings – all the produce and refuse of civilisation announced in staring letters, in daubed effigies, base, paltry, grotesque. A battle-ground of advertisements, fitly chosen amid subterranean din and reek; a symbol to the gaze of that relentless warfare which ceases not, night and day, in the world above.[78]

As Andrew Thacker remarks, advertisements that had been an irritation on omnibuses worked on the Underground railways because of the arrangement of visual space: 'at least now one could gaze at images without incurring the potential social embarrassment of exchanged glances with other passengers'.[79] The advertisement provided passengers with the means to escape from the psychopathology of an alienated environment, immersing them in the exotic, if often vulgar pleasures of a commercial fantasy world.

Nor was this the only surrogate landscape offered by the Underground. As we have seen, passengers could purchase newspapers or books or sheet music at the station stalls and may even have chosen to read about the space they were trying to block out, underlining the extent to which the subsurface railway was a mediated space. Henry Mayhew's pamphlet on *The Metropolitan Railway* (1865) was one such text: the pamphlet carries information on the back cover about trains and stations, and the full-length book from which it was extracted, *The Shops and Companies of London* (1865), includes a prominent advertisement for the railway's station bookseller, J. Willing.[80] As well as containing a history of the Underground, this pamphlet provides a unique insight into the conditions in the third-class carriage. Mayhew closes with a rosy account of a journey on the 'Workmen's Train' – a special off-peak service for working men – which leaves Bishop's Road at the 'burglarious' hour of 5.15 a.m.[81]

> Early as was the hour, we found the platform all of a bustle with men, a large number of whom had brass-buckets in their hand, or tin flagons, or basins done up in red handkerchiefs. Some few carried large saws under their arms, and beneath the over-coat of others one could just see a little bit of the flannel

jacket worn by carpenters; whilst some were habited in the grey and clay-fustian suit peculiar to ground-labourers.[82]

As on the conventional railways, the third-class carriage is revealed to be open plan and subject to none of the alienation of the first- and second-class compartmental carriage; the passengers talk to one another and even cut into other conversations. In this respect, the pamphlet resembles those sources cited by Schivelbusch that suggest the primitive carriages into which proletarian passengers were crowded promoted continuous communication: 'How often', reflected the writer P.D. Fischer, '[have I] while traveling alone or with people with whom it was impossible to start a conversation, envied the travelers of the third or fourth class, from whose heavily populated carriages merry conversation and laughter rang all the way into the boredom of my isolation cell'.[83] Mayhew's pamphlet clearly caters for such bourgeois envy, permitting the middle-class passenger to exchange his cell for the imagined warmth of a working-class community on its way to work.

Later texts indicate that the workmen's trains failed to retain this imaginative appeal. In Arthur Conan Doyle's *A Study In Scarlet* (1887) it is a third-class carriage, rather than a first- or second-class carriage, that is picked out as a symbol for the unreadable nature of the modern metropolis, indicating that the working-class passenger had succumbed to the psychopathology of alienated space: 'I should like to see [Sherlock Holmes] clapped down in a third-class carriage on the Underground, and asked to give the trades of all his fellow-travellers', rumbles an exasperated and as yet unenlightened Doctor Watson: 'I would lay a thousand to one against him'.[84] It seems that the centrifugal force unleashed by the construction of the Underground homogenised even as it segregated, breaking tightly knit slum communities into their component parts and scattering them throughout the city's suburbs on the middle-class pattern, providing working-class families with the fresh air and privacy but imposing upon them that feeling of alienation from the lived environment that had previously been the sole preserve of the bourgeois. In an engraving of the workman's train by Gustave Doré published in *London* (1872), the passengers are shown to be morose and hunched, in the gloom of a tunnel that seems a composite image of the station at Baker Street and the converted Thames Tunnel at Wapping, as anonymous in their round hats as any crowd of office clerks.[85] In George Gissing's novel *Demos* (1886), passengers on the workmen's train no longer talk to one another but are silent through sheer exhaustion: 'Between station and station there's scarcely a man or boy in the carriage who can keep awake; there they sit, leaning over against each other, their heads dropping forward, their eyelids that heavy they can't hold them up. I tell you it's one of the most miserable sights to be seen in this world.'[86] In fact, far from providing the subject for escapist railway literature, the working-class passenger is himself identified as a potential target market in Gissing's *New Grub Street* (1891):

> I would have the paper address itself to the quarter-educated; that is to say, the great new generation that is being turned out by the Board schools, the young men and women who can just read, but are incapable of sustained attention. People of this kind want something to occupy them in trains and on 'buses and trams. As a rule they care for no newspapers except the Sunday ones; what they want is the lightest and frothiest of chit-chatty information – bits of stories, bits of description, bits of scandal, bits of jokes, bits of statistics, bits of foolery. Am I not right? Everything must be very short, two inches at the utmost; their attention can't sustain itself beyond two inches. Even chat is too solid for them: they want chit-chat.[87]

It seems that the Underground was highly effective in fabricating its own clientele. Temporarily eliminating the complicities of language, local references and communal identity that constitute place, in order to establish an individual contract with everyone entering it, the Underground imposed upon each the shared identity of the 'passenger'. 'The non-place is the opposite of utopia', concludes Augé: 'it exists, and it does not contain any organic society'.[88] But, as Pike points out, the same space that regimented the daily routine of the workforce held liberating potential for those not subject to that routine: 'the same carriages that shuttled commuters endlessly back and forth could contain in their seats passengers on a different itinerary'.[89] The network remained peculiarly open to the tactics of *guerrilla consumption* examined by Michel de Certeau: 'a rationalized, expansionist, centralized, spectacular and clamorous production is confronted by an entirely different kind of production, called "consumption" and characterized by its ruses, its fragmentation (the result of its circumstances), its poaching, its clandestine nature, its tireless but quiet activity, in short by its quasi-invisibility, since it shows itself not in its own products (where would it place them?) but in an art of those imposed on it'.[90] In *Subterranean Cities*, Pike cites a passage that perfectly illustrates this form of illicit consumption taken from Rose Macaulay's novel *Told by an Idiot* (1923), in which two teenagers exploit the endless amusement offered by the perpetual motion of the newly completed Inner Circle:

> They knew what they meant to do. They were going to have their money's worth, of underground travelling. Round and round and round and all for a penny fare.... This was a favourite occupation of theirs, a secret, morbid vice.

They indulged it at least twice every holidays. The whole family had used to do it, but all but these two had outgrown it.... Sloane Square. Two penny fares. Down the stairs into the delicious, romantic, cool valley. The train thundered in. Inner Circle its style. A half empty compartment; there was a small run on the underground this lovely August Sunday....

And so on, past King's Cross and Farringdon Street, towards the wild, romantic stations of the east: Liverpool Street, Aldgate, and so round the bend, sweeping west like the sun. Blackfriars, Temple, Charing Cross, Westminster, St James's Park, Victoria, SLOANE SQUARE. O joy! Sing for the circle completed, the new circle begun.

> 'Where great whales come sailin by,
> Sail and sail with unshut eye,
> Round the world or ever and aye.
> ROUND THE WORLD FOR EVER AND AYE....'

Round the merry world again. Put a girdle round the earth in forty minutes. Round and round and round. What a pennyworth! You can't buy much on an English Sunday, but if you can buy eternal travel, Sunday is justified.[91]

Perhaps the figure with the greatest potential for such play was the woman passenger. Unfettered by the daily grind of production, the woman passenger travelling off-peak came to represent a freedom of movement that provided a source of vicarious pleasure for male passengers on their forced march, occupying a central position in the nineteenth-century discourse of the Underground. Long before the Metropolitan Railway even opened, the female passenger can be seen to feature prominently in the speculative images of the stations that appeared in the press. Serving to obscure the Metropolitan Railway's primary role as mass-transportation for the workforce, the well dressed women in these pictures represent a positive vision of circulation and consumption, uncompromised by the production process, and soon caught the public imagination. In a long-forgotten farce by L.H. du Terreaux, performed at the Royal Strand Theatre on Boxing Day 1863, middle-class women passengers are shown travelling on the Metropolitan Line as though long accustomed to such freedom of movement in the capital. The elderly Mrs Paddles enters loaded with purchases for her niece's wedding, and one Mrs Manilla Pumpkin later reveals that she is planning a trip to her dress-maker. In contrast, the gentleman protagonist, Mr Percy De Binks, is paralysed by his inability to deal with tickets, porters, passengers and platforms – and complains that he feels unmanned as a result: 'I couldn't be more unfortunate in the matter of trains if I were a court lady at a Queen's drawing room'.[92] As Pike points out, intrepid women passengers soon began to appear in the novel of society, taking advantage of the exciting combination of accessibility, adventure and romance to be found in the Underground. In Anthony Trollope's *The Way We Live Now* (1875), Hetta Carbury's increasingly independent spirit is signalled by her use of the Metropolitan: 'That afternoon Hetta trusted herself all alone to the mysteries of the Marylebone underground railway, and emerged with accuracy at King's Cross'.[93] In Henry James's novella *A London Life* (1888), a visiting American, Laura Wing, asserts her freedom from British notions of propriety with an excursion in the company of a gentleman compatriot from Victoria Station to Holborn on the Underground:

> Mr. Wendover called for his charming guide and they agreed to go in a romantic Bohemian manner – the young man was very docile and appreciative about this – walking the short distance to the Victoria Station and taking the mysterious underground railway. In the carriage she forestalled the question she knew he would presently put: 'No, no, this is very exceptional; if we were both English – and both what we are otherwise – we wouldn't go so far.'
>
> > 'And if only one of us were English?'
> > 'It would depend on which one.'
> > 'Well, say me.'
> > 'Oh in that case I certainly – on so short an acquaintance – wouldn't go sight-seeing with you.'
> > 'Well, I'm glad I'm American,' said Mr. Wendover, sitting opposite her.
> > 'Yes, you may thank your fate. It's much simpler,' Laura added.[94]

And in H.G. Wells's novel *Tono-Bungay* (1909), Marion begins her relationship with George Ponderevo on an omnibus and is horrified to find that he intends to pursue it in an empty compartment on the Underground:

> One night I was privileged to meet [Marion] and bring her home from an entertainment at the Birkbeck Institute. We came back on the underground railway and we travelled first-class – that being the highest class available. We were alone in the carriage, and for the first time I ventured to put my arm about her.
>
> > 'You mustn't,' she said feebly.
> > 'I love you,' I whispered suddenly with my heart beating wildly,

> drew her to me, drew all her beauty to me and kissed her cool and unresisting lips.
> 'Love me?' she said, struggling away from me, 'Don't!' and then, as the train ran into the station, 'You must tell no one.... I don't know.... You shouldn't have done that....'
> Then two other people got in with us and terminated my wooing for a time.⁹⁵

Pike notes in relation to this passage that the first-class compartment could be a space of propriety and transgression, by turn private and public: and this is a significant point, as the shift in the relationship between the opposition of private and public is the very essence of the modern. As Beatriz Colomina has observed, the technologies that define the space of the modern city – the railway, newspapers, photography, electricity, advertisements, reinforced concrete, glass, the telephone, film and radio – must be understood as mechanisms that disrupt older boundaries between inside and outside, public and private, night and day, depth and surface, here and there, street and interior, and so on.⁹⁶ In entering a first-class compartment, the female passenger was committing herself to a space that embodied the unbound potential of the modern, the possibility that the seeds of an authentic collective life might lie dormant within the illusion of being together, that the illusion might have some real basis in fact, that there was a utopia waiting to be realised in the alienated space of subterranean transit, as Situationist Raoul Vaneigem believed:

> On public transport, which throws them against one another with statistical indifference, people assume an unbearable expression of mixed disillusion, pride and contempt – an expression much like the natural effect of death on a toothless mouth. The atmosphere of false communication makes everyone the policeman of his own encounters. The instincts of flight and aggression trail the knights of wage-labour, who must now rely on subways and suburban trains for their pitiful wanderings.... People touch without meeting; isolation accumulates but is never realised; emptiness overcomes us as the density of the crowd grows.... But we only need to hold out our hands and touch one another, to raise our eyes and meet one another, and everything suddenly becomes near and far, as if by magic.⁹⁷

Perhaps the most striking fantasy of this sort occurs in Henry James's *The Wings of the Dove* (1902), in which Kate Croy chances to find herself in a crowded compartment with Merton Densher as she travels from Sloane Square to Queen's Road by Underground. Densher is on the other bench – at the furthest angle – and yet she is sure of him before the train starts: 'The day and the hour were darkness, there were six other persons and she had been busy seating herself; but her consciousness had gone to him straight as if they had come together in some bright stretch of a desert'.[98] In a psychopathological environment in which social relations should be impossible, there is immediate and meaningful communication: 'they looked across the choked compartment exactly as if she had known he would be there and he had expected her to come in; so that though in the conditions they could only exchange the greeting of movements, smiles, abstentions, it would have been quite in the key of these passages that they should have alighted for ease at the very next station'.[99] The very constraints that prevent them from speaking with strangers present impress the significance of this encounter upon Kate and Merton as nothing else could: 'If the fact that their opportunity had again come round for them could be so intensely expressed without a word, they might very well feel on the spot that it had not come round for nothing. The extraordinary part of the matter was that they were not in the least meeting where they had left off, but ever so much further on, and that these added links added still another between High Street and Notting Hill Gate, and then worked between the latter station and Queen's Road an extension really inordinate'.[100] As they travel swiftly beneath the capital, Merton tries to secure a seat that will permit conversation without appearing to do so, and a silent game of musical chairs ensues, which foreshadows the tortuous and distasteful jockeying for social position that subsequently wrecks their relationship. 'Never in life before had she so let herself go', remarks James; but this freedom is immediately defined by Kate as a loss of caste that she will work hard to overcome, reflecting the economic character of the modern space they occupy, its strict limits as a site for meaningful human interaction. 'He had walked with her to Lancaster Gate, and then she had walked with him away from it – for all the world, she said to herself, like the housemaid giggling to the baker'.[101]

Material by women writers themselves provides a more nuanced understanding of the female passenger's redemptive potential. American journalist Elizabeth Robins Pennell, for instance, confesses that she was initially bewildered and alarmed by the mediated nature of the space. Her first modest expedition from Charing Cross to St John's Wood took a number of hours either way, and she is unable to explain quite how she managed it: 'I have always wondered at my skilful evasion of so simple a journey's commonplace'.

> The advertisements on the station walls may have had something to do with it. Today I can afford to recognize their value as color and decoration. But

as long as my sole anxiety was to know exactly where the train was when it stopped, there was no leisure to note harmonies in the casual arrangement of posters. The one important inscription – in modest white letters on a blue ground – was that which my eyes sought; they were confronted, instead, with flamboyant notices of soap and mustard, with the cast of the newest play, and the sensation of the latest 'special.'[102]

In spite of this, middle-class women were soon using the network to travel throughout the capital. As Ana Parejo Vadillo has observed in her remarkable study of women poets at the *fin de siècle*, recent studies show female passengers 'hard at work in the British Museum Reading Room, visiting galleries and exhibitions, attending lectures, doing philanthropic work at the East End, working as journalists, strolling around the East End, promenading in Hyde Park, going to the theatre and to restaurants, visiting salons, and shopping, among many other activities'.[103] The emancipatory power of the new urban mass-transport systems consequently began to emerge as an important motif in texts by women writers. In the story 'A Worldly Woman' (1892) by Vernon Lee (Violet Paget), Leonard Greenleaf offers to call a hansom cab for his pottery student, wealthy modern woman Valentine Flodden, but is told that she would prefer to go by Underground: 'She spoke the words 'bus and Underground, he thought, with a little emphasis. She was determined to have her fill of eccentricity, now that she had gone in for pottery, and for running about all alone to strange places....'[104]

But as women embraced the economic independence offered by the Underground, their enviable status as consumers uncompromised by the production process vanished. In Ella Hepworth Dixon's *The Story of a Modern Woman* (1894), the protagonist's journey on the Underground is presented as yet another joyless component in the daily grind, as alienated consumption. Mary is a professional writer, travelling in heavy rain to interview the painter Perry Jackson for an article that will earn her a mere threepence per line:

> In the underground railway it was at any rate dry, and Mary could rest her back, tired with bending over a desk since nine o'clock. For a long time she had felt wretchedly weak. The strain of writing was intense; there were whole mornings which she spent staring at a sheet of white paper on her desk. The only ideas she had, came at night, when she ought to have been asleep, and after hours of insomnia she would get up and go to her desk with every nerve in her body quivering. Mary told herself severely as the train rattled on its way to Kensington that she could not afford to break down now. She wanted so much to retain her position on the *Fan*; if she gave it up for a month there

would be a dozen women ready to snatch it from her. Then, too, she was getting on with her three-volume novel, which was to appear in *Illustrations*, and there was the Perry Jackson article for the same paper, over which she had taken a deal of trouble, and to finish which she was on her way to the new Associate's house.[105]

The utopian glamour women passengers held for male and female writers would therefore ultimately diminish. In novels by Gissing, the urban rail network is connected to his unsympathetic depiction of the 'new woman': fissiparous but forceful Ada Rolfe uses the system throughout *The Whirlpool* (1897) and it is in the confines of King's Cross Underground that bookish but imbecilic Jessica Morgan betrays her friend Nancy Lord in *In the Year of the Jubilee* (1894).[106]

THE MAKING OF A METAPHOR

But as Vadillo has shown, in spite of this fact, the novel freedom of movement that public transport offered women writers spurred them to create an innovative and influential urban aesthetic of flux and movement: 'these vehicles for mass transport were optical devices which poets such as Amy Levy, Alice Meynell, Graham R. Thomson and Michael Field used for the observation of modern life'.[107] Instead of indulging in escapist fantasies, female poets of the *fin de siècle* perceived that a network circulating the signs of commerce might be turned into a vehicle for significant transport, a moving picture that might convey the beauty of the modern metropolis. As Certeau points out, the packed isolation of the railway carriage produces pleasurable thoughts as well as separations, the birth of unknown landscapes and the strange fables of our private stories: 'In modern Athens, the vehicles of mass transportation are called *metaphorai*. To go to work or come home, one takes a "metaphor" – a bus or a train.'[108] Like narrative, public transport traverses and organises places, selects and links them together, makes sentences and itineraries from them: 'subway lines, like lifelines on the hand, meet and cross – not only on the map where the interlacing of their multicolor routes unwinds and is set in place, but in everyone's lives and minds', reflects Augé.[109] Though the Paris Metro, for instance, is a *non-lieu* in its 'collectivity without festival and solitude without isolation', Augé points out that we superimpose on its map our private memories of every journey we make, until it is ultimately the tangle of our own lives that confronts us in the Metro: 'the itineraries of daily work are not the only ones we held in memory, and the name of this or that station that, for a long time, was for us merely one name among others, a common point in an invariable series, could suddenly acquire a meaning, a symbol of love or of misfortune'.[110]

Female poets of the *fin de siècle* inaugurated a tradition in which the Underground becomes the metaphor for such intense impressions of individual life in the capital. In Alice Meynell's *London Impressions* (1898) the Underground is shown to enhance the beauty of the capital, while itself remaining an abstract presence in the cityscape.

> London at night has begun, of late, so to multiply her lights that they make all her scenery. A search-light suddenly draws the eye up to the chimney-pots (sweetly touched, they too, on the westernmost of their squalid sides) and to the unbroken sky; and then at once the eye travels down its shaft, revealing clouded air; and here a puff of steam from some machine at work on the new underground railway takes colour on its curves.[111]

And in Elizabeth Robins Pennell's article for *Harper's New Monthly Magazine* (1896), the Underground is said to be picturesque in its combination of commodity culture and the beautiful interplay of light and shadow, making rich atonement for vile atmosphere.

> Rembrandt would have exulted in the rich darkness of the nearest distance; in the way the daylight filters in through the glass roof or skylight above and mingles with the glare of gas and the red and green glow of signals; in the bits of color that tell so well in the sombre surroundings – here the posters on the walls, here the books on the stalls, and there it may be the gay gown and flaunting feather of a lingering passenger; and, above all, in the wonderful effects of the trailing, outspreading smoke, as the train comes thundering in.[112]

But the finest representation of a late-Victorian woman passenger in the Underground produced in this intense impressionist style was written many years later, by the novelist Dorothy Richardson. In *The Tunnel* (1919), the fourth instalment of the epic *Pilgrimage*, Richardson's protagonist Miriam Henderson travels in the late 1990s by Underground to a lecture on Dante; and is entranced by the familiar sulphurous gloom of Gower Street Station, the platform lights shining murkily from the midst of rolling clouds of grey smoke, the dark forms and phantom white faces of waiting passengers emerging suddenly as she weaves through the darkness.[113] Returning in an empty compartment, Miriam meditates feverishly on the nature of divine love and its implications for this moment of her own life on the Underground.

> All the people in the world, full of goodwill without troubling or even thinking about it, were away somewhere else. Just as she had learned what people were, there was nobody. There was no love in her nature. If there were, she would not have been sitting here alone.[114]

The isolation of the compartment is translated into religious idiom and in the paragraphs that follow the psychopathology of mediated space is conflated with the evil of self-will that Miriam must strive to overcome with love. As the compartment starts to fill with people at Praed Street, she realises that her fellow passengers are, like herself, living from within through their contact with Christ: 'I *love* all these people, she murmured in her mind, and felt a glow that seemed to radiate out to all the corners of the compartment'.[115] But her victory over the alienation produced by modern space does not outlast her interest in the face of the woman sitting opposite her – thin and ravaged, strained and fatigued, and wearing an expression of undaunted sweetness and patience:

> Children and housework and a selfish husband and nothing in life of her own. She was at the disposal of every one for kind actions. She would be *really* sympathetic and shocked about an earthquake in China. Was that it? Was that being *inside*? Was that all there was? The woman did not see the wonderful gold-brown light in the carriage; nor the beauty of the blackness outside.

Confronted with the choice between a life of self-less love that might overcome the evil of the modern world and the immense pleasure she derives from her unique personal experience of its beauty, Miriam opts for the latter:

> [To choose the first] meant that now at this moment one must give up the sense of the train going along in the darkness and the sense of the dark streets waiting lamplit under the dark sky and go out to the people in the carriage and then on to the people at Tansley Street. She thought of people she knew who did this, appearing to see nothing in life but people, and recoiled.[116]

The passage above illustrates Certeau's point that the isolation of the railway carriage produces pleasurable thoughts as well as separations – the fables of our private stories.[117] This aspect of subterranean travel is also integral to the fiction of Richardson's contemporary Virginia Woolf. In her seminal prose-poem 'The Mark on the Wall' (1919), Woolf reflects upon that state of isolation observed by Augé: 'As we face each other in omnibuses and underground railways we are looking into the mirror; that accounts for the vagueness, the gleam of glassiness, in our eyes'.[118] But that which was the symbol for the unreadable modern world in the work of Conan Doyle is here transformed into a metaphor for the phantasmal and fluid nature of individual life in the capital, for the 'reflections' that Woolf believed the novelist of the future had a duty to interrogate in the wake of that momentous change that occurred in or around 1910. The Underground is declared to be the single symbol that might convey 'the rapidity of life, the perpetual waste and repair'.[119]

> Why, if one wants to compare life to anything, one must liken it to being blown through the Tube at fifty miles an hour – landing at the other end without a single hairpin in one's hair! Shot out at the feet of God entirely naked! Tumbling head over heels in the asphodel meadows like brown paper parcels pitched down a shoot in the post office![120]

In this remarkable passage, the simile of the parcel that so upset the Victorians is turned into an emblem for the fluid form in which Woolf wrote 'The Mark on the Wall' and that provided the template for the aesthetic of flux and movement that characterised *Jacob's Room, Mrs Dalloway, To the Lighthouse* and *The Waves*: 'I see immense possibilities in the form I hit upon more or less by chance 2 weeks ago', she remarked in January 1920, in relation to 'The Mark on the Wall'. 'Suppose one thing should open out of another … only not for 10 pages but 200 or so – doesn't that give the looseness & lightness I want: doesn't that get closer & yet keep form & speed, & enclose everything, everything?'[121]

In seeking to develop an aesthetic form that might refine the urban pleasures offered by the Underground, Woolf was participating in an endeavour that became an integral part of the modernist project in Britain. Setting aside for a time the hope that an authentic collective life might lie dormant within this non-place, London-based modernists set out to map the thrilling impressions the network could afford to those passengers prepared to embrace the modern world. The history of this bold enterprise is the subject of Chapter 3, 'Blueprints for Babylon'. But before looking at the formulation of abstract space, it is necessary to explain something of the complicated history of the deep-level Tube-railways that began to multiply in the capital around the turn of the century. It will be seen that the development of this important component of London's Underground represents the next stage in the development of that new category of space considered by Augé: an infrastructure of national resonance that opened the capital to the terrifying levelling potential of a new, American, international order.

NOTES

1 'The Mysterious Death on the Underground Railway' was the third in a series of six short stories on 'London Mysteries', first published in the *Royal Magazine* in 1901 (pp. 220–229) and republished as *The Old Man in the Corner* in 1909. Hugh Greene chose to feature the story in his anthology of early crime fiction *The Rivals to Sherlock Holmes* (Harmondsworth: Penguin, 1971) and E.F. Bleiler included the story in his compilation *The Old Man in the Corner* (New York: Dover, 1980). Subsequent passages from 'The Mysterious Death' are from this latter publication: pp. 15–28.
2 *Ibid.*, p. 16.
3 *Ibid.*, p. 24.
4 *Ibid.*, p. 25.
5 *Ibid.*, p. 28.
6 David L. Pike, *Subterranean Cities: The World Beneath Paris and London, 1800–1945* (New York: Cornell University Press, 2005), p. 14.
7 Robert Barr, 'The Doom of London', *Idler Magazine*, Vol. 2 (1892–93), pp. 397–409.
8 David Welsh, *Underground Writing: The London Tube from George Gissing to Virginia Woolf* (Liverpool: Liverpool University Press, 2010), p.23.
9 David L. Pike, 'Underground Theater: Subterranean Spaces on the London Stage', *Nineteenth Century Studies*, Vol. 13 (1999), p. 113, p. 128.
10 Pike, 'Underground Theater', p. 111.
11 Pike, *Subterranean Cities*, p. 43.
12 Wolfgang Schivelbusch, *The Railway Journey: The Industrialization of Time and Space in the Nineteenth Century* (Leamington Spa: Berg Publishers, 1986), p. 79.
13 *Ibid.*, p. 74.
14 *Ibid.*, p. 79.
15 *Ibid.*, p. 83.
16 Dolf Sternberger, *Panorama, oder Ansichten vum 19. Jahrundert*. Quoted in Schivelbusch, p. 62.
17 Pike, *Subterranean Cities*, p. 41.
18 John Oxenham, 'A Murder of the Underground', *To-Day*, 27 February–10 April 1897. Reprinted in Peter Haining, *Murder on the Railways* (London: Orion, 1996), pp. 262–285.
19 Mecca Ibrahim, *One Stop Short of Barking: Uncovering the London Underground* (London: New Holland, 2004), p. 36.
20 Oxenham, pp. 262–285.
21 Ibrahim, p. 36.
22 John Galsworthy, *The Man of Property* (1906), in *The Forsyte Saga, Volume One* (London: Penguin, 1978), p. 265.
23 Ibrahim, pp. 64–65.
24 Schivelbusch, p. 73.

25 *Ibid.*, p. 73.
26 *Ibid.*, p. 120.
27 Karl Marx, *Grundisse: Foundations of the Critique of Political Economy (Rough Draft)*, trans. Martin Nicolaus (London: Penguin, 1977), pp. 692–693.
28 Schivelbusch, p. 122.
29 Karl Marx, *Capital*, trans. Samuel Moore and Edward Aveling (London: George Allen and Unwin, 1971), p. 584.
30 Marx, *Grundisse*, p. 534.
31 Lynda Nead, *Victorian Babylon: People, Streets and Images in Nineteenth-Century London* (New Haven, CT, and London: Yale University Press, 2000), p. 39.
32 John Hollingshead, *Underground London* (London: Groombridge and Sons, 1862), p. 209.
33 Nead, p. 39.
34 *Illustrated London News*, Supplement, 7 April 1860, p. 337.
35 *Illustrated London News*, 2 February 1861, p.98.
36 *Illustrated London News*, 15 February 1862, p. 182.
37 *Illustrated London News*, 28 June 1862, p. 647, p. 648.
38 *Ibid.*, p. 648.
39 David Trotter, *Circulation: Defoe, Dickens, and the Economics of the Novel* (Basingstoke: Macmillan, 1988), p. 67.
40 Schivelbusch, p. 195.
41 Sir Joseph Paxton, 'Evidence to the Select Committee on Metropolitan Communications', *Parliamentary Papers*, Vol. 10 (1854–55), p. 86, p. 92.
42 Nead, p. 32.
43 *Ibid.*, p. 40.
44 Henry Mayhew, *The Metropolitan Railway: From 'The Shops and Companies of London'* (London: C.P. Nicholls, 1865), p. 2.
45 Anthony Trollope, *The Prime Minister* (1876; Oxford: Oxford University Press, 1983), Vol. 2, p. 51.
46 Arthur Conan Doyle, 'The Adventure of the Bruce-Partington Plans' (1908), in *The Original Illustrated 'Strand' Sherlock Holmes: The Complete Facsimile Edition* (Ware: Wordsworth, 1989), p. 781.
47 Arnold Bennett, *Riceyman Steps* (London and New York: Cassell and Company, 1923), p. 318.
48 *Ibid.*, p. 90.
49 *Ibid.*, p. 162.
50 *Ibid.*, p. 11.
51 *Ibid.*, pp. 11–12.
52 *Ibid.*, p. 5.
53 Marshall Berman, *All That Is Solid Melts Into Air: The Experience of Modernity* (London: Verso, 1982), p. 15.
54 *Parliamentary Papers*, Vol. 10 (1854–55), p. 158.
55 See Plan Nos XXXIIa, XXXIIb and XXXIIc, *Parliamentary Papers*, Vol. 10 (1854–55).

56 Walter Benjamin, *The Arcades Project*, trans. Howard Eiland and Kevin McLaughlin (Cambridge, MA, and London: Harvard University Press, 1999), p. 37.
57 Schivelbusch, p. 193.
58 *Parliamentary Papers*, Vol. 10 (1854–55), p. 52.
59 *Ibid.*, p. 80.
60 T.C. Barker and Michael Robbins, *A History of London Transport* (London: George Allen and Unwin, 1963), Vol. 1, p. 102.
61 Mayhew, p. 3.
62 *Illustrated London News*, 18 November 1865. Quoted in Derek A. Bayliss, *The Post Office Railway* (London: Turntable Publications, 1978), p. 15.
63 Virginia Woolf, 'The Mark on the Wall', in *The Complete Shorter Fiction*, ed. Susan Dick (London: Harper-Collins, 1991), p. 84.
64 Schivelbusch, p. 23.
65 Nead, p. 36.
66 George Eliot, *Felix Holt, The Radical* (1866), ed. William Baker and Kenneth Womack (Ontario: Broadview, 2000), p. 26.
67 'The Metropolitan Railway Monitor', *Punch*, Vol. 55 (3 October 1868), p. 146.
68 *Ibid.*
69 Edmondo de Amicis, *Jottings About London*, trans. Robert S. Minot (Boston, MA: Alfred Mudge and Son, 1883), Part 2, pp. 24–25. First published as *Ricordi di Londra* in 1874.
70 Christian Wolmar, *The Subterranean Railway* (London: Atlantic Books, 2005), pp. 87–88.
71 E.V. Page and Vincent Davies, *Timothy Tott or The 'Metropolitan Railway'* (London: Willey and Co., 1883), p. 5.
72 Marc Augé, *Non-Places: Introduction to an Anthropology of Supermodernity*, trans. John Howe (London and New York: Verso, 1995), p. 96.
73 *Ibid.*, p. 77.
74 *Ibid.*, p. 103.
75 *Ibid.*
76 Wolmar, p. 56.
77 Augé, *Non-Places*, p. 106.
78 George Gissing, *In the Year of the Jubilee* (1894), ed. John Halperin (London: Hogarth Press, 1987), p. 309.
79 Andrew Thacker, *Moving Through Modernity: Space and Geography in Modernism* (Manchester: Manchester University Press, 2003), p. 91.
80 Wolmar, p. 56.
81 Mayhew, p. 2.
82 *Ibid.*, p. 29.
83 Quoted in Schivelbusch, p. 70.
84 Arthur Conan Doyle, *A Study in Scarlet* (1887), in *The Original Illustrated 'Strand' Sherlock Holmes*, p. 17.
85 Gustave Doré, 'The Workman's Train' (1872), in *London* (Newton Abbott: David and Charles Reprints, 1971), p. 113.

86 George Gissing, *Demos: A Story of English Socialism* (1886), ed. Pierre Coustillas (Brighton: Harvester Press, 1972), p. 96.
87 George Gissing, *New Grub Street* (1891), ed. Irving Howe (Boston, MA: Houghton Mifflin, 1962), p. 378.
88 Augé, *Non-Places*, p. 111.
89 Pike, *Subterranean Cities*, p. 45.
90 Michel de Certeau, *The Practice of Everyday Life*, trans. Steven Rendall (London: University of California Press, 1988), pp. 30–31.
91 Rose Macaulay, *Told by an Idiot* (1923) (New York: Doubleday, 1983), pp. 200–202.
92 L.H. du Terreaux, *Waiting on the Underground: A New Farce* (Royal Strand Theatre, 1863; Lord Chamberlain's Plays, British Library, No. 53052).
93 Anthony Trollope, *The Way We Live Now* (1875), ed. John Sutherland (Oxford: Oxford University Press, 1982), p. 377, p. 385.
94 Henry James, *A London Life and The Reverberator* (1888), ed. Phillip Horne (Oxford: Oxford University Press, 1989), p. 78.
95 H.G. Wells, Tono-Bungay (1909), ed. Patrick Parrinder (London: Penguin, 2005), p. 123.
96 Beatriz Colomina, *Privacy and Publicity: Modern Architecture as Mass Media* (Cambridge, MA: MIT Press, 1994), p. 12.
97 Raoul Vaneigem, *The Revolution of Everyday Life* (1967), trans. Donald Nicholson-Smith (London: Rebel Press, 1994), pp. 39–40.
98 Henry James, *The Wings of the Dove* (1902), ed. Cheryl B. Torsny (London: J.M. Dent, 1997), pp. 50–51.
99 *Ibid*.
100 *Ibid*.
101 *Ibid*.
102 Elizabeth Robins Pennell, 'London's Underground Railway', *Harper's New Monthly Magazine*, Vol. 92, No. 548 (January 1896), p. 278.
103 Ana Parejo Vadillo, *Women Poets and Urban Aestheticism: Passengers of Modernity* (Basingstoke: Palgrave Macmillan, 2005), pp. 13–14.
104 Vernon Lee, 'A Worldly Woman', *Vanitas* (London: Heinemann, 1892), pp. 128–129.
105 Ella Hepworth Dixon, *The Story of a Modern Woman* (London: Heinemann, 1894), pp. 154–155.
106 Gissing, *In the Year of the Jubilee*, p. 309.
107 Vadillo, p. 34.
108 Certeau, p. 112, p. 115.
109 Marc Augé, *In the Metro*, trans. Tom Conley (Minneapolis, MN: University of Minnesota Press, 2002), p. 6.
110 *Ibid*., p. 30, p. 9.
111 Alice Meynell, 'The Trees', in *London Impressions: Etchings and Pictures in Photogravure by William Hyde and Essays by Alice Meynell* (Westminster: Archibald, Constable and Co., 1898), p. 15.
112 Pennell, p. 278.

113 Dorothy Richardson, *Pilgrimage, Vol. 2: The Tunnel, Interim* (1919) (London: Virago, 1979), p. 353.
114 *Ibid.*, p. 355.
115 *Ibid.*, p. 356.
116 *Ibid.*, p. 358.
117 Certeau, p. 112.
118 Virginia Woolf, 'The Mark on the Wall', in *The Complete Shorter Fiction* (1985), ed. Susan Dick (London: Triad, Grafton Books, Harper-Collins, 1991), p. 85.
119 *Ibid.*, p. 84.
120 *Ibid.*
121 Virginia Woolf, *The Diary of Virginia Woolf, Vol. 2, 1920–1924*, ed. Anne Olivier Bell (London: Hogarth Press, 1978), pp. 13–14.

2

THE LORD OF THE DYNAMOS

The American Invasion of the Tube-Network in Theodore Dreiser's *The Stoic* (1947)

> A nationalism that bristles with resentment and is all astrain with the passion of self-defence is only less perverted from its natural genius than the nationalism which glows with the animus of greed and self-aggrandisement at the expense of others.
>
> (J. Hobson, *Imperialism*, 1902)[1]

In the course of his trip to Europe in November 1911, US novelist Theodore Dreiser followed the Thames 'to the giant plant of the General Electric Company, not unlike those which supply the power to drive the subway trains in New York, and thought of Sir Thomas More and Henry VIII, who married Anne Boleyn at the Old Church near Battersea Bridge, and wondered what they would think of this modern powerhouse!'[2] The plant at Lots Road had been built by the American transport magnate Charles Tyson Yerkes, in the final phase of his extraordinary career, when he boldly attempted to monopolise the emerging London Tube-network; the model for Frank Algernon Cowperwood, the hero of Dreiser's magnum opus the Cowperwood trilogy, Yerkes was thus the chief reason for Dreiser's presence at Lots Road in 1911: 'since the last one-third of my story was laid in London', he explained, 'I thought that possibly in February or March I would run over to that city, look up my data, run right back and complete my book'.[3] With the final instalment of his trilogy in mind, Dreiser gazed upon the immense American power-station, with its two chimneys nearly twice as tall as Nelson's Column, and was struck by the fact that there seemed to be no continuity between the new American force represented by Yerkes and the pageant presented by British history, only conflict. 'What a change from Henry VIII and Sir Thomas More', he concluded, 'to vast, whirling electric dynamos and a London subway system!'[4]

This perception was not without foundation: the period of Anglo-American interaction that Dreiser had set out to chronicle was in fact one of tremendous antagonism, a significant low point in the history of the relationship between the two countries. But the remark seems prophetic, too – for Dreiser's political views were to become increasingly dominated by the national binary formulated at Lots Road, a process that culminated in a visceral Anglophobic outburst shortly after America's entry into the Second World War. The final, long-delayed novel in the Cowperwood trilogy, published posthumously as *The Stoic* in 1947, is thus an extraordinary palimpsest of Anglo-American hatred – the history of an American financier's ruthless invasion of a transport network at the heart of the British Empire – told by a pre-eminent American novelist who deeply resented the two countries' political alliance in the First World War and who wished to prevent a recurrence of this in the Second. This chapter will examine the historical events upon which *The Stoic* is based, explain the circumstances that compelled Dreiser to re-inscribe the fraught history of the space in his long-delayed novel and reveal how the crude national binary that animates the biographical and historical background suffers an enriching complication in the finished work – a work that should be recognised as a key text in the cultural history of the non-places of global consumer capitalism, providing an insight into a formative period in which the balance of economic and political power shifted decisively from the British Empire to the United States.

'A LONDON SUBWAY SYSTEM'

London's Tube-network was excavated by a tunnelling technology called the Greathead Shield – the development of an experiment that had been at the forefront of Britain's Industrial Revolution, the Thames Tunnel Shield. The first patrons of the Tube-railways would have been aware of this fact. They may even have travelled on the East London Railway that had run through the Thames Tunnel since 1869, or on Peter Barlow's Tower Subway, a cable-operated railway that was operational for a mere three months, in 1870. The Tube-railways that began to multiply in London through the 1890s and 1900s should have felt familiar, the next stage in Britain's industrial heritage. It is therefore curious to find that, for the Victorians and Edwardians, the creation of the Tube-network was fraught with patriotic technological and economic anxiety, to find that the early Tube-railways were, in fact, considered to be symptomatic of the threat posed by American innovation and investment.

Consider the opening of the City and South London Line, the first Tube-railway, in 1890. The Prince of Wales switched on the electric current with an 'elaborately chased gold key', before riding to a banquet in a spacious marquee resonant with imperial splendour: 'It was noticeable', remarked *The Times*, 'for the Oriental character of its internal decoration, in which Madras palampores were largely used.'[5] But the Indian silk failed to conceal the anxieties associated with this Tube-railway in the late-Victorian mind, stemming from its reliance upon foreign technology. The City and South London, for instance, was the first British railway to introduce open-plan American *cars*: the passengers sat on benches that ran the whole length of a carriage, cushioned throughout. Furthermore, the railway made the bold decision 'to adopt what has not hitherto been tried in this country, although in force on the high-level railways in New York – namely, a uniform fare'.[6] The working man would travel, for the first time in Britain, in the same space as his social superiors. Such innovations were perceived – with elation or with horror – to impose a foreign vision of social equality upon the city. Eric Banton praised the levelling effect of the Tube in an article called 'Underground Travelling London', in George R. Sims's *Living London* (1901–03): 'the office boy, finding that these trains have no third-class carriages, has sat down in great content beside the City magnate, and still the heavens do not fall!'[7] The *Railway Times* was not so salutary: 'we are not prepared to say that the one class will not be found to have its disadvantages as well as its advantages, as we have scarcely yet been educated up to that condition of social equality when lords and ladies will be content to ride side by side with Billingsgate "fish fags" and Smithfield butchers'.[8]

The motive power for this railway provoked further fears of foreign innovation. *The Times* complained that 'It is, indeed, not a little remarkable how completely we have been left behind by America in the use of electric motors'.[9] And, in his speech at the opening ceremony, the electrical engineer to the railway, Mr Mather, was reported to say that he had 'entered heartily into the enterprise, trusting to redeem the reputation of England, which had been somewhat left behind by Germany and America in the practical application of electrical science'.[10] This fear of international competition might even have been a contributory factor in the tremendous public unease at this time with regard to electricity. The technology was literally foreign to the British people – outside their experience or control.

> Supposing, it has been asked, a train breaks down in a tunnel what will become of the passengers? Will they have to walk through the tunnel with the knowledge that, if at any moment they should come into contact with the electric conductor, they will meet the gruesome fate which, to judge from American newspapers, seems to be the common lot of those who have to do with electric wires in the States?[11]

As this 1890 article in *The Times* goes on to explain, in the event of a breakdown the power is immediately switched off. But passengers were not reassured. When a Central London train broke down in a tunnel ten years later, 'nervous lady passengers were almost terrified into hysterics by vague fears of a horrible death caused by touching the electric rail'.[12]

The terrifying alien power in the new Tube-railways was to provide the inspiration for H.G. Wells's story 'The Lord of the Dynamos' (1895) – which is set in the power plant for the City and South London in Stockwell. The title refers to the largest and noisiest of the three dynamos there, which, through the course of the story, becomes an object of worship for a 'savage' known as Azuma-zi, who comes from an unspecified region of the world and now performs menial tasks in the engine shed: '[the chief attendant] expatiated upon its size and power to Azuma-zi until heaven knows what odd currents of thought that and the incessant whirling and shindy set up within the curly black cranium'.[13] Azuma-zi comes to believe he should offer his boss as a human sacrifice to the machine, and pushes him onto the naked terminals: 'Never had Azuma-zi seen a man killed so swiftly and pitilessly. The big humming machine had slain its victim without wavering for a second from its steady beating. It was indeed a mighty god.'[14] Following the failure of a subsequent attempt to sacrifice the scientific manager, Azuma-zi chooses to commit suicide, hurling himself at the big dynamo: 'So ended prematurely the worship of the Dynamo Deity, perhaps the most short-lived of all religions. Yet withal it could at least boast a Martyrdom and a Human Sacrifice.'[15] The premise of the story is ostensibly the terror and awe a savage might feel 'brought into abrupt contact with the crown of our civilisation', but 'The Lord of the Dynamos' provides a rather better insight into the way the English had come to regard electrical technology.[16] It was Wells who first conceived the idea that one might make a fetish of the machines in Stockwell – which he likens to such exotic entities as the Buddha at Rangoon and the devils of

Solomon – and his narrator is very clearly as captivated by their tumultuous power as Azuma-zi: 'If it were possible we would have the noises of that shed about the reader as he reads, we would tell all our story to such an accompaniment'.[17]

The Times concluded its special report on the City and South London with the remark that 'no Englishman can be satisfied to think that the country which invented railways may perhaps be falling behind the United States in carrying railways forward to their fullest and most perfect development'.[18] But subsequent Tube-railways in London were to exacerbate, rather than allay, such fears. The carriages for the Central London Railway were 'open from end to end, after the American fashion'.[19] And the 'American fashion' was to be followed by every subsequent Tube-railway, where the carriages are to this day referred to as *cars* – even though the American open-plan layout has long since been taken up by the mainline railways. The uniform fare was also a feature of each new Tube-railway in the capital. The Central London Railway, for instance, was soon nicknamed the Twopenny Tube, and was referred to as such in the Gilbert and Sullivan opera *Patience* (1881). And, in spite of the hopes expressed by Mr Mather, when he opened the City and South London, later Tube-railways were to import technology from the United States. General Electric fitted out the Central London Railway, and Jackson and Sharp supplied the Waterloo and City with rolling stock. What's more, this reliance on American technology was to increase enormously in the next century, when two rival American financial tycoons began to buy up the capital's transport infrastructure.

'A novel feature in connexion with the enterprise', observed *The Times* in 1890, concerning the projected electric Tube-railway from Charing Cross to Hampstead, 'is that it will be entirely in the hands of American capitalists, and it will also be the first of such a nature that has ever been carried out in Europe by Americans'.[20] In fact, American capital had played a considerable part in the creation of earlier Tube-railways; as historian Christian Wolmar states, 'it is no exaggeration to say that London's Tube system owes its existence almost entirely to American finance'.[21] But the English became widely aware of this fact only with the take-over in 1900 of the Hampstead Tube by Charles Tyson Yerkes, the model for Frank Algernon Cowperwood. An English associate later recalled how he had accompanied the American to Hampstead Heath in order to look over the proposed site for the railway's terminus. 'It was a very wet day, but when they alighted near Jack Straw's Castle, the sun came out and illuminated the spires and towers of London below'. On the spot where the peasant rebel is said to have mustered his men for the overthrow of the established order, Yerkes contemplated the capital, and turned to a companion with the forceful words, 'Davis, I'll make this railway'.[22]

His first step was to buy up, and electrify, the existing steam-powered subsurface lines – thereby rendering these earlier railways a further object for nationalist anxieties. In fact, they feature as such in Arthur Conan Doyle's 'The Adventure of the Bruce-Partington Plans', where they play a central part in a plot that involves other invisible, trans-national entities that threaten the British Empire, such as Irish-American submarines and German spies (see Chapter 1).[23] The weak financial condition of these companies had been exacerbated by the opening of the Central London Railway, which ran right through the Inner Circle. The consequent fall-off in passenger numbers is mentioned in a contemporary short story by Baroness Orczy, who observes that 'the old Underground was being deserted for the time being for the sake of the novelty of the other line'.[24] If the Metropolitan and the Metropolitan District were to survive, the steam engines clearly had to be replaced with some form of electrical traction. To this end, Yerkes formed the Metropolitan District Electric Traction Company on 15 July 1901, and with the assistance of Robert William Perks (the model for Elverson Johnson in *The Stoic*) soon took control of the Metropolitan District Railway. His rejection of the inexpensive (and highly hazardous) electrification scheme favoured by the Metropolitan soon prompted accusations that Yerkes's 'American friends were financially interested as manufacturers in the scheme adopted by the District Company'.[25] In fact, even the power-station that Yerkes planned to build at Lots Road was interpreted by some as an assault upon England's cultural heritage. James Whistler raged that 'Yerkes proposes to put up a gigantic power house in Chelsea for the electrification of the Underground, and as it is to have enormous chimneys towering far into the sky, it will completely ruin the bend of the Thames made famous by Turner'. Unlike Dreiser, Whistler found little pleasure in this clash, concluding that 'They ought to be drawn and quartered'.[26]

The satirical magazine *Punch* echoed these sentiments when in 1906 it expressed the hope 'that Chelsea, with its Artists' Quarter, will take advantage of the magnificent opportunity offered by the four [*sic*] Chimneys of the Generating Station'. Recalling the savage comments of the historian Thomas Carlyle on the career of an earlier 'railway king' in the essay 'Hudson's Statue' in *Latter-Day Pamphlets* (1850), *Punch* proposed that Yerkes' power-plant should be surmounted by an immense 'Equestrian Statue of Carlyle, reading his own works', and provided an artist's impression of this ironic monstrosity that reeked with black smoke.[27] In fact, the cartoon was the latest in a long line of satirical images and lyrics in *Punch* expressing the widespread bafflement and outrage at American innovation and investment in the Underground. The preface to the one hundred and twentieth volume of the magazine depicted one 'Jonathan M. Yankes, of New York City (M. for Monroe, Sir), and Agent of the great Amurican Pioneer and British Isles Development Trust', as a relentless hustler who had grasped 'the reverse of the medallion' somehow missed by President Monroe: 'And let me tell you there is a future before your country, Sir, soon as we start in under the Pond with our Pan-Anglo-Saxon Submarine Toob'.[28] In another cartoon, published on 6 February 1901, the subterranean menace is shown toppling the capital's national monuments, and in that same issue a lyric in music-hall doggerel bemoaned the impact it was believed the Tube would have upon Hampstead Heath.[29]

> Oh! sive us 'Appy 'Amstid!
> It's Parrydice, you bet!
> Theer ain't no smoke ter 'arm a bloke,
> Nor yet no smuts as yet.
> An' so I opes they'll tell
> This bloomin' Yanky swell
> Ter send 'is toobs ter – well,
> Not 'Appy 'Amstid![30]

However, it was Yerkes's sharp business practices which ultimately unleashed the full force of this pent-up national outrage, following his sabotage of the Morgan Tube, a Tube-railway financed by the American millionaire J. Pierpont Morgan, considered vital to London's future development. (The struggle between Cowperwood and 'Stanford Drake' is outlined with infectious excitement in Chapter 51 of *The Stoic*.) The MP for Luton 'doubted whether for a long time, if ever, such a very dirty transaction was ever done by parties coming before Parliament'; 'Parliament had been tricked' and the District Railway 'had been stretching out its arms like an octopus over these tube railways'.[31] The Member for West Edinburgh felt 'that the House should not allow the public interest to be made a counter in a game of this sort – for it was a game in which it was proposed to make the London roads pawns on the chequer board of Wall Street'.[32] The national technological and economic anxieties that had, through twelve years, become increasingly tangled with the Tube reached its height, with MPs heaping ignominy on the Yerkes Group in the House of Commons, 'prompted', suggests Wolmar, 'by a xenophobic attitude towards the American financiers who were pressing to develop railway lines in the capital'.[33]

'RADICALLY AMERICAN'

The death of Yerkes at the Waldorf-Astoria Hotel on 29 December 1905, and the widely reported, albeit tenuous, claim that his company was now back in British hands, in no way served to abate the public's anxiety at American involvement in the Tube-network, for when the Baker Street and Waterloo, the Great Northern Piccadilly and Brompton, and the Hampstead Tube were opened in 1906 and 1907, the tunnels built by the American engineer James Chapman were found to be replete with technical innovations imported from the United States.[34] The system possessed the first railway escalators in London, 170 elevators supplied by Otis Elevator Co., American-style advertisements and (on the surface) station buildings built to a formulaic pattern, in a prescient attempt at corporate branding. In fact, the Underground presented London with a heavily Americanised environment, one which anticipated, in many respects, what the French anthropologist Marc Augé has since christened the non-places of late capitalism: those international, text-generated spaces that seem everywhere and nowhere, such as motorways or airports or supermarkets.[35] The American character of the London Underground was not lost upon Dreiser, who claimed, in the course of an argument in a Tube-car, that the network was incontrovertible proof that America was remaking England in its own image:

> The subway system on which we were riding was due to the influence of an American who came to London to make a fortune. The car advertising, as one saw it displayed everywhere, had been borrowed absolutely from America. A large number of the car advertisements which our eyes studied in an effort to obtain corroboration concerned American-made products. I recall distinctly the Walk-Over Shoe, Armour's Extract of Beef, the Gillette Safety Razor, the Eastman Kodak, the Waterman Pen, the Ingersoll Dollar Watch and a half-dozen other things, all of which were shown in the particular car in which we were travelling.[36]

In the travel book in which this passage occurs, Dreiser postulated a binary opposition between 'America – its raw force' and 'that vast established order, which is England' – he asserted that the latter would 'unquestionably be made over radically by United States experience'.[37]

For much of his time in England, Dreiser found this a highly pleasurable thought. Choosing to travel everywhere by Tube, he reflected that the only fault he could find with the system was that the people in the cars were not Americans: 'Naturally that was a great defect'.[38] 'This whole nation had been and is still being shot through with American influence', he concluded.[39]

But elsewhere the novelist confessed to feelings of ambivalence, expressing pleasure in elements that would surely be lost in an England remade in America's image, and horror at the callousness and crudity of the American forcefulness embodied by men like Yerkes. For instance, while professing admiration for the benefits capitalist 'sharks' such as Morgan, Rockefeller and Yerkes had conferred upon America, Dreiser also blamed the 'lawlessness of the men at the top' for the widespread belief that it was 'the privilege of every living, breathing American [to be] rude and brutal every other',[40] and contrasted the courtesy possessed by English railway employees to the coarseness and inattentiveness on the part of their American counterparts, whose forcefulness precluded the possibility of service.[41] The scales seem to have fallen from the writer's eyes in a conversation with an Englishwoman who claimed to have cried the first time she was compelled to undress openly in an American Pullman. 'The enormity of the Pullman system came home to me at once', recalled Dreiser; 'It was like a flash of lightening. Being purely American raised, I had always imagined, as Americans always do, that the American Pullman system, like the American everything else, was the best in the world.' He explained that he had seen the English sleeping cars, and that these furnished a single section to each person, with a bed, washstand, small table, dressing mirror and clothes hook, and all for no more money than the American Pullman Company charges. 'After that, my eyes began to open to some other defects of the American railway system.'[42] But it was in the course of his contemplation of the English countryside (from the vantage provided by the 'string of baby carriages' on the English mainline system) that the gravest doubts occurred to Dreiser concerning Britain's exposure to the raw forcefulness that had driven titans like Morgan to lay mighty railways across the American continent. 'Somehow, now, you feel only the absence of the railroad', he wrote, 'the fact that it cannot endure, that rooms are damp and dark and that bathrooms, telephones, electric lights and phonographs are somehow inappropriate, crude, new and destructive of all this quaintness'.[43] The 'delicious little streets' should be covered with glass, he insisted, to protect them from modernity's encroachment.[44] 'My father was a German, my mother of Pennsylvania Dutch extraction, and yet there is a pull here in this Shakespearean–Wordsworthian–Hardyesque world which is precisely like the call of a tender mother to a child. I can't resist it. I love it. I love it so much that it even hurts me – and I am not English but radically American.'[45]

The publication of *The Financier* and *The Titan*, the first two volumes in the Cowperwood trilogy, following Dreiser's return to America in 1912, served to highlight the fundamentally problematic nature of the writer's faith in American force, as embodied by Yerkes and his power-station at

Lots Road. In his recent biography, Jerome Loving notes that Dreiser clearly identified with his creation Cowperwood, filling out the tycoon's turbulent private life with elements taken from his own epic sexual history, and Loving observes that this 'fantasized identification with the hero' was strange, given the writer's professed political beliefs concerning the financial abuse of the poor. 'Admirers of *Sister Carrie* and *An American Tragedy* find it odd that Dreiser should have devoted so much time and effort to this Tamburlaine of American business.'[46] Dreiser himself was not unaware of this apparent discrepancy, expressing with amused incredulity that 'at the same time that I am interesting myself in our social conditions, I am concluding the last volume of the Trilogy which, I am sure, most of my critics will pounce on as decidedly unsocial and even ridiculous as coming from a man who wants social equity'. He was seemingly unable to explain why, merely remarking that 'Nevertheless, I am writing it just that way'.[47] In fact, the position occupied by Cowperwood within the wider context provided by his creator's political and social convictions was to become increasingly marginal over time, as Dreiser embraced both Quakerism and communism. This may account for his startling failure to engage with *The Stoic* sufficiently to complete the Cowperwood trilogy in the thirty years that followed the publication of *The Titan*.

The end to this thirty-year hiatus was brought about by the transformation of what was once a vague, ambivalent irritation with the 'vast, established order that is England' into a virulent all-out Anglophobia in the run-up to the Second World War. Born into a family of immigrants from Germany, Dreiser had made a pilgrimage to his father's childhood home an integral part of the European expedition he recounted in *A Traveler At Forty* – and was no less ambivalent in his response to 'the blazing force' of the newly unified German Empire than to the crumbling established order in England: 'a vital, glowing life, entirely superior and more ominous than that of Switzerland, and in many ways less pleasant'.[48] America's entry into the First World War had served to clarify his perspective. Having only recently achieved a hard-won sense of connection with the Fatherland, Dreiser was horrified to find his own nation taking up arms on the side of the English, plunging the once proud German Empire into chaos and ruin. He came to blame the English for inveigling the Americans into the First World War; and the looming possibility of a second conflict between the European powers stoked this long smouldering resentment into new flame. Confused for a time by the threatening stance Germany had taken in relation to the Soviet Union, Dreiser's private hatred for the English at last seemed vindicated when Stalin and Hitler signed the non-aggression pact in 1939. Now that the Third Reich posed no threat to his beloved Soviet Union, England was once again the natural enemy of both International Communism and the German people, and Dreiser felt free to ally himself with Charles Lindbergh's America First Movement – venting his Anglophobia in a political tract called *America Is Worth Saving* in 1941. Following Operation Barbarossa, and the attack on Pearl Harbor, Dreiser was compelled to change tack, but his political activism came to an abrupt halt when, shortly before a speech called 'Democracy on the Offensive', Dreiser told a reporter that 'Should Russia go down to defeat, I hope the Germans invade England'. He explained, 'I would rather see Germans in England than those damn, aristocratic, horse-riding snobs there now'. Subsequent remarks made by Dreiser to the newspapers the following day suggest that his Anglophobic comments were closely related to his perception that England lacked the vital force that distinguished America and Germany: 'the English have done nothing in this war thus far except borrow money, planes and men from the United States. They stay at home and do nothing. They are lousy.'[49] Crucified by the newspapers and denied an active role in politics, Dreiser was beaten back into fiction, where he sought to reconcile his fascination with the amoral forcefulness that had blighted his public life with his late faith in the fundamentally benevolent nature of the cosmos, which may well have frustrated for so long the completion of the Cowperwood trilogy.

Such a reconciliation takes place in the closing chapters of *The Stoic*, in which Cowperwood's lover Berenice comes to perceive through the study of Indian philosophy that the millionaire's rapacity, or rather his 'worship and constant search for beauty in every form, and especially in the form of a woman, was nothing more than a search for the Divine design behind all forms – the face of Brahman shining through'.[50] But such a conclusion would seem flimsy and facile without the skilful presentation of Cowperwood's struggle for power in England in the earlier part of the book: in order for the conclusion reached by Berenice to convince, Cowperwood's movement into Nirvana had to seem inherent to the man rather than imposed, a genuine synthesis rather than an arbitrary settlement. In *The Stoic*, Dreiser would show how Cowperwood might make his own conclusion, how America's raw force might come to know Nirvana through a paradoxical, all-out assault on that vast, established order that is England.

Such a project had previously seemed impossible, thwarted by Dreiser's inability to engage sympathetically with the raw, amoral forcefulness of the American millionaire. But the suppression of Dreiser's political activism had served to electrify with new partisan passion the Anglo-American binary he had formulated long ago on the bank of the Thames overlooking Lots Road. The millionaire's intervention in the Tube-network is repeatedly referred to as an 'invasion', and Berenice even compares the millionaire's passage across the Atlantic to Caesar's crossing of the Rubicon.[51] The nationalist opposition to be expected from the English to the American financier is emphatically asserted by the characters Cowperwood, Sippens and Johnson: 'I know very well no American millionaire is going to be allowed to come in here and take charge of our undergrounds', Johnson declares; 'we do not like outsiders to come in and manage our affairs for us'.[52] And such predictions are borne out by the subsequent action of the novel in which Cowperwood's proposed invasion of the London underground field is said to have provoked a furore: 'With but few exceptions directors and shareholders of both of the old loop companies were against him'.[53]

Moreover, Cowperwood encounters Englishmen who fulfil in every possible respect the controversial characterisation that generated such public outrage in 1942. The financier's opponents include fierce, and highly ineffectual, figures such as Sir Hudspeth Dighton, 'seventy-five years of age, ultraconservative, and not at all interested to enter upon radical railway changes', and Lord Colvay, who has his breakfast 'with the *Times* to the right of him, for reasons of mental dignity principally', while 'reading the *Daily Mail*, his favourite paper'.[54] And even those Englishmen who choose to support Cowperwood are shown to suffer from that 'strong sense of individual and racial superiority' which Dreiser believed 'not an uncommon trait in Englishmen'.[55] Johnson, for instance, has risen from the position of a baker's apprentice to become a partner in a firm of solicitors, but continues to feel that 'there should be a ruling class which should advance and maintain itself by a desirable if not always justifiable cunning'.[56] His friend, Lord Stane, for all his progressive views, is also 'content that they should travel different social levels'.[57] There is one possible exception to the negative stereotype, in the mysterious figure of Abington Scarr, who sells Cowperwood the Baker Street and Waterloo Line. But Scarr's character is said to have been shaped by his time in the colonies, which Dreiser believed to possess vigour that England lacked.[58] Otherwise, every Englishman in *The Stoic* only serves to confirm that 'damn, aristocratic, horse-riding snobs' rule the 'vast established order, which is England'.[59] The lack of vital force upon which Dreiser blamed the alleged failure of the English to achieve anything of note in the Second World War is also a feature in *The Stoic*, in which England's inertia is such that the shareholders of the Metropolitan and Metropolitan District Railways cannot bring themselves, even in the face of the threat posed by Cowperwood, 'to unite the two loop lines, let alone electrify them and operate them as a unit'.[60] On the other hand, the American is 'a man who could, if he wished, become a great *force* in London's affairs' (my italics) with only the interests of those 'millions of Londoners who have never been able to travel beyond the limits of their own neighbourhoods' at heart.[61]

When you recall that Dreiser believed that America and Germany were characterised by the same raw, vital force it can be no coincidence that this benevolent and amoral, invading force arrives on a ship called the *Kaiser Wilhelm der Grosse*.[62]

The political animus on the part of the author that launched his antihero's final financial venture can hardly be considered sympathetically, but it clearly enabled Dreiser to engage with the most striking elements in the history of the creation of the Tube-network, and to thereby complete the trilogy. The Tube-related chapters in *The Stoic* remain valuable because they are an accurate portrayal of how often vicious nationalist energies operated, and continue to operate, in the transactions of an international financial system that should work to render such energies obsolete. They remind us of the extent to which a nation's prestige can become invested in transport infrastructure, the public property that most constitutes the collective sense of national or civic territory, and reveal the consequences that follow when this property threatens to fall into the control of perceived outsiders. When one considers the uproar in the United States, for which there were no rational reasons, following Arab investment in American port facilities, it is clear that the representation of the irrational impulses that animate big business and the resistance to its activities in *The Stoic*, indeed in the Cowperwood trilogy as a whole, remains highly instructive and richly resonant today.[63]

But by far the most important achievement to stem from the writer's unrighteous indignation is the reconciliation of those mighty opposites first perceived in the vital force of the power-station and in the moribund historical order embodied by the Thames. In the final part of the trilogy, Cowperwood is very much aware of his own mortality, feeling 'that he owed it to himself, to his life, to his reputation as representing an immense creative force, a financial figure of the first rank, to go forward and round out his career in some such climactic fashion as this'.[64] The most obvious expression of this impulse is the magnificent tomb he plans for himself and for his wife Aileen, one of the few objects to survive the fall of the Cowperwood estate following the millionaire's death at the Waldorf-Astoria Hotel. His invasion of England is likewise an attempt to shape the circumstances of his own, imminent non-existence, in a country that is shown to be not unlike Nirvana.

First encountered in the course of a visit to Lord Haddonfield's sixteenth-century stately pile Beriton Manor, the immense peacefulness of England is keenly felt by Aileen. 'Oh, to have such a place as this, with the social security and connections of this man!', she thinks. 'Not to have to struggle any more. Forever to be at peace.' Cowperwood, on the contrary, is 'not overawed or even impressed by either title or unearned increment', having 'created wealth and fame for himself'.[65] Similarly, it is his mistress Berenice who views Canterbury, 'that exquisite poem in stone', and thinks 'not only of the faded memories and jumble of hopes and fears that had produced all this, but also of the mystery and immensity of voiceless time and space'.[66] By contrast Cowperwood is said to be 'but little interested in the affairs of bygone men and women, being so intensely engaged with the living present'. Though he is 'somehow touched with the futility of so much that was still so beautiful', Cowperwood perceives little in the Cathedral other than 'the hands and brains, aspirations and dreams of selfish and self-preserving creatures like himself'.[67] In fact, his epiphany only comes towards the end of the book, at the party held by Lord Stane in his manor house, Tresgasal Hall in Cornwall. In this English stately home, Cowperwood at last experiences for himself the peace that prefigures Nirvana – and this is made possible by the peculiar courtesy that Dreiser had noted to be such a marked feature of English life thirty years before. Earlier in *The Stoic*, Berenice remarks that 'Americans haven't the manners or courtesy or tolerance of these people over here', and in response Cowperwood observes that this is because 'Americans have taken an undeveloped continent, and are developing it, or trying to, in a very few years, whereas these people have been working on this little island for a thousand years'.[68] The ancient orderliness of English society has produced a courtesy which might serve as a respite for such world-weary outcasts as Cowperwood and Berenice. England's full potential, in this respect, becomes apparent when the adulterous couple are introduced to the Queen. 'She evinced particular interest in Berenice, and made various inquiries, which, if Berenice had answered them truthfully, might have resulted in great injury to herself, but since she did not, resulted in the wish, expressed by the Queen, that she might see more of her in London; in fact, that she hoped she would be free to attend her next Court reception'.[69] Thwarted by the healthy lack of civility in the United States, where he was deprived the social prestige that should have resulted from his fortune, Cowperwood has thrust himself by main force into the pattern of a moribund society, and has found there, by some cosmic paradox, the peace he has hunted, with his raw force, throughout the trilogy. 'You, this place, these people!' he exclaims to Berenice at Lord Stane's party in Tresgasal Hall. 'This is what I've been seeking all my life!'[70]

The moment of fulfilment marks the reconciliation of the productive force embodied by Cowperwood with the peace later interpreted by Berenice as Nirvana, and is the culmination of the trilogy. Cowperwood has nothing left to live for and is therefore stricken down the moment he has uttered these words with an attack of the illness that soon claims his life. But the epiphany at Tresgasal was to mark the culmination of his creator's career too. For over thirty years Dreiser's life and life work had been frustrated by his intense but ambivalent feelings towards the mighty opposites he had once perceived in an American power-station and an English river. Having finally resolved this conflict (in characteristically paradoxical fashion), Dreiser passed away exactly forty years to the day after the death of the model for the man he had just killed off in *The Stoic*, on 28 December 1945.[71]

The writer had lived just long enough to witness the balance of power in the Anglo-American relationship entirely inverted since the days when American millionaires like Charles Tyson Yerkes had first begun to impact upon Britain's imperial prestige. This radical shift had shaped the turbulent events behind the final volume in the Cowperwood trilogy, and its creator had himself sought to hasten the process, sacrificing much to do so. For these reasons *The Stoic*'s vision of conflict and a lethal reconciliation possesses a significant and shocking position in the history of the relationship between the United States and the British Empire. The novel reveals that the industrial spaces brought about by the latter were peculiarly open to aggressive intervention on the part of writers and businessmen from the nation soon to establish a novel form of empire which eschewed the classic imperial model of military control for an economic and cultural hegemony. The Tube-network is the first of the new spaces to emerge in that Empire of Desire; and Theodore Dreiser was the first to recognise it as such when he gazed at that power-plant in Lots Road and imagined the dynamos whirling.

NOTES

1. J. Hobson, *Imperialism* (1902) (London: George Allen and Unwin, 1905), p. 11.
2. Theodore Dreiser, *A Traveler at Forty*, ed. Renate von Barbeleben (Urbana and Chicago, IL: University of Illinois Press, 2004), p. 209. This is the first complete version of the text to be published. The original edition was published in 1913 in an excessively truncated form, following the threat of legal action from the English publisher Grant Richards. All subsequent references to *A Traveler at Forty* are to this new edition, published by the University of Illinois Press.
3. *Ibid.*, p. 7.
4. *Ibid.*, p. 209.
5. *The Times*, 5 November 1890, p. 12.
6. *Ibid.*
7. Eric Banton, 'Underground Travelling London', in *Living London: Its Work and Its Play. Its Humour and Its Pathos. Its Sights and Its Scenes* (1901–03), ed. George R. Sims, reprinted as *Edwardian London*, 4 vols (London: Village Press, 1990), vol. 4, pp. 60–63, at p. 62.
8. *Railway Times*, 8 November 1890, p. 545.
9. *The Times*, 4 November 1890, p. 13.
10. *The Times*, 5 November 1890, p. 12.
11. *The Times* 4 November 1890, p. 13.
12. *The Times*, 4 September 1900, p. 8.
13. H.G. Wells, 'The Lord of the Dynamos' (1895), in *Complete Short Stories* (London: A. & C. Black, 1987), p. 286.
14. *Ibid.*, p. 291.
15. *Ibid.*, p. 293.
16. *Ibid.*, p. 284.
17. *Ibid.*, p. 286.
18. *The Times*, 4 November 1890, p. 13.
19. *The Times*, 28 June 1900, p. 10.
20. *The Times*, 20 September 1890, p. 6.
21. Christian Wolmar, *The Subterranean Railway* (London: Atlantic Books, 2004), p. 147.
22. Sir H.H. Dalrymple Hay, as reported by Alan A. Jackson and Desmond F. Croome in *Rails Through the Clay: A History of London's Tube Railways* (London: George Allen and Unwin, 1962), p. 66.
23. Sir Arthur Conan Doyle, 'The Adventure of the Bruce-Partington Plans', in *The Original Illustrated 'Strand' Sherlock Holmes: The Complete Facsimile Edition* (Ware: Wordsworth, 1989), pp. 765–781.
24. Baroness Orczy, 'The Mysterious Death on the Underground Railway', in *The Old Man in the Corner* (New York: Dover, 1980), p. 17.
25. *The Times*, 30 October 1901, p. 10.
26. R.D. Blumenfeld, *R.D.B.'s Diary* (London: William Heinemann, 1930), 7 November 1900, p. 132.

27 *Punch*, 11 April 1906, p. 259.
28 *Punch*, 26 June 1901, pp. iii–iv.
29 *Punch*, 6 February 1901, p. 122.
30 *Ibid.*, p. 121
31 *Parliamentary Papers*, Vol. 113 (16 October–3 November 1902), col. 1145, col. 1146, col. 1147.
32 *Ibid.*, col. 1156.
33 Wolmar, p. 180.
34 Insular irritation frequently manifested itself in fury at the supposed bastardisation of the English language perpetuated by the American management. See the *Railway Magazine*, July 1906, and *The Times*, 2 October 1911.
35 See Marc Augé, *Non-Places: Introduction to an Anthropology of Supermodernit*, trans. John Howe (London and New York: Verso, 1995).
36 Dreiser, *A Traveler at Forty*, p. 156.
37 *Ibid.*, p. 14, p. 160.
38 *Ibid.*, p. 156.
39 *Ibid.*, p. 160.
40 *Ibid.*, p. 784.
41 *Ibid.*, p. 86.
42 *Ibid.*, p. 267–268.
43 *Ibid.*, p. 213.
44 *Ibid.*, p. 213.
45 *Ibid.*, p. 92.
46 Jerome Loving, *The Last Titan* (Los Angeles, CA: University of California Press, 2005), pp. 225–226, p. 221.
47 Theodore Dreiser, *Letters of Theodore Dreiser*, ed. Robert H. Elias (Philadelphia, PA: University of Pennsylvania Press, 1959), p. 583.
48 Dreiser, *A Traveler at Forty*, p. 591.
49 See Loving, pp. 385–389.
50 Theodore Dreiser, *The Stoic* (1947) (New York: Apollo Edition, Thomas Y. Crowell, 1974), p. 305. Subsequent references are taken from this edition.
51 *Ibid.*, p. 24, p. 129, p. 165, p. 201, p. 97.
52 *Ibid.*, p. 73, p. 79.
53 *Ibid.*, p. 201.
54 *Ibid.*, p. 126.
55 Dreiser quoted by Loving, p. 230.
56 Dreiser, *The Stoic*, p. 67.
57 *Ibid.*, p. 76.
58 *Ibid.*, p. 199. Abington Scarr appears to be modelled on Whitaker Wright, an Englishman who left the country to make his fortune from mining in the United States, a millionaire by the age of thirty-one. He returned to England in 1899 (where he was assumed to be American) and began to establish a business empire on the back of the Australian gold rush. He also started to build a 'Xanadu' in the style of Citizen Kane, at Lea Park in south-west Surrey, levelling hills and raising new hills, creating a vast artificial lake with

a subterranean conservatory beneath it so that guests could watch fish and swimmers while they smoked. Following bankruptcy in 1900 Wright fled to New York, but was captured, extradited and put on trial in 1904 for larceny. Wright was found guilty and sentenced to seven years' hard labour. But he was never to serve his sentence – having swallowed prussic acid immediately after his removal from the court. See David McKie, 'The Fall of a Midas', *Guardian*, 2 February 2004. Some years later H.G. Wells was to incorporate Whitaker Wright's career into his novel *Tono-Bungay* (1909) – a book that appears to have had a profound influence on the first two novels in the Cowperwood trilogy.

59 Dreiser, *A Traveler at Forty*, p. 14.
60 Dreiser, *The Stoic*, p. 127.
61 *Ibid.*, p. 123, p. 239.
62 *Ibid*, p. 87. Cowperwood's mistress, Berenice, arrives on the *Saxonia*.
63 Heather Timmons, 'Dubai Port Company Sells Its U.S. Holdings to A.I.G.', *New York Times*, 17 February 2006.
64 Dreiser, *The Stoic*, p. 154.
65 *Ibid.*, p. 100.
66 *Ibid.*, p. 138.
67 *Ibid.*, p. 137.
68 *Ibid.*, p. 107.
69 *Ibid.*, p. 210.
70 *Ibid.*, p. 233.
71 Loving, p. 399.

3

BLUEPRINTS FOR BABYLON

Modernist Mapping of the London Underground

Beneath the pavement, sunk in the earth, hollow drains lined with yellow light for ever conveyed them this way and that, and large letters upon enamel plates represented in the underworld the parks, squares, and circuses of the upper. 'Marble Arch – Shepherd's Bush' – to the majority the Arch and the Bush are eternally white letters upon a blue ground. Only at one point – it may be Acton, Holloway, Kensal Rise, Caledonian Road – does the name mean shops where you buy things, and houses, in one of which, down to the right, where the pollard trees grow out of the paving stones, there is a square curtained window, and a bedroom.

(Virginia Woolf, *Jacob's Room*, 1922)[1]

The historian Eric Hobsbawm once made the startling claim that the most original work of avant-garde art produced in Britain between the wars was Harry Beck's Tube Map (Figure 1).[2] In a fascinating essay published in the book *Imagined Londons*, David L. Pike examined the basis for this polemical assertion, and concluded that 'By simplifying the complex network of urban railway lines into a visually pleasing and easily legible map bearing little or no relation to either the experiential or the physical metropolis of London, Beck codified a particularly modernist conception of space'.[3] In Pike's view, the Tube Map fits into a genealogy of modernist space that originated in the mid-nineteenth century with the blue and red and yellow lines Baron Haussmann imposed upon a map of Paris. 'Such projects undertook, in the physical space of Paris, to control the chaotic, ungraspable reality of the modern city through color-coding, straight lines, and diagonal cuts.' Beck's Map achieved this same goal but, in a manner symptomatic of the history of such schemes in London, through its impact upon the representational, rather than physical, space of London.[4] The tangle of subsurface railways, Tube-railways and light railways, built at multiple times and at various levels, had been flattened out and homogenised in a totalising vision of what French sociologist Henri Lefebvre termed *abstract space*, that is to say, the conception of space as a coherent, homogenous whole, which can consequently be bought and exchanged in the same manner as any other commodity: 'Abstract space is a planned and organised space, thought rather than lived, and known conceptually rather than directly experienced'.[5] But while modernist space is typically understood to have had no place for the individual, everyday contingency of the city dweller, the Tube Map can be seen to have perpetuated the possibility of individual reverie even as it constrained its limits – and according to Pike it is to this factor that the phenomenal popularity of the Tube Map is to be attributed. 'While it makes the Tube into a closed system, the map also retains the possibility of such an infinite journey through an alternate London space.'[6] In concluding, Pike speculates that this freedom was facilitated by the primary feature borrowed from its failed predecessors: the bright colours that remain a Victorian trace in Beck's modernist work of art.

> They are, after all, what attracts the eye no matter how many times one has seen it; they are what inspires the reverie that makes the tedious minutiae of each ride bearable; they are, in the end, what remains utopian about this space, just as it is the primary colors in Mondrian's grids that make the space of his paintings mystical as well as rationalizing, and just as, conversely, it was the grayness of postwar architecture that came to epitomize the intolerability of its architectural uniformity.[7]

Thus, in Pike's analysis, the Tube Map owes its success to a variation on mainstream modernist practice – the conservation of an oneiric pleasure in an otherwise abstract, rationally organised space. But the Tube Map is, of course, merely the best-known product of the history of modernist innovation in relation to the London Underground, opening up the possibility that the synthesis embodied by Beck's Map might represent the culmination of a specifically London-based modernist aesthetic. In spite of the fact that the patronage of postimpressionist artists in the inter-war years by the Underground is now common knowledge, having featured in many beautiful, profusely illustrated, books published by Capital Transport, there is surprisingly little criticism on the English avant-garde's intense interaction with the Tube-network. Richard Cork provided only a brief overview in an essay on Eduardo Paolozzi's mosaics at Tottenham Court Road; and, though Michael Saler has produced a remarkable and comprehensive reassessment of the nature and extent of the modernist achievement in England, the focus in his work is very much on the personality of Frank Pick, the executive officer of the Underground and the man behind the company's innovative design and publicity between the First and Second World Wars. This top-down approach tends to perpetuate the fixed ideas about modernism that Pike has shown to occlude alternative approaches to modern urban space. The specific aesthetic that persuaded artists and architects to channel their energies into the transformation of the London Underground is subsumed into that totalising vision pursued by Frank Pick, who was in any case prepared to take up any product, modernist or not, if it proved to be conducive to the unity of the Tube-network. In the present chapter I will establish what the English avant-garde hoped to achieve in participating in the creation of Pick's earthly paradise. I will show that their involvement in this project resulted from a commitment to refashioning the non-places of modernity on a pattern, like that of their continental counterparts, that would impose order on the modern age, but which would preserve that spirit of euphoric reverie that is missing from the schemes of Le Corbusier and Mies van der Rohe. In so doing I reveal common ground for future consideration of the fissiparous modernisms that occupied London at this time, facilitating the ongoing reappraisal of this collective achievement in relation to the international mainstream centred in Paris.

MAPPING THE FUTURIST CITY

'I travelled by a tube train yesterday', enthused F.T. Marinetti in the *Evening News* in March 1912. 'I got what I wanted – not enjoyment, but a totally new idea of motion, of speed.'[8] Since the thought that the Tube might excite such a sensation seems somewhat ridiculous today, these remarks should be put in their historical context. The deep-level Tube-railways were for the most part less than six years old in 1912[9] and were excavated not with the tried-and-tested 'cut-and-cover' technique, whereby a street was uprooted, the railway put in and covered over and the street replaced (the technique used to build the Paris Metro), but with an innovative mechanical shield that forced the tunnels right through the London clay, in a vigorous manner that might have been calculated to please a Futurist. ('I had, of course, travelled by tube [*sic*] in Paris', remarked Marinetti, 'but it was not the same sensation at all'.) In 1912, the Tube-railway was simply the last word in urban transit. Powered by the largest electrical plant in the world at Lots Road, Marinetti's Tube-car would have rattled and swerved through narrow tunnels far below London: the same ecstatic sensation of power and speed he had taken from automobiles, imparted to the Futurist through a mechanism that constituted an entire urban environment!

In Marinetti's view these new sensations were a reproof to the artists of England. 'Turner once painted an engine, but it was a dead engine, just its outside appearance, not its soul, the soul of power and speed.' They had failed to capture the spirit of the modern that Marinetti perceived in the Tube-railways and in the brilliant-hued motor-buses and in the enormous glaring posters. 'London itself is a Futurist City!' Marinetti declared, and the Futurist aesthetic was therefore perfectly adaptable to English conditions. Marinetti himself claimed to be preparing a picture that would show what an English Futurism might look like: 'I have an idea which may be developed by one of our artists. But I cannot tell you any more about it yet.' It is entirely possible that this cryptic remark referred to a painting that has since been lost, called *The Non-Stop*, by C.R.W. Nevinson, shown at the London Group exhibition in March 1914. Although no visual record of the work has survived, Richard Cork has observed that contemporary reviews indicate that the piece was a literal fulfilment of Marinetti's exhortation to the artists of England two years before in *Evening News*. The critic Frank Rutter recalled that the piece was 'a circular picture of the interior of a compartment in a "Tube" in which the vibration of seated figures and strap-hangers was kaleidoscopically expressed in vivid bright colours'.[10] According to the *Westminster Gazette*, *The Non-Stop* was a 'mixture of streaks of light, and fragments of advertisements, and curves, and colour, with lines that suggest straphangers here and there'.[11] And with *The Non-Stop* in mind, P.G. Konody in the *Observer* declared of Nevinson that 'He is obsessed with the idea of speed, devotes himself to conveying by pictorial means the sensation of speed in railway trains, and other means of movement by displacing objects, making them penetrate each other, in fact, making several movements simultaneous'.[12] Having garnered more newspaper attention than any other work at the London Group exhibition, *The Non-Stop* rendered the Tube a key symbol of that spirit of modernity that the English avant-garde would have to engage with if they were to take up the challenge posed by Marinetti.

Such straightforward application of Futurist theory to English material was untypical. In fact, the single instance in which the Tube is used as a symbol for a straightforward Futurist vision of urban modernity occurs in a story by Russian science fiction novelist Yevgeny Zamyatin, written in

1917, shortly after his sojourn in Britain. In 'The Fisher of Men', the Tube is the sweltering belly of an urban organism brimming over with physical vitality, wherein 'the frenzied blood pulsated and sped more frantically along the resounding concrete tubes'.[13] When London is subjected to aerial bombardment it is to the white-tiled catacombs of the Tube that the city's vigorous inhabitants retreat: 'They clung on to the footboards and then with a roar sped along the tubes, without caring where they were going and got off without caring where they were. They crowded together in the delirious underground world with its concrete sky hanging over them, its confusion of caves, staircases, suns, kiosks, vending machines.'[14]

The English avant-garde were to take up the challenge of Marinetti very much on their own terms. In fact, Nevinson's *The Non-Stop* seems to have received so much press coverage only because it was already considered relatively intelligible compared with the latest work shown at the London Group exhibition by artists such as Wyndham Lewis and David Bomberg, who were moving towards the new aesthetic that was soon to be called Vorticism. Lewis believed that Futurism had its points, but as he explained to the incredulous Marinetti in a water-closet one day: 'We've had machines here in England for a donkey's years. They're no novelty to *us*.'[15] In Lewis's view the Futurist's ecstasy at Tube-railways and automobiles could only appear naïve or romantic or even absurd in England, where the impressionism of speed had been memorably expressed by Mr Toad of Toad Hall some years earlier, in that decidedly un-modernist text *The Wind in the Willows* (1908): 'Here to-day – in next week to-morrow! Villages skipped, towns and cities jumped – always somebody else's horizon! O bliss! O poop-poop! O my! O my!'[16] Marinetti's rapturous response to the Tube is precisely a case in point. The Italian had perceived merely a new idea of motion and speed. His English counterparts would have been better informed. As previous chapters have indicated, the creation of the Tube represented a particularly traumatic event in the socio-economic history of Britain, and English artists held few illusions regarding the political significance of the Tube-network. In his mural for the Omega Workshop *Scenes of Contemporary London Life* (1916–17), Roger Fry depicted the Underground as the opposite of everything that Marinetti had celebrated. The mural shows a weary woman slogging up the steps of a Tube-station under the company's roundel. Excessively large and oppressive, the scarlet circle presses down upon the woman's hat, the angular border pushing into her face. Far from being caught up in a new idea of speed, the woman passenger is hampered by the bleak confluence of angular planes produced by wall and stair-rail. And on the blocked-up doorway in the room's wall, Fry painted a railway bookstall, fitted out with newspapers and publicity material (including an advertisement for the

Omega Workshop!), reinforcing the corporate connotations carried by the roundel, and reflecting the fact that the Tube is a heavily mediated space produced by a new global brand of consumer capitalism.[17]

If the English avant-garde were to successfully capture the spirit of the modern world they would first have to take into account their own problematic perception of the space picked out by Marinetti as its embodiment. This struggle surfaces in a cluster of Imagist poems published shortly before the First World War, reproduced by Andrew Thacker in his book *Moving Through Modernity* (2003). As Thacker notes, Marinetti may have influenced the Imagists, but the latter group never quite eulogised machinery in the manner of the Futurists: 'For Imagism transport represented a modern world redolent with anxieties as well as mechanical delights'.[18] F.S. Flint's lyric 'Tube' was first published in *The Egoist* in January 1914, and presents an unspoken address to a second person who examines his or her fellow passengers in vain for a sign, for a light in their eyes. But the passengers are said to sit stolid, lulled by the roar of the train in the Tube, content with the electric light, assured, comfortable, warm: 'this is the mass, inert; / intent on being the mass, / unalarmed, undisturbed'.[19] The speaker's despair is momentarily alleviated by the reflection that he and his companion are a 'spirit that moves'. The phrase possesses a Futurist flavour, and this suspicion is confirmed by the subsequent lines, in which the speaker claims that this spirit of movement is imbued with a transformative potential: 'we leaven the mass, / and it changes; / we sweeten the mass, / or the world / would stink in the ether'. The new idea of motion and speed celebrated by the Italian is resituated in the figure of the intellectual – providing him with the means to humanise non-place. As in Dorothy Richardson's *The Tunnel* (1919), the Underground is depicted by Flint as a psychopathological space that might be rendered a habitat through something rather like Marinetti's urban aestheticism.

Thacker is, therefore, not entirely correct to say that 'What Imagist poetry celebrated in the machinery of the Underground was not necessarily speed, but rather its ability to stage a poetic encounter which could stress fixity amid the vertiginous bustle of modernity'.[20] On the contrary, Flint's Tube is rather like Marinetti's 'dead engine' – a technological space that has to be transformed into a *metaphor* through the moving spirit of the artist. According to the Imagist Richard Aldington, what is new in Flint's poetry is not the objective so much as the rigour of the form through which the poet seeks to reconcile us to a forced existence in a 'gloomy-market-prison-metropolis'.[21] In an article published in *The Egoist* in May 1915, Aldington writes, 'The escape is not to be found in chanting of abstract chimneys and racing automobiles, in ecstatic sentimentalizing over super-aeroplanes and turbines, and such-like romantic balderdash'. Instead, 'there is an escape from artificiality and sentimentality in poetry, and that is by rendering the moods, the emotions, the impressions of a single, sensitized personality confronted by the phenomena of modern life, and by expressing these moods accurately, in concrete, precise, racy language'.[22] And in a poem printed in that same issue, Aldington proceeded to show exactly what he meant. 'In the Tube' begins with the poet-protagonist stumbling into a Tube-car and surveying

> A row of advertisements,
> A row of windows,
> Set in brown woodwork pitted with brass nails,
> A row of hard faces,
> Immobile,
> In the swaying train,
> Rush across the flickering background of fluted dingy tunnel....[23]

These faces once again lack the spirit of movement; and this phenomenon is heightened by their juxtaposition with a material environment so dynamic it even serves to lend these apparitions the illusion of vitality. But where Flint's passengers were merely inert, Aldington's express their antipathy to the poet through their very fixity.

> Eyes of greed, of pitiful blankness, of plethoric complacency,
> Immobile,
> Gaze, stare at one point,
> At my eyes.
>
> Antagonism,
> Disgust,
> Immediate antipathy,
> Cut my brain, as a sharp dry reed
> Cuts a finger.
>
> I surprise the same thought
> In the brasslike eyes:
>
> 'What right have you to live?'[24]

As well as an Imagist, Aldington was a signatory of the Vorticist Manifesto published in the journal *BLAST* in June 1914, and his poem could be interpreted as a polemical illustration of the variation in the Futurist and Vorticist response to the mediated spaces of the modern world. The opposition between the inert passengers content to be carried by the mechanical means of conveyance laid on by their market-prison-metropolis, and the moving spirit of the artist, which refashions modern life in concrete, precise and racy language, occurs in the following passage by Ezra Pound, where he contrasts those who think of man 'as the TOY of circumstance, as the plastic substance RECEIVING impressions' with people like himself who 'think of him as DIRECTING a certain fluid force against circumstance, as CONCEIVING instead of merely observing and reflecting'.[25] As Rod Mengham has demonstrated, this is in fact the fundamental difference between Futurism and Vorticism: 'an antithesis that might help to differentiate between two very different artistic enthusiasms for the machine, the one accompanied by a zest for adrenalin, the other by a respect for order; between the Futurist embrace of sheer dynamism and what we might now think of as the kinematic priorities of Vorticism'.[26]

Rather than feeling awe for the new idea of motion and speed embodied by the Tube, the Vorticists followed Flint in situating the moving spirit of the modern world within the artist: 'In a Vorticist Universe we don't get excited at what we have invented', Lewis, the ringleader of the Great English Vortex, declared in *BLAST*; 'If we did it would look as though it had been a fluke.'[27] Thus, in Lewis's highly experimental play *Enemy of the Stars*, the spirit of movement in the Tube is a symbol for the creativity possessed by the artist. The play is set just south of the Arctic Circle, where the characters Arghol and Hanp live together in a hut at the bottom of a pit. Arghol is the artist: he has fled from the city to the wilderness, and now dwells in abject poverty and is beaten regularly with a character called Hanp, who stands for the hateful mass of humanity that both envies and hates the artist. The Tube is referred to in the stage arrangements: 'A GUST, SUCH AS IS MET IN THE CORRIDORS OF THE TUBE, MAKES THEIR CLOTHES SHIVER OR FLAP, AND BLARES UP THEIR VOICES'.[28] In addition to reinforcing the bleakness of the locality, this reference to the unseen forces at work in the Tube serves to evoke Arghol's 'underworld of energy and rebellious muscles', which ultimately initiates the action of the play.[29] And the Tube was to serve again in Lewis's work as the locus for the violent but potentially redemptive force of the modern artist in a sketch published in *The Egoist* in March 1916 that depicts a young soldier in the Tube:

> This young man was strung to a proud discipline. He was a youthful favourite of Death's something like a sparring partner. He had the equivalent of chewing-gum, too, in the cynical glitter of his face, and his lazy posing.[30]

Lewis compares the 'profound and sinister business' of the soldier to the 'functional existence' of the woman, and concludes that our vigorous world would 'certainly maul the Constellation of Hercules if that misguided organisation should come in our direction'.[31] Given the polemical stance taken by *BLAST 2* against the German Empire, it seems likely that this militant constellation is a symbol for the Kaiser, and the playful, aggressive, disciplined force of the soldier (problematic in the notorious short story 'Cantleman's Spring-Mate') is here a straightforward paradigm for the Vorticist.

But the clearest expression of the Vorticist response to the forces at work in the new urban spaces exemplified by the Tube is to be found in Lewis's short-story collection *The Wild Body* (1927), in an essay called 'The Meaning of the Wild Body'. Seeking to explain his theory of the comic, Lewis remembers how, one day in the Underground, as the train was moving out of the station, 'I and those around me saw a fat but active man run along, and deftly project himself between the sliding doors, which he pushed to behind him'.[32] Although there was nothing especially funny about his face or general appearance, 'his running, neat, deliberate, but clumsy embarkation, *combined with the coolness of his eye*, had a ludicrous effect, to which several of us responded'. According to Lewis it was *the eye* that was the key to the absurdity of the effect:

> It seemed to say, as he propelled his sack of potatoes – that is himself – along the platform, and as he successfully landed the sack in the carriage: – 'I've not much "power", I may just manage it: – yes just!' Then in response to our gazing eyes, 'Yes, that's me! That was not so bad, was it? When you run a line of potatoes like ME, you get the knack of them: but they take a bit of moving.'[33]

This incident perfectly illustrates Lewis's view that the root of the comic is to be found in detachment. The new idea of motion that Marinetti experienced in the Tube was less marvellous than the fact that sacks of potatoes like ourselves should move of our own will at all. The Tube can only reinforce our sense of ourselves as fundamentally material objects: and this can result either in the slavish response of Marinetti and Aldington's passengers, or in the liberating detachment of the fat man who has not made the mistake of identifying 'himself with his machine'.[34] The modern urban space of the Underground therefore possessed, in Lewis's view, the potential for profound human comedy: where Aldington's precise language had tried to neutralise a threat, the polished sides of the Great English Vortex would instead celebrate its comic mastery of the material world.

> We hunt machines, they are our favourite game.
> We invent them and then hunt them down.[35]

The result was a highly cartographic art – one has only to flick through the journal *BLAST* to see that this reordering of the forces at work in the space of the modern world increasingly came to resemble the two-dimensional format of the map or schematic plan. The process is incomplete in the first issue, where the image that best illustrates this tendency is Lewis's 'Plan of War', but by July 1915 'The Island of Laputa' and 'Atlantic City' by H. Sanders, 'Hyde Park' by Frederick Etchells, 'Design for "Red Duet"' by Lewis and 'Rotterdam' by Edward Wadsworth (that is, every image of a modern landscape featured in the second issue) can be seen to evoke the form of the map or diagram. In this respect, the Vorticist aesthetic rather recalls the urban redevelopment projects of the modernist mainstream, which, it will be remembered, set out 'to control the chaotic, ungraspable reality of the modern city through color-coding, straight lines, and diagonal cuts'.[36] In fact, the momentous introduction of Le Corbusier's architectural theories to the English-speaking world might have been a consequence of its perceived resemblance to the Vorticist aesthetic. The English translation of Le Corbusier's *Vers Une Architecture* and *Urbanisme* were both undertaken by the Vorticist Frederick Etchells, who believed that the main thesis of the book translated as *The City of To-morrow and Its Planning* (1929) 'is that such a vast and complicated machine as the modern great city can only be made adequately to function on the basis of a strict order'.[37] Le Corbusier had denied that his theories indulged the mere fancy of some neurotic passion for speed, noting that speed is now a brutal necessity and that Western cities must reorganise these mechanical forces on an orderly rational plan, like that for a 'City of Three Million Inhabitants'.[38] 'This is no dangerous futurism, a sort of literary dynamite flung violently at the spectator', Le Corbusier explained. 'It is a spectacle organized by an Architecture which uses plastic resources for the modulation of forms seen in light'.[39] It must have seemed that Le Corbusier was fulfilling in the field of town planning what the Vorticists had hoped to achieve in graphic art. Etchells' eagerness to resituate Le Corbusier's thought within the framework of the English discourse of the London Underground is signalled by his curious decision to change the word 'metro' to 'tube' throughout and to reproduce a full-page sectional image of the rebuilt Piccadilly Circus Tube Station in his introduction, as an illustration of the menace posed by mechanised forces lacking in organisation.

But having remarked this shared emphasis on mapping, one should note that the effect the Vorticists hoped to achieve was rather different to that which Le Corbusier sought with his City of Three Million Inhabitants. For, if the Vorticists rejected the Futurism of Marinetti, they were equally unsatisfied with the lifeless formalism that they believed characterised the Cubism which inspired Le Corbusier: 'Picasso's structures are not ENERGETIC ones, in the sense that they are very static dwelling houses', wrote Lewis. 'They are inappropriate in the construction of a man, where however rigid the form may be, there should be at least the suggestions of life and displacement that you get in a machine.'[40] As Andrzej Gasiorek observes (in an essay that contrasts Lewis's views on the role modernist architecture should play in regenerating society with Le Corbusier's), if Lewis argues in favour of reordering and regulating life, he also fears that the process of rationalisation may have dystopian consequences, and speculates that society 'might become as mechanical as a tremendous insect world, all our awakened reason entirely disappeared', that we might be 'overpowered by our creation'.[41] In contrast, as Paul Edwards notes, the typical Vorticist design was not directly transferable to architecture: 'To be true to the two-dimensional multivalency of the pictures, the architecture would need its own form of three-dimensional multivalency, preserving the pictures' suggestion of multiplying life's possibilities instead of imposing on the user of the building a univalent experience'.[42] According to Edwards, where the International Style was solemn, uniform and closed, a Lewisian architecture would have been zestful, pluralistic and open, 'would have as its aim to increase gusto and belief in life, to use our inventions to enjoy all the possibilities of organic life experienced by other species without being reduced to animal or mechanical functionalism'.[43] In calling for the forces that constitute the modern metropolis to be reorganised in line with the brash, colourful, open-ended forms developed by the Vorticists, in *BLAST* and *The Caliph's Design* (1921), Lewis's primary objective was to enhance the oneiric urban pleasures celebrated by Marinetti, which would turn out to have no place in the functional International Style.

'SETS FOR A MOVIE ABOUT BABYLON'

Lewis believed the Vorticist movement should aim for nothing short of a physical reordering of the visible part of the modern world. 'A man might be unacquainted with the very existence of a certain movement in art, and yet his life would be modified directly if the street he walked down took a certain shape, at the dictates of an architect under the spell of that movement, whatever it were', he noted in 1922 in his journal *The Tyro*.[44]

'To take a small example, the posters on the hoardings and in the tubes to-day would not be quite what they are ... if painters and draughtsmen in their studios had not done paintings ... of a certain type, during the last ten years.'[45] In Lewis's opinion this programme of renewal would do well to begin with the reinvention of commercial art, particularly the commercial art that appeared in the Tube: 'if Tube Posters, Magazine Covers, Advertisement and Commercial Art generally, were ABSTRACT, in the sense that our paintings at present are, they would be far less harmful to the EYE, and thence to the minds, of the Public'.[46] Lewis had intuitively understood that our day-to-day experience of modernity is heavily mediated by corporate images and text, and believed that, in imposing their orderly aesthetic upon the medium of the advertisement, the Vorticists could move very far very quickly towards the production of a space conducive to cultural revolution.

Of course, the reordering of the Tube would possess a particular symbolic resonance for the Vorticists – as it would constitute a final victory over the Futurist city in the very space that Marinetti had declared a paradigm of the modern world. By the time Lewis published *The Caliph's Design*, the Tube's status as such in the discourse of the English avant-garde had been confirmed time and time again by those writers who wished to express their own view on the proper relationship that should exist between the space of modernity and the art of the moderns. Perhaps the most notable instance occurs in T.S. Eliot's famous review of *Sacre du Printemps*, published in *The Dial* in 1921. Eliot was careful to include the 'roar of the underground railway' among the 'barbaric cries of modern life' that Igor Stravinsky had related to the rhythm of the steppes and transformed into music. Since this emphasis on 'interpenetration and metamorphosis' has been interpreted as an important preliminary to the mythic method of *The Waste Land*, it is interesting to note that in praising this reorganisation of modern barbarity into a formally ordered composition, Eliot is merely echoing a central element in the Vorticist aesthetic.[47]

In fact, the symbolic resonance of the Tube for self-consciously modern writers and artists was such a commonplace that it was even subjected to satire in Aldous Huxley's *Crome Yellow* (1921). In this novel, the monstrous intellectual Mr Scogan explains that he prefers the modern style of painting because he likes to see pictures from which nature has been completely banished – exclusively the product of the human mind – and this is why he always chooses to travel by Tube.

> For, travelling by bus, one can't avoid seeing, even in London, a few stray works of God – the sky, for example, an occasional tree, the flowers in the

window-boxes. But travel by Tube and you see nothing but the works of man – iron riveted into geometrical forms, straight lines of concrete, patterned expanses of tiles. All is human and the product of friendly and comprehensible minds. All philosophies and all religions – what are they but spiritual Tubes bored through the universe! Through these narrow tunnels, where all is recognizably human, one travels comfortable and secure, contriving to forget that all round and below and above them stretches the blind mass of earth, endless and unexplored. Yes, give me the Tube and Cubismus every time....[48]

However, it must have appeared far from probable that the Vorticists would in fact have the chance to make over this richly resonant space in line with their aesthetic. Frank Pick, the publicity manager for the Underground Group, had certainly achieved something of a reputation for innovative design. Pick had commissioned the radical sans serif typeface and the roundel for the station signs (which subsequently became one of the earliest corporate logos) from typographer Edward Johnston. He had ventured into the hitherto disreputable poster industry, commissioning posters from E. McKnight Kauffer and F. Gregory Brown. But Pick's interest in modern art had hitherto extended no further than the Impressionists. Moreover, the vast bulk of the pictorial material he had commissioned prior to the end of the First World War was in exactly that sentimental style of poster art (by Frank Brangwyn and his ilk) that Lewis had attacked in *BLAST* and *The Caliph's Design*: 'the sugary couple on the walls of the Tube, that utter their melancholy joke and lure you to the saloons of the Hackney Furnishing Company'.[49]

But set aside for one moment the style in which such early posters were produced, and one can see much the same preoccupation with movement, modernity and mapping that had so preoccupied the avant-garde. The emphasis upon movement and modernity is particularly evident in two posters by Charles Sharland: *Light, Power and Speed* (1910) depicts new trains brought into use following the electrification of the system in 1905, while *Paddington New Station* (1913) presents a sectional image of the first moving staircase in Britain, introduced at Earl's Court Station in 1911.[50] And in a famous image by John Hassall an elderly couple ask their way of a policeman who silently jerks a thumb to a map of the system on the wall of a Tube-station.[51] As Michael T. Saler shows, Pick believed London was a terrifying sprawl, and sought to promote a public image of the Tube-network as an integrated entity, in order to achieve in microcosm that organic unity he had failed to find in urban modernity.[52]

Pick's objectives thus had much in common with those of the Vorticist aesthetic. Perhaps Pick realised this when he saw an image by Nevinson on a poster to advertise that artist's exhibition of war paintings in the Tube in 1918. In this image Nevinson's fluid Futurism had hardened into the angular energy that is such a marked characteristic of Vorticist art. The arresting impact of this poster is reflected in the prominent reference to the artist in Walter Bayes' painting of exhausted Londoners sheltering from aerial bombardment in the station at Elephant and Castle called *The Underworld* (1918).[53] However this may be, soon after the appearance of this poster Pick began to commission designs from E. McKnight Kauffer that reflected that artist's intense involvement in the Vorticist movement.

McKnight Kauffer came to England in 1914 and found work with the Underground Group through the commercial artist John Hassall, producing posters that depict rural landscapes near London in a style that combines elements from Van Gogh, Fauvism and Art Nouveau. McKnight Kauffer's engagement with the Vorticist movement first became evident in 1917, following the creation of a striking image called *Flight* (subsequently converted into the poster that launched the *Daily Herald* in March 1919). The first version of this image is in the form of a woodcut, a vehicle favoured by several Vorticist artists, such as Edward Wadsworth and David Bomberg, and the final version perfectly exemplifies the incorporation of the Futurist impressionism of speed into a formal geometric pattern.[54]

In that same spring McKnight Kauffer became secretary to the London Group and produced posters for their exhibitions and for commercial clients that reflected his increasing fascination with Vorticism, such as *Winter Sale at Derry & Toms* and *Vigil the Pure Silk* for Walkers Brothers, and was instrumental in encouraging Wyndham Lewis to resurrect the English Vortex as X Group in 1920.[55] According to Mark Haworth-Booth, the X Group exhibition was 'the last flourish of Vorticism', but while the failure of the X Group certainly marks the end of the Great English Vortex as an organisation, it also heralded the period in which the peculiar aesthetic developed by the Vorticists enjoyed its greatest popularity.[56] In fact, some of the most brilliant, and by far and away the most influential, plastic art in the style came in the years following the fall of the X Group, as Pick permitted former Vorticists to realise their ambitions for the reordering of the metropolis through the patronage of the Underground Group. Not least among these belated works of art were the striking posters wherein McKnight Kauffer found an outlet for his interest in the Vorticist aesthetic. As Lewis later remarked, McKnight Kauffer 'disappeared as it were belowground, and the tunnels of the "Tube" became thenceforth his subterranean picture galleries'.[57]

McKnight Kauffer's *Winter Sales Are Best Reached Underground* (1921) was the first produced for Pick in the Vorticist style, and was described by Roger Fry as a 'fascinating silhouette of dark forms to begin with, and out of these forms gradually disengage themselves hints of the flutter of mackintoshes blown by a gusty wind, of the straining forms pushing diagonally across the driving rain'. According to Fry, this poster marked a move towards abstract form: 'the familiar shapes of such a scene are taken as the bricks to build up a most intriguing pattern'.[58] McKnight Kauffer's Vorticist aesthetic soon manifested itself again in a series to promote various museums commissioned by the Underground Group between 1922 and 1923. Angular patterns convey the inorganic growth of crystal in the poster for the London Museum of Practical Geology and recall images produced by Lewis shortly before the First World War. And as Haworth-Booth observes, the spectacular stylised flames that evoke the Great Fire of London in the poster *London History at the London Museum* are almost certainly derived from Edward Wadsworth's woodcut *Black Country, Blast Furnace* (1918).[59] But the final poster with the title *Winter Sales Are Best Reached by Underground* (1924) (Figure 2) is by far the most successful application of the Vorticist aesthetic to the commercial medium of poster art. Inessentials are stripped from bold blocks of colour held in a tense network of forces. Two female shapes barely sheltered by umbrellas – swept about like the folds of their coats – move between bars of rain that are slanted to strike them; are sustained by curves of brown and red that move the eye on to what seems a Tube-station. In *Winter Sales* McKnight Kauffer perfectly captures the spirit of movement embodied by the metropolis in a colourful two-dimensional plan, thereby enhancing, through the change posters effected in the representational space through which the passenger moved, the element of reverie in travel Underground.

Inevitably, these experiments provoked a ferocious backlash from reactionaries. Following the appearance of the first *Winter Sales* poster, the advertising manager at Pear's, took McKnight Kauffer to task in an attack that seems to have extended to the artist's earlier work. 'Impossible ducks, futurist trees, vermilion grass, and such like absurdities may appeal to what, as I have no wish to be offensive, I will call the "higher thought", but believe me, Sir, those people who live their lives in the ordinary, conventional way, as do the bulk of the general public, need nothing more subtle in a poster than a straightforward appeal to their sense of pleasure, duty, or whatever it be'.[60] The hostility rumbled on throughout McKnight Kauffer's Vorticist period, culminating in the coinage of the term 'McKnightmare' in a trade journal in 1924.[61] This constant criticism may have provoked McKnight Kauffer's retreat into a tamer style. Though it is impossible to tell whether this retreat took place at Pick's instigation or on the artist's own initiative, it is certainly the case that some years were to pass before he again produced posters in as strident a modernist style as that employed in *Winter Sales*.

Fortunately, the advertising manager at Pear's was correct in at least one respect. McKnight Kauffer's Vorticist period had indeed proven very popular with the 'higher thought'. The wry tone in which Evelyn Waugh's Charles Ryder confesses to hanging McKnight Kauffer posters on his college wall in *Brideshead Revisited* (1945) may even suggest that, in the early 1920s, McKnight Kauffer possessed something like the highly paradoxical combination of mass popularity and countercultural cool status currently enjoyed by the street artist Banksy.[62] And this support may well have encouraged McKnight Kauffer to work back towards a modernist style in the posters he produced for the Underground Group from the late 1920s – a style more rigorously oriented to the medium than his early efforts, but which retained that peculiar fusion of mapping and movement that had characterised the Vorticist aesthetic. The most perfect example in this new style is *Power – The Nerve Centre of London's Underground* (1931). In this poster, text and image are integrated into a design wherein a rudimentary representation of the power-station that generated electricity for the network is shown superimposed upon what seems a swirling dynamo about the corporate logo, from which lashes out, sinuous and sinewy, a black- and blue-veined forearm and a fist that strikes a bolt of jagged energy at the word 'Underground'.

The triumph of the Vorticist aesthetic in the Tube opened the medium of the poster to other members of the avant-garde in England. Clive Gardiner, C.R.W. Nevinson, Edward Bawden, Eric Ravilious and Edward Wadsworth, and leading figures with an international profile, such as Man Ray, Zero (Hans Schleger) and Lazslo Moholy-Nagy, were all commissioned to produce posters for the London Underground.[63] And soon other corporations, such as Cunard and Shell-Mex, began to emulate the Underground Group's success, commissioning innovative poster art from McKnight Kauffer throughout the 1930s.[64] Through McKnight Kauffer's Tube-posters, Vorticism achieved an immeasurable impact on the field of commercial art, and on the mediated spaces that are such an important component in the non-places of the modern world more generally. Without the example of McKnight Kauffer, Beck's Tube Map, with its bright colours and orderly abstraction, would have been unthinkable, and such schematic maps have, of course, become an integral element in the non-place.

McKnight Kauffer's success also paved the way for the reordering of the physical space of the metropolis in line with the Vorticist aesthetic – as Pick sought to apply the modernist principles McKnight Kauffer exemplified in poster art to the architectural composition of the city itself. The most highly publicised instance of this process was the fateful decision to commission sculpture from Jacob Epstein, for the Underground Group's headquarters building at 55 Broadway, in 1928. Epstein had been a leading member of the Vorticist movement. As Cork has noted, the sculptor had in fact been instrumental in persuading Ezra Pound that a new initiative in modern British art was worth supporting: 'So far as I am concerned', Pound wrote, 'Jacob Epstein was the first person who came talking about "form, not the *form of anything*"'.[65]

Epstein's sculptures for the Underground Group were to achieve an international exposure unlike that previously accorded to any other work of modernist art produced in Britain. As Henry Moore later observed, 'he took the brickbats, he took the insults, he faced the howls of derision ... and as far as sculpture in this century is concerned, he took them first'.[66] The unveiling of *Night* on 24 May and *Day* on 1 July 1929 provoked a barrage of philistinism and xenophobia that was immediate and ferocious. The *Daily Telegraph*, for instance, described *Night* as 'a great coarse object in debased Indo-Chinese style, representing a creature half-Buddha, half mummy, bearing on its knees a corpse-like child of enormous proportions', and this report was reprinted in newspapers as far away as Melbourne in Australia and Christchurch in New Zealand.[67] The sculpture *Day* was too extreme even for Pick. 'I have only seen pictures of it, and in these I must say it looks awful', Pick confessed in the *Evening Standard*. 'But you cannot get the right perspective by taking it by itself. It must be judged in relation to the whole building, and then I think people will not find fault with it.'[68] The architect Charles Holden himself believed in secret that Epstein had failed to take 'full cognizance of the capabilities of the block to serve for a figure in the round which was my intention', asserting that this resulted in 'the round-shouldered effect to preserve the necessary attachment to the background' and that this 'was obviously a miscalculation on Epstein's part and perhaps a mistake on my part not to have given him more explicit instructions, but it is alive and vigorous like much Mediaeval sculpture and that is what I most value'.[69] Fortunately, both Pick and Holden were prepared to defend *Day* and *Night* in public whatever their private misgivings; the former even threatened to resign if the company directors chose to cut the figures off the building.[70] And the controversy had ultimately served to bring Epstein's work for the Underground Group to the attention of millions: when a failed attempt to 'bomb' *Day* and *Night* with tar and feathers took place in October 1929 this non-event achieved news coverage around the world.

Epstein's two monumental works closely echo the stepped form of 55 Broadway. Each group features a seated figure whose legs suggest the pillars on either side of the door beneath and the first tier of the building, behind which loom the high-rise blocks set back from the street. The seated woman in *Night* is a mother figure, remote and sombre, who supports the head of a male figure lying in her lap, over whom she passes a huge and powerful hand. The seated man in *Day* (Figure 3) is a father figure with a flat fierce face that stares implacably out, who shelters – and seems about to raise – a male child, its head improbably but expressively twisted to face the father, its crotch pushing out at the street, as though rising with the father's massive hands. Contrary to what Holden believed, each sculpture is responsive to the possibilities presented by its environment. *Day* is flattened towards the front to take full advantage of the noon sun: the figures stand apart from the façade, the effect of their mass amplified by the light, the outline unbroken by shadow. The rounded back serves to emphasise the volume, the latent power of the father figure, when the sculpture is viewed from an angle. Combined with the child's recessive chest, and the forward thrust of the father's arms, the sculpture seems to have swollen open to the sun, as though the father figure's back were some tremendously thick, stony husk. *Night* is also very well suited to its situation: positioned on the north side, banished from sunlight, the sculpture is stained now with streaks of moisture and tarnished with patches of moss and lichen that lend the piece a fitting atmosphere of human neglect and inhuman vitality. To have 'stuck' any group on 55 Broadway that paid no regard to Holden's design would have produced 'a very restless effect', Epstein explained to the *Manchester Guardian*.[71] Epstein's sculptures therefore interpret the purpose of the headquarters building for the Underground Group – and what they show are elemental, godlike figures that rouse and lay to rest. Epstein revealed that he had first considered representing the traffic moving in and out of stations, and his final work clearly conveys the powerful, pervasive and parental control the Underground Group had assumed in the life of the capital.

The sculptures of the Four Winds by Eric Gill, Eric Aumonier and Henry Moore, high above *Day* and *Night*, serve to reinforce this message. Facing the four points of the compass, the figures emphasise the totalising cathedral-like element in the headquarters building, which, with its cruciform plan, immediately opposite Westminster Abbey, is at once in continuity and in conflict with that embodiment of English history. Though Holden later claimed that the cruciform plan was purely functional, permitting the pedestrian to cut across the site, the monumentality was surely a factor – as Sir William Holford observed – or why the masonry cladding when he might have chosen to highlight his functional steel-frame with glass curtain-walls?[72] With the headquarters building, Holden re-enacted the cultural *tour de force* effected by the English cathedral, but through an architecture of horizontal bands and small vertical setbacks that evoked the Babylonian ziggurat or the bristling energy of the New York skyline: the *Evening News*, for instance, thought 55 Broadway 'perhaps the nearest approach to a skyscraper in London'.[73] Similarly, while Holden commissioned avant-garde sculptors who would celebrate the Tube's modernity, power and speed, he insisted that Epstein carve directly onto the building, after the practice in the Middle Ages. Thus, 55 Broadway is the culmination of an astonishing, London-based variation on the modernist aesthetic. The cathedral skyscraper embossed with the four winds, with day and night, expresses a harmonious totality, a mastery of time and space, even as it evokes the Futurist city praised by Marinetti and the atavistic urban fantasy Lewis had wanted to capture in his plans for a city that would have looked like 'sets for a movie about Babylon'.[74]

In fact, Holden had come as close as conceivably possible to realising Lewis's ambition to transform the architectural space of modernity in a style congruent with the Vorticist aesthetic. Holden had worked with Epstein when the two collaborated on the building for the British Medical Association: he would therefore have been aware of his associate's involvement with the Vorticist movement and must have read its pronouncements on the future of architecture with interest. However that may be, it is clear that Holden evolved a singular architectural style that is rather more closely related to the spirit of McKnight Kauffer's poster art, for instance, than to the constructions of the Bauhaus (Figure 4). Though his stations on the Morden extension are in the International Style previously little known in England, they possess a historical and topographical resonance absent from the universalist designs of the European mainstream. The folding screens that bear the corporate logo are framed by façades built not in concrete but in Portland stone, a building material possessing historic associations with London. And the station buildings on the extensions to Cockfosters and Uxbridge follow a similar procedure. These functional box-like structures, with their enormous square windows, might have been created by Le Corbusier had they not been constructed in the beautiful brick common to southern England. This humane modern architecture is probably inspired by the fusion of German Bauhaus and American Organic Architecture practised by the Dutch modernist Willem Dudok, but other elements in these stations remain hard to explain. Holden's supposedly functional station architecture is invested with the historically resonant and the futuristically fantastical. Medieval stained glass, wheels with leaf springs, narrow, fin-like towers, a spire like an electrical tesla coil, the figure of an archer like a car's hood ornament by Eric Aumonier – each emphasises the magic of the machine-age metropolis, in a manner that evokes a specifically Vorticist aesthetic.

This fantastical functionalism found full expression in the rebuilt Piccadilly Circus. Though entirely practical, facilitating passenger flow by opening out cramped passages into a single circular space, Holden's subsurface interchange still fires the imagination. The futuristic ambulatory is plated in Travertine marble, the building material synonymous with Rome; over the escalators a map of the world, painted by Stephen Bone, highlighted the territories controlled by the British Empire; and a clock on a wall showed the time in metropolitan centres throughout the world.[75] The *New York Times* declared that the renovated space had been 'utterly transformed by modern architecture and modern art into a scene that would make a perfect setting for the finale, or indeed, the opening chorus of an opera'.[76] With this triumphant reordering of an architectural space at the heart of the metropolis, in a form that combined functional and fantastical, Holden had, in fact, fulfilled the final objective in the Vorticist manifesto:

> WE WHISPER IN YOUR EAR A GREAT SECRET.
> LONDON IS NOT A PROVINCIAL TOWN.
> We will allow Wonder Zoos. But we do not want the
> GLOOMY VICTORIAN CIRCUS in
> Piccadilly Circus.
> IT IS PICCADILLY'S CIRCUS![77]

THE ART OF BEING RULED

By the mid-1930s the English avant-garde had transformed the London Underground into Europe's pre-eminent modernist space, avoiding the pitfalls that awaited the grand plans of Le Corbusier and Mies van der Rohe, at a time when these, for the most part, remained on the drawing board. The brightly coloured but rational map, the fanciful but forceful commercial art, the playful but functional architecture: according to any criteria, the Vorticist project in the Tube must be considered a success that put the achievement of the Parisian Purists into the shade. According to any criterion, that is, other than that of the movement itself. The Vorticists had really believed that the revolution of material reality would bring about a cultural revolution, transforming the way in which the public perceived and interacted with the modern world. As Lewis himself later acknowledged, in this they had not been correct. 'Though one Kauffer does not make an Underground summer, poster art is somewhat more alive than it was, and a few shop-fronts, here and there, give a "modern" flavour', he remarked, in an influential review of the Vorticist achievement in Britain:

'*We are the first men of a Future that has not materialized.* We belong to a "great age" that has not "come off". We moved too quickly for the world. We set too sharp a pace. And, more and more exhausted by War, Slump, and Revolution, the world has *fallen back*.'[78] In the essay 'Plain Homebuilder: Where Is Your Vorticist?' (1934), Lewis speculates that the reason for this failure might be that, though they had tried hard to preserve the element of utopian reverie that found no place in the International Style, Vorticist art had still lacked sufficient sensual appeal, resulting in interiors 'obviously designed for a particularly puritanic athlete of robotic tastes, with an itch for the rigours of the anchorite, and a sentimental passion for metal as opposed to wood'.[79] But, as Andrzej Gasiorek has convincingly argued, the real fault is surely that, in spite of its sane and humane aesthetic, Vorticism ultimately shared Le Corbusier's conception of the modern city as a problem, envisaging 'a scenario in which *design* (order) was pitted against the *everyday* (formlessness) on which it sought to bestow meaning'.[80] For all its attention to the contingency of the passenger, the transformation of the London Underground was still a totalising plan imposed on the capital by a central authority – a design caliph – which in rationalising only served to reinforce the nascent spaces of consumer capitalism. Henri Lefebvre's critique of the International Bauhaus can therefore equally be applied to the Vorticist movement: 'The curious thing is that this "programmatic" stance was looked upon at the time as both rational and revolutionary, although in reality it was tailor-made for the state – whether of the state-capitalist or the state-socialist variety'.[81] Lewis later confessed that, at the time he wrote *The Caliph's Design*, he had not appreciated the extent to which the 'hideous foolishness of our buildings, our statues, our interiors' was matched by the 'hideous foolishness' of our social and economic life: 'nor how impossible it is, until that core of bottomless foolishness is altered for the better, to acquire the kind of gay intellectual shell that I wished'.[82] In creating a bright, new and enchanting capital, the Vorticists had produced the blueprint for a Babylon that was more functional than if had it been functionalist. They had perpetuated the spaces of the market-prison-metropolis. They had formulated the art of being ruled.

This might explain why the English avant-garde persisted in depicting the Tube as a symbol for an as yet unredeemed modern world. In W.H. Auden's 'Letter to Lord Byron' (1937), it is 'The bowler hat who strap-hangs in the Tube / And kicks the tyrant only in his dreams, / Trading on pathos, dreading all extremes'.[83] In Aldous Huxley's *Point Counter Point* (1928), a naïve young member of the intelligentsia called Walter Bidlake is shown to approve the nationalisation of the mines, but is unable to stomach sitting next to an elderly man who spits on the floor of the Tube and smokes a pipe that stinks: 'Walter looked away; he wished that he could personally like the oppressed and personally hate the rich oppressors'.[84] And as Hugh Kenner pointed out in *The Mechanic Muse*, it is the Tube that T.S. Eliot turns into a metaphor for descent to the Underworld in *Four Quartets* – drawing upon his own experience travelling from South Kensington to Russell Square everyday well into his mid-forties: 'To change from the one line to the other he had to "descend lower," as he puts it in *Burnt Norton*. One way down was by spiral stairs, on which you turned and turned the narrow gyre in half-darkness.' Or he could take the lift, an abstention from movement, while the world moved, 'in appetency on its metalled ways'.[85] In the Underground, Eliot had found a space of alienation that could provide him with a modern objective correlate for the mystical 'way of negation':

> Or as, when an underground train, in the tube, stops too long
>   between stations
> And the conversation rises and slowly fades into silence
> And you see behind every face the mental emptiness deepen
> Leaving only the growing terror of nothing to think about ...
> I said to my soul, be still, and wait without hope
> For hope would be hope for the wrong thing; wait without love
> For love would be love of the wrong thing; there is yet faith
> But the faith and the love and the hope are all in the waiting.
> Wait without thought, for you are not ready for thought:
> So the darkness shall be the light, and the stillness the dancing.[86]

Descent into this unredeemed modern space is staged again and again in texts such as Louis MacNeice's *Autumn Journal* (1939), Louis-Ferdinand Céline's *Guignol's Band* (1945) and George Orwell's *Keep the Aspidistra Flying* (1936). The following passage from Jean Rhys's nightmarish novel *Good Morning, Midnight* (1939) perfectly illustrates the impasse in which members of the English avant-garde found themselves – trapped by a space that a modernist aesthetic had helped to shape.

> I am in the passage of a tube station in London. Many people are in front of me; many people are behind me. Everywhere there are placards printed in red letters: This Way to the Exhibition, This Way to the Exhibition. But I don't want the way to the exhibition – I want the way out. There are passages to the right and passages to the left, but no exit sign. Everywhere the fingers point and the placards read: This Way to the Exhibition.... I touch the shoulder of the man walking in front of me. I say: 'I want the way out.'[87]

But by far the most striking of these descents into the Underground as Underworld takes place in Virginia Woolf's *The Waves* (1931), when Jinny enters the renovated interchange at Piccadilly Circus. Since the revisionist postcolonial reading performed by Jane Marcus, this remarkable novel has been read as a subversive narrative about culture-making, which exposes the false premises that underpin fascism at home and imperialism abroad.[88] Having uncovered modernist involvement in this space of descent, I can take Marcus's interpretation one step further. In comparing the great avenues that meet beneath Eros to sanded paths of victory driven through jungle, Jinny is implicating the modernist reorganisation of the Tube in the imperial project.[89] The crowds moving through the ambulatory are characterised as a 'triumph of life' that even the committed consumerist Jinny cannot but feel terrifying, if only for an instant: 'I admit, for one moment the soundless flight of upright bodies down the moving stairs like the pinioned and terrible descent of some army of the dead downwards and the churning of the great engines remorselessly forwarding us, all of us, onwards, made me cower and run for cover'.[90] This is the perception of the Tube expressed in the oil painting *Underground* by Gladys Hynes, in which the bowler-hatted and blank-faced commuters are mere appendages to the Machine.[91] It would seem that many modernists in England shared Lewis's belief that the Vorticist project in the London Underground had consolidated rather than revolutionised the non-places of the modern world, sustaining the nineteenth-century imperium and paving the way for our twenty-first-century economic emporium.

> Look how they show off clothes here even under ground in a perpetual radiance. They will not let the earth even lie wormy and sodden. There are gauzes and silks illumined in glass cases and underclothes trimmed with a million close stitches of fine embroidery. Crimson, green, violet, they are dyed all colours. Think how they organize, roll out, smooth, dip in dyes, and drive tunnels blasting through the rock. Lifts rise and fall; trains stop, trains start as regularly as the waves of the sea. This is what has my adhesion. I am a native of this world, I follow its banners.[92]

Far from being beaten by the extraordinary impasse brought about by the Vorticist transformation of the London Underground, Lewis was among the first to move beyond the centralising impulse behind *The Caliph's Design* in order to call for a revolt against the strictures of the modernist spaces produced by the Vortex: 'You should not be afraid of *desecrating* these spotless and puritanic planes and prudish cubes; and it is up to you, after all, to refuse to be made into a sedate athletic doll – into an exhibit, like a show-piece for a lecturer'.⁹³ In this startling passage from 'Plain Homebuilder: Where Is Your Vorticist?', Lewis sets out the practice of *détournement*, the playful misuse of functional space, nearly thirty years before it received attention in the theory of Michel de Certeau, Guy Debord, Raoul Vaneigem and Henri Lefebvre. ⁹⁴ As Gasiorek observes in relation to this passage, Lewis is encouraging the consumer to resist the control of the architect and designer by showing disrespect for their pristine blueprints: 'The habitable is now associated (whisper it) with the disorder of the everyday, which refuses the cold sublime of Mies, the technocratic purism of Le Corbusier, and the authoritarian fantasy of Lewis's own caliph'.⁹⁵ In insisting on the everyday as the site of the unplanned and open-ended creativity of the consumer, Lewis had initiated a new phase in the struggle to make a home of the modern world.

THOSE THINGS THAT GO TO MAKE UP WHAT WE CALL 'LIFE'

From the invasion of the station platforms in the Blitz depicted by Henry Moore and Bill Brandt, to the station busking celebrated by Eduardo Paolozzi, to the graffiti art memorialised by novelist John Healy – every subsequent desecration of the ordered space of the network has found champions among writers and artists in the modernist tradition. Even Metroland, an environment formerly reviled by the English intelligentsia, found champions who recognised it, at last, as a significant triumph over the non-places of the modern world. But in the final section of this chapter I would like to draw attention to a modernist masterpiece produced in the inter-war period that already seems to exhibit the shift in perspective prescribed by Lewis.

Anthony Asquith's *Underground* (1928) is an innovative motion picture that shares the Vorticist preoccupation with the reordering of urban impressions of speed into a rigorously stylised aesthetic. But this little-known piece is also a celebration of cinema's long love affair with urban transport. The long opening shot, in which a point of light opens up in the darkness like the iris of a camera to reveal a Tube-station rushing to fill the screen, echoes the Lumières' short of a train arriving and (swiftly followed by a shot in which elevator steps slide up over the screen like a film reel) serves to impress forcibly upon the viewer the intimate bond that exists between the motion picture and the railroad. As Lynne Kirby notes, 'As a machine of vision and an instrument for conquering space and time, the train is a mechanical double for the cinema and for the transport of the spectator into fiction, fantasy, and dream. It is a metaphor in the Greek sense of the word: movement, the conveyance of meaning.'[96] Kirby speculates that directors were quick to seize on the train for the 'sense in which the railway journey provides a contained space and time, a special "nowhere" outside the sphere of normal rules and codes of conduct'.[97] And this observation seems particularly suggestive, given the formative role the Tube has played in the development of the *non-lieu*. In associating the camera with the train, the elevator with the film reel, Asquith implied that the modern medium of the motion picture can best represent and make meaningful a non-place that more traditional art forms had failed to comprehend. Shots that recall the primitive short films of sensation and spectacle are incorporated into a piece with the haunting symbolism of Expressionist cinema. Importing a lighting specialist from Germany, and choosing a lead actress 'with the face of a Modigliani', Asquith produced what is perhaps Britain's single important contribution to modernist cinema in the silent period.[98]

But what sets the film apart from other modernist representations of the Underground by English writers and artists in the inter-war period is the unprecedented interest evinced in the everyday lives of the people who use the space: 'The "Underground" of the Great Metropolis of the British Empire, with its teeming multitudes of "all sorts and conditions of men," contributes its share of light and shade, romance and tragedy and all those things that go to make up what we call "life"'. It is for this reason, the opening title card explains, that the Underground is the setting for a 'story of ordinary work-a-day people'. The sensational shot that opens the movie is thus followed with an intimate sequence set in a packed Tube-car that attempts to convey something of the subtle interactions that take place between passengers while they travel to work.

There is too little space for a full account of Asquith's extraordinary motion picture. But the scene in which Bill and Nell fall in love (following the shot of the elevator steps rising like a film reel) merits special mention: walking in opposite directions, the wrong way up parallel elevators, half-way along the shaft, Bill and Nell appear to be holding back time as they flirt over the barrier as well as gloriously abusing the most functional of spaces in a Tube-station. Later, as they stand next to one another apart from the crowd, innovative lighting reveals the passion seething beneath their humdrum conversation. The camera pans back to show us what they would like to be doing – when they part, Bill and Nell leave their titanic shadows locked in a fierce kiss.

And the finale is of particular interest. At this crucial moment in the film, Asquith once again chose to mount the camera on a mechanism for movement (in this instance, a lift), thereby transforming the transport system into an optical instrument for observing the capital that serves to heighten rather than marginalise our imaginative and emotional engagement with the space; and thereby realising that experience of the city that the Vorticists had sought to capture and refine in their art. In this, his first solo project, Asquith had proven that film might achieve that end for which more traditional media such as painting had struggled so hard: *Underground* testifies to the unprecedented power of an effortlessly *kinematic* art.[99]

NOTES

1 Virginia Woolf, *Jacob's Room* (1922) (London: Hogarth Press, 1980), pp. 65–66.
2 Eric Hobsbawm, *Behind the Times: The Decline and Fall of the Twentieth-Century Avant-Gardes* (New York: Thames and Hudson, 1999), p. 39.
3 David L. Pike, 'Modernist Space and the Transformation of London', in *Imagined Londons*, ed. Pamela K. Gilbert (New York: State University of New York Press, 2002), p. 101.
4 *Ibid.*, pp. 104–105.
5 *Ibid.*, p. 107.
6 *Ibid.*, p. 112.
7 *Ibid.*, pp. 112–113.
8 *Evening News*, 4 March 1912.
9 The earliest tube-railway was created at least five years later than the first true automobile.
10 Quoted in Richard Cork, *Vorticism and Its Allies* (London: Arts Council of Great Britain, 1974), p. 19.
11 *Westminster Gazette*, 6 March 1914, p. 5.
12 *Observer*, 8 March 1914, p. 7.
13 Yevgeny Zamyatin, *Islanders and The Fisher of Men* (1917), trans. Sophie Fuller and Julian Sacchi (Edinburgh: Salamander Press, 1984), p. 84.
14 *Ibid.*, p. 90.
15 Wyndham Lewis, *Blasting and Bombardiering* (1937) (London: John Calder, 1982), p. 34.
16 Kenneth Grahame, *The Wind in the Willows* (1908) (London: J.M. Dent, 1993), p. 39.
17 Roger Fry, *Omega Mural* for Arthur Rack, 4 Berkeley Street, London 1916. See Richard Cork, *Eduardo Paolozzi Underground* (London: Royal Academy of Arts, 1986).
18 Andrew Thacker, *Moving Through Modernity: Space and Geography in Modernism* (Manchester: Manchester University Press, 2003), p. 86.
19 F.S. Flint, 'Poems', *The Egoist*, Vol. 1 (1 January 1914), p. 14.
20 Thacker, p. 86.
21 Richard Aldington, 'The Poetry of F.S. Flint', *The Egoist*, Vol. 2 (1 May 1915), p. 81.
22 *Ibid.*, p. 80.
23 Aldington, 'In the Tube', *The Egoist*, Vol. 2 (1 May 1915), p. 74.
24 *Ibid.*
25 Ezra Pound, 'Vortex', *BLAST 1* (1914), ed. Wyndham Lewis (Santa Rosa: Black Sparrow Press, 2002), p. 153.
26 Rod Mengham, 'From Georges Sorel to BLAST', *The Violent Muse*, ed. Jana Howlett and Rod Mengham (Manchester: Manchester University Press, 1994), p. 40.
27 Wyndham Lewis, 'Our Vortex', *BLAST 1* (1914), p. 148.

28 Lewis, 'Enemy of the Stars', *BLAST 1* (1914), p. 60.
29 *Ibid.*, p. 74.
30 Wyndham Lewis, 'A Young Soldier', *The Egoist*, Vol. 3 (1 March 1916), p. 46.
31 *Ibid.*, p. 46.
32 Wyndham Lewis, 'The Meaning of the Wild Body', in *The Wild Body* (London: Chatto and Windus, 1927), p. 248.
33 *Ibid.*, p. 249.
34 *Ibid.*, p. 249.
35 *Ibid.*, p. 148.
36 Pike, p. 104–5.
37 Le Corbusier, *The City of To-morrow and Its Planning* (1929), trans. Frederick Etchells (New York: Dover, 1987), p. vii.
38 *Ibid.*, p. 190.
39 *Ibid.*, p. 178.
40 Wyndham Lewis, ed., *BLAST 2* (1915) (Santa Rosa: Black Sparrow Press, 2002), p. 44.
41 See Andrzej Gasiorek, '"Architecture or revolution"? Le Corbusier and Wyndham Lewis', in *Geographies of Modernism: Literature, Cultures, Spaces*, ed. Peter Brooker and Andrew Thacker (London and New York: Routledge, 2005), pp. 136–145.
42 Paul Edwards, 'Afterword', in Wyndham Lewis, *The Caliph's Design* (Santa Barbara: Black Sparrow Press, 1986) p. 156.
43 *Ibid.*, p. 158.
44 Wyndham Lewis, *The Tyro*, No. 2 (London: Egoist Press, 1922), p. 5.
45 *Ibid.*, p. 6.
46 Lewis, *BLAST 2*, p. 47.
47 T.S. Eliot, 'London Letter: September 1921', *The Dial*, Vol. 71 (1921), p. 453.
48 Aldous Huxley, *Crome Yellow* (1921) (London: Chatto and Windus, 1974), p. 170.
49 Lewis, *The Caliph's Design*, p. 132.
50 Reproduced in Oliver Green, *Underground Art* (London: Laurence King, 1999), pp. 24–25.
51 Reproduced in Green, pp. 22–23.
52 Michael T. Saler, 'The "Medieval Modern" Underground: Terminus of the Avant-Garde', *Modernism/Modernity*, Vol. 2, No. 1 (January 1995), p. 129.
53 Walter Bayes, *The Underworld* (1918), oil on canvas, Imperial War Museum.
54 See Mark Haworth-Booth, *E. McKnight Kauffer* (London: V&A Publications, 2005), pp. 17–20.
55 *Ibid.*, p. 22.
56 *Ibid.*, p. 26.
57 Lewis, *Blasting and Bombardiering*, p. 212.
58 Quoted in Haworth-Booth, p. 28.
59 *Ibid.*, p. 34 and p. 6.
60 *Ibid.*, p. 36.
61 *Ibid.*, p. 36.

62 'On my first afternoon I proudly hung a reproduction of Van Gogh's Sunflowers over the fire and set up a screen, painted by Roger Fry with a Provencal landscape, which I had bought inexpensively when the Omega Workshops were sold up. I displayed also a poster by McKnight Kauffer and Rhyme Sheets from the Poetry Bookshop, and, most painful to recall, a porcelain figure of Polly Peachum which stood between black tapers on the chimney-piece'. Evelyn Waugh, *Brideshead Revisited* (1945) (Harmondsworth: Penguin, 1951), p. 27.
63 Reproduced in Oliver Green, *Underground Art* (London: Laurence King, 1990), p. 57, p. 64, p. 14, p. 83, p. 108, p. 88, p. 77, p. 76 and p. 85.
64 Haworth-Booth, pp. 72–73 and pp. 76–85.
65 Quoted in Richard Cork, *Jacob Epstein* (London: Tate Gallery Publishing, 1999), p. 34.
66 *Ibid.*, p. 8.
67 Quoted in Stephen Gardiner, *Epstein* (London: HarperCollins, 1993), p. 300.
68 Quoted in Michael T. Saler, *The Avant-Garde in Interwar England* (Oxford: Oxford University Press, 1999), p. 112.
69 Charles Holden, letter to Christian Barman, 19 August 1953, Box 4, AHP 1894–1992, Victoria and Albert Museum, London.
70 Christian Barman, *The Man Who Built London Transport* (North Pomfret, VA: David and Charles, 1979), p. 130.
71 Quoted in Gardiner, p. 296.
72 See Charles Holden, AHP/26/18/1, Box 26, Victoria and Albert Museum, London; and Sir William Holford, 'Charles Holden, Craftsman-Architect', *The Listener*, 19 May 1960, pp. 879–880.
73 *Evening News*, 29 August 1939.
74 Wyndham Lewis, *Rude Assignment* (1950), ed. Toby Foshay (Santa Barbara: Black Sparrow Press, 1984), p. 169.
75 See Saler, *The Avant-Garde in Interwar England*, p. 109.
76 Kathleen Woodward, 'Art Descends into the London Subway', *New York Times Magazine*, 13 October 1929, p. 12.
77 Lewis, 'Manifesto', *BLAST 1*, p. 19.
78 Lewis, *Blasting and Bombardiering*, p. 254.
79 Wyndham Lewis, 'Plain Homebuilder: Where Is Your Vorticist?' (1934), in *Creatures of Habit and Creatures of Change: Essays on Art, Literature and Society, 1914–1956*, ed. Paul Edwards (Santa Rosa: Black Sparrow Press, 1989), p. 284.
80 Gasiorek, p. 143.
81 Henri Lefebvre, *The Production of Space* (1974), trans. Donald Nicholson-Smith (Oxford: Blackwell Publishers, 1991), p. 124.
82 Lewis, *Rude Assignment*, p. 169.
83 W.H. Auden, 'Letter to Lord Byron' (1937), in *Collected Longer Poems* (London: Faber and Faber, 2002), p. 52.
84 Aldous Huxley, *Point Counter Point* (1928) (London: Random House, 2004), p. 16.

85 Hugh Kenner, *The Mechanic Muse* (Oxford: Oxford University Press, 1987), pp. 24–25.
86 T.S. Eliot, 'East Coker' (1940), in *The Complete Poems and Plays* (London: Faber, 1969), p. 180.
87 Jean Rhys, *Good Morning, Midnight* (1939) (London: Penguin, 1969), p. 12.
88 Jane Marcus, 'Britannia Rules the Waves', in *Decolonizing Tradition*, ed. Karen R. Lawrence (Urbana and Chicago, IL: University of Illinois Press, 1992), pp. 136–162.
89 Virginia Woolf, *The Waves* (1931), ed. Gillian Beer (Oxford: Oxford University Press, 1992), p. 160.
90 *Ibid.*, p. 161.
91 Gladys Hynes, *Underground* (c.1925). See Cork, *Eduardo Paolozzi Underground*, p. 30.
92 Woolf, *The Waves*, p. 161.
93 Lewis, 'Plain Homebuilder: Where is Your Vorticist?', p. 285
94 Lefebvre, pp. 167–168.
95 Gasiorek, p. 145.
96 Lynne Kirby, *Parallel Tracks: The Railroad and Silent Cinema* (Exeter: University of Exeter Press, 1997), p. 2.
97 *Ibid.*, p. 242.
98 R.J. Minney, *Puffin Asquith, The Biography of the Honourable Anthony Asquith: Aristocrat, Aesthete, Prime Minister's Son, and Brilliant Film Maker* (London: Leslie Frewin, 1973), p. 39.
99 Mengham, p. 40.

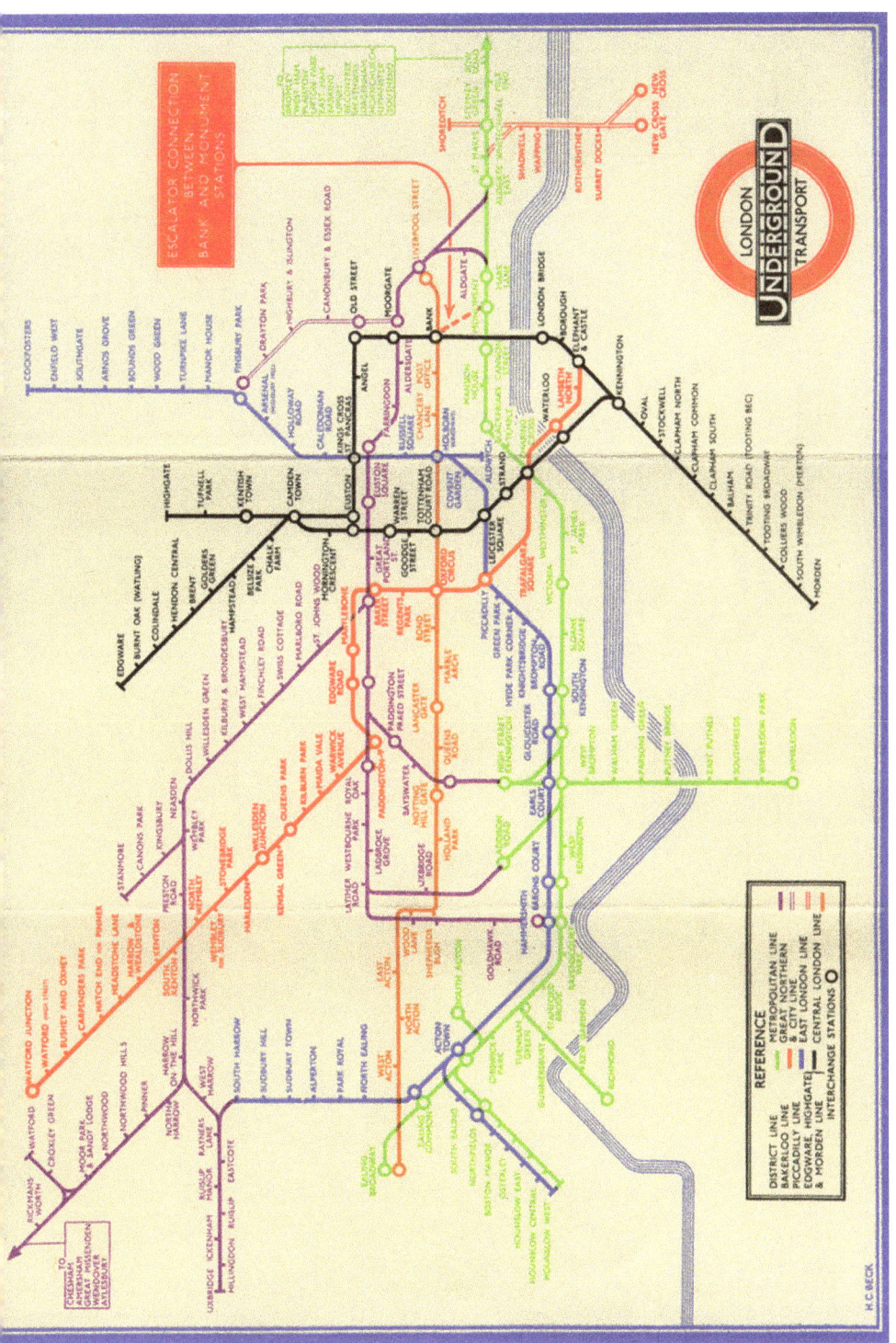

Figure 1. Harry Beck's Tube Map (1933).
© TfL from the London Transport Museum collection.

Figure 2. Poster art by E. McKnight Kauffer: *Winter Sales Are Best Reached by Underground* (1924).
© TfL from the London Transport Museum collection.

Figure 3. Jacob Epstein's sculpture on 55 Broadway, *Day* (1929).
© TfL from the London Transport Museum collection.

Figure 4. Charles Holden's Tube-station at Arnos Grove (1932).
© TfL from the London Transport Museum collection.

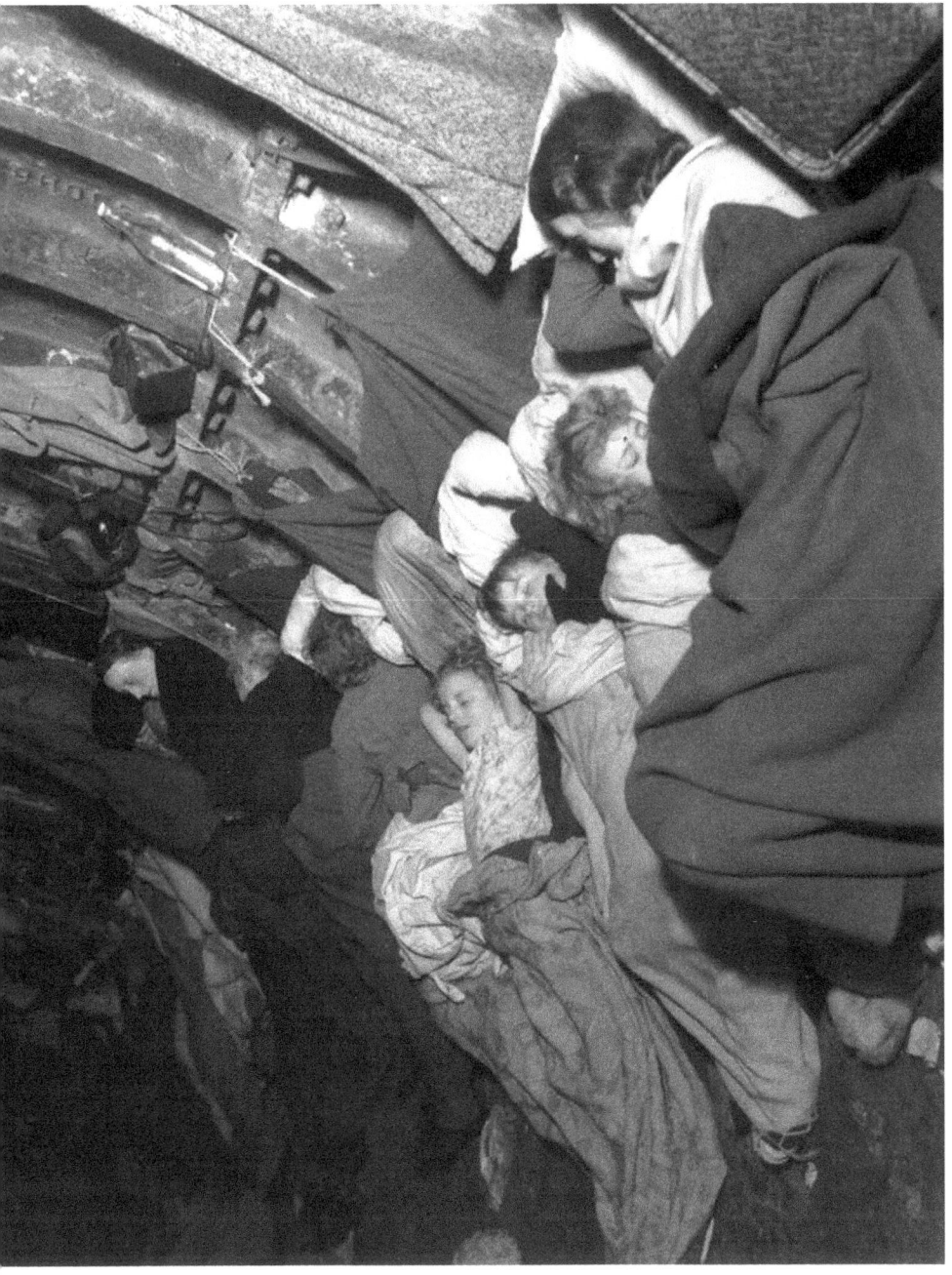

Figure 5. Bill Brandt's photograph of a family sheltering in the Liverpool Street extension (1940).
From the Imperial War Museum Photography Archive, negative number D1578.

Figure 6. M. McNeill's photograph of children sheltering in the Tube during the Blitz published anonymously in the *Evening Standard* in 1940. Hulton Archive, ref. 149606564. © Getty Images.

Figure 7. Henry Moore, *Women and Children in the Tube*, 1940 (HMF 1726). Reproduced by permission of the Henry Moore Foundation.

Figure 8. Henry Moore, *Group of Draped Figures in a Shelter*, 1941 (HMF 1807). Reproduced by permission of The Henry Moore Foundation.

4

MAKING A HOME IN MODERNITY

The Conceptual History of Metroland

'J 'habite Metroland', declares Julian Barnes's protagonist in the novel of that name, explaining that it 'sounded better than Eastwick, stranger than Middlesex; more like a concept in the mind than a place where you shopped'.[1] And this is precisely what Metroland is, as one of the booklets produced by the Metropolitan Railway to promote the region explained: 'Metro-Land is a country with elastic borders which each visitor can draw for himself, as Stevenson drew his map of Treasure Island'.[2] From the start, Metroland has been a territory that exists primarily in the imagination. The moniker 'Metro-land' was coined in 1915 in order to impart integrity to a thin corridor of land that lay to the north-west of London along the Metropolitan Railway In the inter-war years, spacious and leafy housing estates began to be built in this region, constructed in a syncretic style, incorporating elements from Tudor, Queen Anne and Art Nouveau. And the word remains evocative long after it lost this tenuous connection with reality, flourishing in poetry and fiction, and entering the language as a 'generic expression of suburban life', representative of at least one-third of the total housing-stock in Britain immediately prior to the Second World War, the archetypal commuter belt.[3] But, in fact, 'Metro-land' represents a paradoxical combination – a locality, a region, a place that is defined entirely by its relation to a non-local transit system – a non-place. In previous

chapters I have argued that the London Underground was taken by the avant-garde to be a symbol of the exciting new mediated spaces brought into being by the rise of international circulatory networks. To study Metroland is, then, to consider how people have managed to inhabit a space that would not seem to lend itself to habitation; it is to examine how and with what success people have attempted to make a home in modernity. The present chapter will attempt to chart this virtual space, considering its antecedents in the fiction of H.G. Wells and G.K. Chesterton, exploring its unrelentingly negative portrayal in the inter-war years – as a failure to meet modernity with modernism – and then looking at the subsequent reassessment of the Underground garden suburb's success in meeting its own objectives following the Second World War, with special attention to Julian Barnes's first novel, *Metroland* (1980).

BEDFORD PARK IN THE YEAR 12203AD

The critic Samuel Hynes once described the Morlocks in H.G. Wells's *The Time Machine* (1895) as the best representation of the lower classes in turn-of-the-century fiction.[4] Given that the Morlocks are subhuman mutant cannibals, this view has always seemed to me utterly incomprehensible! But few would choose to question the Time Traveller's identification of the Morlocks as the brutalised progeny of the working classes – that is to say, the Time Traveller's assertion that the gradual widening of the social difference between capitalist and labourer is 'the key to the whole position'.[5] As a result, *The Time Machine* has become an important text for those critics interested in the vertical city. In her seminal work *Notes on the Underground*, Rosalind H. Williams interpreted the book as a classic example of a journey into the social underworld, 'a movement from the comfortable but deceiving social surface down into the grim, dark world of the underclass'.[6] But this interpretation has recently been challenged by David L. Pike, who has observed that the Time Traveller's final explanation is subject to the same failing as the rest, that is, his failure to explore the space thoroughly before coming to a conclusion: 'For all his pioneering spirit, he proves unable to draw any knowledge from his journey to the future, treating it instead as any tourist would'.[7] The Time Traveller is perfectly open about this – he insists upon his previous hermeneutic failures and states that this final hypothesis is as likely to be as erroneous as the rest: 'It may be as wrong an explanation as mortal wit could invent'.[8] He even seems to anticipate the criticism levelled at his story by Pike, pointing out that 'while such details are easy enough to obtain when the whole world is contained in one's imagination, they are altogether inaccessible to a real traveller amid such realities as I found here'.[9] Pike concludes that the process behind the evolution of late-Victorian society in the polarised world of 802701AD could therefore be absolutely anything: 'it is not apparent whether the Morlocks are descended from underground workers, from a technocratic elite, or simply from a random group of survivors who sheltered underground'.[10] In fact, the little evidence there is would seem to point to another hypothesis altogether, one which the Time Traveller would have every reason to contemplate with reluctance. As Pike notes, the upper-middle-class Richmond-based inventor has considerably more in common with the supposed scions of the working classes than he would like to admit: 'his technological mind, his obsession with action, and a constant craving for the meat denied him by the vegetarian diet of the Eloi'.[11] Here I will elaborate upon Pike's suspicions, proving that Eloi and Morlock were inspired not, as is usually assumed, by the spectacle of class stratification, but rather by the new middle-class suburban sprawl created by London's Metropolitan and Tube Railways. *The Time Machine* is one of the first fictional responses to that peculiar entity the Underground garden suburb and might therefore be read fruitfully within the context provided by the later literature on Metroland.

The first point is easily proven with reference to the original version of the novel, serialised in the *National Observer* between 17 March and 23 June 1894. In that original version, the Time Traveller encounters Eloi and Morlocks in the year 12203 and this comparative proximity to the nineteenth century reflects the ease with which the Time Traveller, in response to questions from his audience, can extrapolate with authority from 'the problems of our own age'.[12] His speculation on the nature of the Morlock underworld, for instance, is subject to few of the caveats that appear in the final novel, and is not undermined by any previous interpretative failure. The Time Traveller explains that humanity's evolution into two species has probably come about through segregation: 'Imagine, for instance, the more refined and indolent class of people to intermarry mainly among themselves, and the operative or business class – the class of operatives aspiring to rise in business influence and business pursuits – also marrying mainly in their own class'. The Time Traveller hastens to add that 'I do not mean any split between working people and rich – families drop and rise from toil to wealth continually – but between the sombre, mechanically industrious, arithmetical, inartistic type, the type of the Puritan and the American millionaire and the pleasure-loving, witty, and graceful type that gives us our clever artists, our actors and writers, some of our gentry, and many an elegant rogue'. The Time Traveller claims to see this split emerging 'even now in our English society' and speculates that, were this to continue, on 'the former line we should get at last a colourless love of darkness, dully industrious and productive', and on 'the latter, brilliant weakness and gay silliness'.[13]

The Eloi and the Morlocks were thus initially conceived as a cautionary allegory for the slow divorce taking place between the arts and the sciences – and this must seem very strange to modern readers. To put it simply, there seems to be no obvious physical prototype for this two-tier space, such as informed readers seemed to have in Upmark House, the typical English stately home where Wells spent his childhood. The text fails to present the contemporary reader with any clear target for this satirical attack. The novel's earliest readers, however, can have suffered no such difficulties: they must have perceived, in this fantastical vision of a garden city sustained by a network of mechanised subterranean tunnels, topical reference to the colony for artists that had recently been built in Bedford Park, Chiswick, following the extension of the District Railway to Richmond, where *The Time Machine* is set.

Bedford Park had been built by the speculator Jonathan Carr to a design by Norman Shaw that had been inspired by the Arts and Crafts Movement – a garden suburb with red-brick bay-windowed semis, which is now better known to readers as Saffron Park in G.K. Chesterton's *The Man Who Was Thursday* (1907), where it is cruelly described as 'the outburst of a speculative builder, faintly tinged with art, who called its architecture sometimes Elizabethan and sometimes Queen Anne, apparently under the impression that the two sovereigns were identical'.[14] Bedford Park was a template for the Underground garden suburbs that were to follow in the wake of the Metropolitan and Tube Railways' expansion into the countryside around London, and the prototype for twentieth-century semidetached suburbia.[15] 'It is difficult', remarked Chesterton years later, 'to explain how there was then something fanciful in what is now so familiar'.[16] At the time, however, Bedford Park was a revolutionary reinvention of urban space that seemed to combine the benefits of town and country. The poet John Betjeman once described this place as 'the most significant suburb built in the last century, probably the most significant in the Western world'.[17] In the early years, poets and artists, playwrights and academics, even anarchist Sergius Stepniak, flocked to Bedford Park to participate in the bohemian lifestyle it could offer. 'Here until just before the war', Betjeman recalled, 'gentle craftsfolk survived making Celtic jewellery in their studios or weaving on hand looms among the faded sun flowers of a now forgotten cult'.[18] The High Priest himself, William Butler Yeats, composed 'The Lake Isle of Innisfree' while living here between 1887 and 1889, and Bedford Park featured as the setting for this particular flight of fancy in the novel he wrote at this time, *John Sherman* (1891), in which the protagonist is said to be 'set dreaming a whole day by walking down on Sunday morning to the borders of the Thames a few hundred yards from his house – and looking at the osier-covered Chiswick eyot'.

> It made him remember an old day-dream of his. The source of the river that passed his garden at home was a certain wood-bordered and islanded lake, whither in childhood he had often gone blackberrying. At the further end was a little islet called Innisfree.[19]

The curious role Bedford Park played as the scene for the composition of Yeats' earliest, and most otherworldly, lyrics did not escape Chesterton: 'it amuses me to think that under those toy trees and gimcrack gables there was already passing a pageant of strange gods and the head-dresses of forgotten priests and the horns of holy unicorns and the wrinkled sleep of Druidic vegetation, and all the emblems of a new heraldry of the human imagination'.[20] Chesterton clearly believed that the unreal nature of Bedford Park was conducive to fantasy and his ambivalent feelings about that are reflected in his novel *The Man Who Was Thursday*, in which it is satanic anarchist poet Lucian Gregory who thrives upon this 'attractive unreality'.[21] Significantly, his fantastical and violent aesthetic is shown to be challenged by the mechanical perfection of the Underground Railway that runs through Bedford Park. Gabriel Symes, champion of rationality, points out that

> Chaos is dull; because in chaos the train might indeed go anywhere, to Baker Street or to Baghdad. But man is a magician, and his whole magic is in this, that he does say Victoria, and lo! It is Victoria.... You say contemptuously that when one has left Sloane Square one must come to Victoria. I say that one might do a thousand things instead, and that whenever I really come there I have the sense of hair-breadth escape.[22]

In this light the 'Time Machine' of 1894 can be recognised as the vehicle for a veiled attack upon the idiosyncratic fusion of socialism, aestheticism and suburban pastoral first realised in the revolutionary landscape at Bedford Park. The passion for sunflowers is reflected in the flowers woven together by the Eloi. The socialist spirit of the suburb is reflected in the large communal buildings. The frugivorous diet echoes the dietary trends at Bedford Park, which possessed at this time a magazine called the *Vegetarian*. And the spirit of the *fin de siecle* is expressed in the Time Traveller's phrase the 'Sunset of Mankind' and in the mysterious White Sphinx.[23] In subsequent versions, of course, the White Sphinx is a symbol for the interpretative challenge posed by this vision of the future, functioning as the enigmatic nexus between the Upperworld and Underworld: 'the sightless eyes seemed to watch me; there was the faint shadow of a smile about the lips'.[24] But in the *National Observer* 'Time Machine' the Sphinx is exclusively an object of the Upperworld which, in the year that saw the publication of Oscar Wilde's poem *The Sphinx* (1894), can hardly have been mistaken for anything other than a symbol for aesthetic decadence. By some coincidence the passage in which the Time Traveller first describes the Sphinx even bears a striking resemblance to the famous frontispiece produced for that book by the artist Charles Rickett: 'a winged sphinx, but the wings, instead of being carried vertically at the sides, were spread so that it seemed to hover'.[25]

It has often been observed that *The Time Machine* of 1895 starts out as a polemical response to William Morris's *News from Nowhere* (1890), but that this theme is halted abruptly when the Time Traveller realises that his Time Machine has been stolen by Morlocks and that the year 802701 is not therefore a Fabian utopia. In the *National Observer* 'Time Machine', this engagement with the perceived inadequacies of *News from Nowhere* is, on the contrary, specific and sustained. The Time Traveller's discovery of the Morlocks serves to reinforce rather than undermine his previous observations. William Morris had presented a bucolic and socialist vision of the future city, inhabited by adherents to the Arts and Crafts Movement (the inspiration for Bedford Park) – and the *National Observer* 'Time Machine' outlines the consequences that might follow from this Luddite retrogression. Wells shows that were the artistic and the scientific impulses to gradually part ways, the former would eventually find itself without a brain, and the latter without a soul. Certainly, the fate that awaits the Time Traveller's progeny is clear enough, in these, his ominous final lines: 'There is that kid of mine upstairs crying. He always cries when he wakes up in the dark. If you don't mind, I will just go up and tell him it's all right.'[26]

The Time Traveller himself, of course, is no Morlock. Though technically minded, he is also highly sensitive to atmosphere and can relate his adventures with a narrative skill that holds his audience spellbound. In fact, with his home in Richmond, the lameness that he develops in the final version of the novel, and the literary coterie that gathers about him, the Time Traveller rather resembles the late-nineteenth-century poet and literary editor W.E. Henley, who lived some 'quarter of an hour's walk from Bedford Park, out on the high road to Richmond', where friends and followers as varied as those in *The Time Machine* would assemble on Sunday nights to hear their chief hold forth.[27] Now best remembered as the inspiration for Robert Louis Stevenson's treacherous swashbuckler Long John Silver in *Treasure Island*, Henley was also a ground-breaking poet, composing a poetry sequence in *vers libre* on his time in the hospital ward where his leg was amputated, and the editor of a series of important periodicals, such as the *Magazine of Art*, which championed artists such as Auguste Rodin and James Whistler, and *New Review*, which published work by writers such as Joseph Conrad, Paul Verlaine and Paul Valéry. According to Elizabeth Robins Pennell, 'Henley had no use for the affectations of William Morris'.[28] He was, in fact, to lead a concerted campaign against the Yellow Nineties, publishing some of the first attacks on Oscar Wilde's *Dorian Gray*, and physically assaulting the man himself, clinching an argument on the steps of a London café with a flying crutch.[29] 'His personality is insistent', recalled Wilde; 'To converse with him is a physical no less than an intellectual recreation'.[30] When one considers that Henley encouraged Wells to write and to rewrite *The Time Machine*, that he published the first and second version in his magazines the *National Observer* and the *New Review*, and that Wells had initially intended to dedicate the novel to his editor and patron, it seems highly probable that the inspirational synthesis of the artistic and scientific impulses represented by the Time Traveller was suggested by W.E. Henley, and that *The Time Machine* was initially intended to be a minor salvo in a much wider war against cultural fragmentation in the *fin de siècle*, orchestrated by the *National Observer*.

One can only speculate why Wells should choose to suppress the story's original purpose in the next version of *The Time Machine* – published in *New Review* in 1895. Certainly, the change was not the result of any equivocation on the part of the novelist, for one can find in his later book *Anticipations* Wells's first experiment in prophecy, initially published as a series of articles in the *Fortnightly Review* in 1901, a vision of the future similar to that expressed in the *National Observer* 'Time Machine'. Wells predicts the rise and sprawl of garden suburbia: 'these suburban railways are the mere first rough expedient of far more convenient and rapid developments', he claimed; 'the London citizen of the year 2000AD may have a choice of nearly all England and Wales south of Nottingham and east of Exeter as his suburb.... It will certainly be a curious and varied region, far less monotonous than our present English world, still in its thinner regions, at any rate, wooded, perhaps more abundantly wooded, breaking continually into park and garden, and with everywhere a scattering of houses'.[31] Wells asserts that 'The old upper class, as a functional member of the State, is being effaced' and the old lower class 'is crumbling down bit by bit towards the abyss.... But, side by side with these two processes, is a third process of still profounder significance, and that is the reconstruction and the vast proliferation of what constituted the middle class'.[32] Within this emerging new society Wells claimed to perceive the 'processes by which men, often of the most diverse parentage and antecedent traditions, are being segregated into a multitude of specific new groups which may presently develop very distinctive characters'.[33] The most economically powerful is what Wells here calls the 'shareholder' or 'leisure class', who will consequently 'dominate the world of art': 'standing apart from the movement of the world, as they will do to a very large extent, the archaic, opulently done, will appeal irresistibly to very many of these irresponsible rich as the very quintessence of art'. In fact, Wells sneered that 'we can pretty confidently foretell a spacious future and much amplification for that turgid, costly, and deliberately anti-contemporary style of which William Morris and his associates have been the fortunate pioneers'.[34] The second group consists of the 'mechanics and engineers', who would probably favour a functional, austere lifestyle, but will instead be compelled to live in houses built to please the shareholding class who are 'saturated with the second-hand archaic': 'that shabby shirking of the truth of things that has given the world such stockbroker in armour affairs as the Tower Bridge and historical romance, will, I fear, worry the lucid mind in a great multitude of the homes that the opening half, at least, of this century will produce'.[35] The passage recalls Wells's own frustrations following his attempt to commission a modern streamlined country house from the architect Charles Voysey, who insisted on peppering the structure with his sentimental signature, the heart motif. The two finally settled on a compromise. Voysey was to have his hearts but Wells wanted them inverted so that people might mistake them for spades – the symbol of industry. (Incidentally, this was not how they were interpreted in the local town, where the Wells living in Spade House was believed to be the professional card-player of the same name who had recently broken the bank at Monte Carlo.) If Wells had even the slightest inkling, when he had first penned *The Time Machine*, exactly how hard a scientifically minded man like himself might find it to commission a house to his liking, it may explain why his Morlocks had chosen to inhabit the one purely functional element in the Underground garden suburb.

Most probably Wells intended that the Time Traveller's earliest interpretation should become a troubling ghostlike presence within the text, implied only by the novel's physical proximity to Bedford Park and the hunger for peptone that the Time Traveller shares with the Morlocks. This open-endedness has certainly stood the novel in good stead. Instead of a polemical text that might, in time, have become a mere historical curiosity, *The Time Machine* is a novel that possesses the indeterminate suggestiveness of myth, permitting highly varied reinterpretations of the story to take place over the past century. In the first film adaptation, the Morlocks are mutant Cold-Warriors, rising from their nuclear bunkers to slaughter peace-loving hippies in their garden paradise; and in the 2002 film version, beautiful young people like Samantha Mumba, in tune with nature, are sacrificed to feed the rapacity of a financial elite twisted over time by its own genetic technology into a biologically stratified society, ruled with an iron fist by a leather-clad Jeremy Irons. The present interpretation of the *National Observer* 'Time Machine' must therefore be considered a critique of merely one application of the mythic components in the tale among many, rather than 'the key to the whole position'; and is interesting primarily for the light it throws on the fictional response to the revolutionary new form of urban space represented by Bedford Park. In the rest of this chapter it will be revealed that Wells's fable anticipates much that is characteristic in the subsequent literature on inter-war garden suburbia, not least its implacable rejection of an urban environment that was very soon to find its apotheosis in Metroland.

THE MORLOCKS ON METROLAND

The earliest reaction on the part of writers to the creation of housing estates modelled on Bedford Park along the branch lines of the Metropolitan Railway echoed the antipathy expressed by their nineteenth-century predecessors to the encroachment of the Victorian railway suburb. As John Carey has noted, in 'The Suburbs and the Clerks' (an essay that focuses upon the Victorian railway suburb but which also includes material on the semidetached inter-war suburb), English writers in the early twentieth century 'were recruited, generally speaking, from the educated and comfortably-off, many of them grew up in old-style green outer suburbs, which were later spoiled by housing development'.[36] The childhood home spoilt by the expansion of Metroland thus came to feature prominently in work with an autobiographical element. In *A Sort of Life* (1971), Graham Greene remembered how the scenery of his 'calf-love', his uncle's country home in Berkhamsted, four miles from the Metropolitan Line, was cleared for a building estate: 'When I see a performance of *The Cherry Orchard* today', he wrote, 'it is on that estate I hear the axes falling'.[37] Evelyn Waugh would later recall how his home was swallowed by the suburb of Golders Green, following the extension of the Hampstead Tube.[38] And in George Orwell's *Coming Up For Air* (1939) the narrator flees Metroland only to discover that his happy childhood home in Oxfordshire has itself been swamped by inter-war suburbia: 'it was buried somewhere in the middle of that sea of bricks'.[39] Even Betjeman, later the champion of Metroland and saviour of Bedford Park, was susceptible to this nostalgia, complaining in his poem 'Middlesex' that in Ruislip Gardens only 'a few surviving hedges

/ Keep alive our lost Elysium – rural Middlesex again'.[40] The area is now the haunt of the facile Elaine, fresh-complexioned with Innoxa, hair delicately drowned in Drene:

> Gentle Brent, I used to know you
> Wandering Wembley-wards at will,
> Now what change your waters show you
> In the meadowlands you fill![41]

As Carey has observed, such horror on the part of those novelists with a commitment to socialist ideals was profoundly problematic – incompatible with their conviction that slums should be cleared and people housed. E.M. Forster confessed that he could not equate the problem, 'It is a collision of loyalties', while J.B. Priestley concluded, with tremendous reluctance, 'We should be content to make the whole country hideous if we know for certain that by doing so we could also make all the people in it moderately happy'.[42] However, the emergence of strident new architectural principles, marked in Britain by the publication of Frederick Etchells's translation of *Vers Une Architecture* by Le Corbusier in 1927, was soon to free writers from any such crisis of conscience. In 1933 a contingent of British architects, including Geoffrey Boumphrey, Wells Coates and Ernö Goldfinger, joined European colleagues, such as Le Corbusier, Fernand Léger and László Moholy-Nagy, on a passenger cruiser sailing from Marseilles to Athens, for the fourth meeting of the International Congress of Modern Architecture, to consider the future of the urban environment. The Congress concluded that the suburb 'is a kind of scum churning against the walls of the city' and that, far from being a necessary evil, the suburb 'constitutes one of the greatest evils of the century'.[43] Boumphrey returned to Britain convinced that 'If half the energy and money poured into the suburbs in the last 17 years had been spent on the towns inside them, the country would be a better place, and the towns more fit to live'.[44] And soon other English intellectuals were persuaded that each person 'who goes to the suburbs seeking the edge of the countryside pushes the countryside away from somebody else and he in turn suffers from having it pushed away from him'.[45] The escape to suburbia was therefore fundamentally 'selfish and anti-social'; what was required was a collective expression of housing that placed the needs of society over those of the individual, such as Le Corbusier's *Unité d'Habitation* in Marseilles.[46] As a result, London's most extensive suburban experiment, Metroland, was henceforth to be represented as a failure of community. Following Le Corbusier's lead, English intellectuals would claim that a corrosive individualism was creating a 'terrible solitude in the crowd of that vast urban agglomeration'.[47]

T.S. Eliot's pageant play *The Rock*, for instance, written to raise money to build forty-five churches in the new suburbs to the north of London, attacked the individualism of Metroland, as expressed in its preference for non-team sports, such as golf and tennis, foretelling that the only monument to the 'decent godless people' who inhabited 'the land of lobelias and tennis flannels' would be 'the asphalt road / And a thousand lost golf balls'. In pounding biblical cadence, Eliot complained that in Metroland 'no man knows or cares who is his neighbour' and insisted that 'There is no life that is not life in community, / And no community not lived in praise of GOD'.[48] Orwell's novel *A Clergyman's Daughter* (1935) presents a similar vision of Metroland: 'labyrinths of meanly decent streets, all so indistinguishably alike, with their ranks of semi-detached houses, their privet and laurel hedges and plots of ailing shrubs at the crossroads, that you could lose yourself there almost as easily as in a Brazilian forest'. There are women in such places suffering from 'utter solitude'.[49] The district is referred to as Southbridge in the novel but is clearly modelled upon Uxbridge, where Orwell worked unhappily as a school-teacher. The writer concludes that 'There is perhaps no quarter of the inhabited world where one can be quite so completely alone as in the London suburbs'.[50] The same paradox emerges in Graham Greene's travel book *The Lawless Roads* (1939), where building lots in bustling Berkhamsted can nevertheless symbolise 'Metro-land loneliness'.[51]

This terrible sense of loneliness in the company of other people is the subject of a short story by Elizabeth Bowen called 'Recent Photograph', in which a journalist sets out to investigate why one 'Mr Joseph Wellington Brindley' should have cut his wife's throat before turning in for the night with his head inside the gas oven, 'having mitigated the inside's iron inclemency with two frilly cushions'.[52] He finds that Mr and Mrs Brindley inhabited a suburban pastoral, where 'laburnum boughs dripped languorously over the pavement, slanting from among the sprightlier grace of Japanese plum', in an area recently embraced by the 'enterprise of the Metropolitan'.[53] A neighbour recalls that their household was one in which the keynote was laughter: 'he never laid hands on anything but it broke, or at any rate tumbled over, and then his wife would laugh'.[54] The wife's intention was far from malicious: 'that was the way Mr Brindley should be treated, just chaffed and laughed at, else he got so morbid'.[55] But her continuous laughter seems only to have served to have closed down conversation, the opportunity to talk through his depression, leaving Mr Brindley utterly isolated. 'Mr Brindley never said anything', recalled the neighbour; 'he would just stand there, looking shyly at his wife out of the corner of his eye'.[56] On one occasion she found Mr

Brindley 'walking with his bag up and down in front of his own house, and sometimes stopping to stare up at the windows [as though] it was a strange house that he was afraid to go into'.[57] When Mr Brindley lost his job he was thus unable to communicate the fact to his wife, but continued to leave the house as before, coming back later and later; the misery pent up, supercharged by the continual friction of a personal relationship that fostered a sense of isolation, finally shattering out in violence when his wife discovered the truth.

The story recalls the random acts of violence in Greene's description of Metroland, in *The Lawless Roads*. 'You couldn't live in a place like this', wrote Greene, 'it was somewhere to which you returned for sleep and rissoles by the 6.50 or the 7.25'; he claimed that, though he called Berkhamsted home, 'it had no real hold'.[58] Much the same point is made satirically in Evelyn Waugh's novel *Vile Bodies*, in an offhand account of the expansion engineered by the property magnate Lord Metroland, in the area beyond Aylesbury, where 'every house seemed to be a garage and filling station'.[59] Christopher Lloyd, the narrator in Julian Barnes's novel, is thus far from the first person to think that people live in Metroland only because it seems an area easy to escape from.[60]

In fact, in the overall picture to emerge from such sources, Metroland bears a striking resemblance to the non-place which had brought it into being. Like the Underground Railway, it too was an intangible environment, everywhere and nowhere, ineffectually tied to topography and history. In each case the managers of the space were compelled to mediate it to the public through images and texts such as those in the *Metro-land* pamphlets produced from 1915 to 1933. And in each case, this detachment had resulted in an isolation that – in the view of the English intelligentsia – was psychopathological. But, as we have seen, the modernists who continually reviled Metroland were fascinated with the London Underground. The network featured as a symbol for the modernist project in work by writers and artists as various as F.T. Marinetti, C.R.W. Nevinson and Virginia Woolf. The relationship was even lampooned by Aldous Huxley in his novel *Crome Yellow*. If the modernists are the spiritual progeny of W.E. Henley, the prophecies in *The Time Machine* must be considered perfectly accurate. The opponents of romantic decadence had rejected the garden suburb for the tunnels of the London Underground. In fact, E. McKnight Kauffer and H.G. Wells came as close as possible to actually living in the Tube when they moved into Chiltern Court, the enormous apartment block built above Baker Street Station in 1929. The suburban pastoral inspired by the Eloi had fallen under a vicious attack from the Morlocks based in the London Underground.

The reason for this negative response to Metroland on the part of those most committed to a modernist aesthetic seems to be that, while the London Underground finally chose to use experimental artists and architects to make its spaces intelligible, Metroland presented the highly unappealing spectacle of modernity without modernism. In every possible respect, the environment must have seemed a fudge and a compromise: where modernism insisted upon a clear boundary between town and country, Metroland offered 101 shades of grey in between, composed of units typically neither house nor apartment block but *semidetached*, and while the keynote of the New Architecture was functionality, a fantastic non-functional mish-mash of Queen Anne, Tudor and Art Nouveau, cobbled together on-site from mass-produced components, was by far and away the most pervasive architectural style in Metroland.

This 'infernal amalgam' is the subject of a series of images in Osbert Lancaster's satirical guide to architecture, *From Pillar to Post* (1938). The variation he christened 'Stockbroker Tudor' is represented in the cartoon images as an absurd bogus antique in the midst of electricity pylons, aeroplanes and motorcars. In the accompanying commentary Lancaster suggests that next time 'the passer-by is a little unnerved at being suddenly confronted with a hundred and fifty accurate reproductions of Anne Hathaway's cottage, each complete with central-heating and garage, he should pause to reflect on the extraordinary fact that all over the country the latest and most scientific methods of mass-production are being utilized to turn out a stream of old oak beams, leaded window-panes and small discs of bottle-glass, all structural devices which our ancestors lost no time in abandoning as soon as an increase in wealth and knowledge enabled them to do so'.[61] Lancaster observes that the greatest ingenuity has been displayed in installing the most incongruous modern technology: 'electrically produced heat warmed the hands of those who clustered enthusiastically round the yule-logs blazing so prettily in the vast hearth; the light which shone so cosily from the old-horn lantern was obtained from the grid; and from the depths of some old iron-bound chest were audible the dulcet tones of Mr. Bing Crosby or the olde-world strains of Mr. Duke Ellington'.[62] Other writers expressed a similar antipathy to such half-way houses through snide reference to the fake 'Tudor Bar' (as in Betjeman's notorious poem calling for the destruction of Slough) and through the use of epithets such as Jacobethan, Tudorbethan and Jerrybethan, which recall Chesterton's early remarks on the syncretic architecture in Bedford Park: 'sometimes Elizabethan and sometimes Queen Anne, apparently under the impression that the two sovereigns were identical'.[63]

Writers in the inter-war period seem to have hated Metroland chiefly because it appeared to represent a failure of nerve. This perception was to persist after the Second World War. As late as 1956 even Betjeman could suggest, in a poem set in the Baker Street Station buffet beneath Chiltern Court, that suburban expansion in Metroland meant the end for the 'radiant hope' placed in the Metropolitan Railway's 'many-branched electrolier', when 'Youth and Progress were in partnership'. A couple who caught the first non-stop train to Willesden Green to 'autumn-scented Middlesex' are now said to be dying of cancer and heart disease. 'The trees are down' and an 'Odeon flashes fire', like the angels that barred the path to paradise, 'Where stood their villa by the murmuring fir'. 'Of their loves and hopes on hurrying feet / Thou art the worn memorial, Baker Street'.[64] And the claim that Metroland represents a failure to meet modernity with a modernist aesthetic provides the premise for Julian Barnes's novel *Metroland* (1980). Only in suburbia, the protagonist Christopher Lloyd complains, could there be orange sodium lights capable of fugging up the primary colours: in the face of such threatening indeterminacy, he and his friend Toni cannot even count on being themselves any more.[65] The underlying cause is soon explained by an elderly commuter who reveals that the region is the result of a failed attempt to connect Manchester and Paris and to crown London with a monument to modernity 150 feet higher than the Eiffel Tower. The development of Metroland is shown to have marked 'the beginning of the end' for a railway that had once had 'confidence *in* ambition'.[66]

The twist is that, in this instance, the narrator's own life will ultimately follow the same narrative arc. Failing to achieve the long sought for connection with Symbolist Paris, Christopher Lloyd settles for Metroland, and so seeks to readjust his earlier parameters for failure and success. The change that facilitates this accommodation with the historically unacceptable unreality of Metroland begins in Paris, when Christopher claims happiness depends 'necessarily upon the unreality of one plane of your life', and is completed by his marriage to Marion, which compels him to accept that he must henceforth move 'further away from the examination of truth'.[67] He soon discovers that he can be happy working on books seemingly calculated to irritate people like Osbert Lancaster – a cook book designed to look like a Coronation cake-tin and a gardening book which is said to look as though it might sprout roots.[68] And even the sodium lights that turn the stripes in his pyjamas brown no longer fret him, because 'there's no point in trying to thrust false significances on to things'.[69]

> It's certainly ironic to be back in Metroland [concludes Christopher]. But isn't part of growing up being able to ride irony without being thrown? Besides, it's an efficient place to live. Next to the record shop is a grocer's which sells eggs

with shit and straw on them; two minutes' walk from where Marion gets her hair done you can see real pigs mucking up a field. Five minutes' drive and you're in open country where only the pylons remind you of town. As a boy, when we drove past these pylons, I would elbow Nigel out of his SF magazine with a whisper of 'Look, nude, giant girls'. Nowadays, when we pass them, I still think of the poem, but find it excited and inexact.[70]

Christopher's conversion is representative of a wider change in the representation of Metroland in the course of the 1970s. The documentary film *Metro-land*, written and presented by John Betjeman, was broadcast in 1973; and it was soon followed by a spate of architectural studies, such as *Semi-Detached London* (1973), *The Design of Suburbia* (1981) and *Dunroamin: The Suburban Semi and Its Enemies* (1981) that sought to re-evaluate the merits of the garden suburb. However, the process of rehabilitation had commenced much earlier, when writers had begun to brace themselves for the Second World War, and had realised that much that they valued in modern England, and wished to see saved, could be found only in Metroland.

SYNTHETIC FANTASY

The clash of totalitarian regimes on the continent encouraged writers to perceive a new and positive significance in the emphasis upon the individual that had so long been regarded a key element in Metroland. Priestley now praised the 'miles of semi-detached bungalows, all with their little garages, their wireless sets, their periodicals about film stars, their swimming costumes and tennis rackets and dancing shoes', because they were 'essentially democratic'.[71] 'Notice how the very modern things', observed Priestley, 'like the films and wireless and sixpenny stores, are absolutely democratic, making no distinction whatever between their patrons'. Orwell too, in *The Lion and the Unicorn* (1941), expressed the belief that, though interwar suburbia presented 'a rather restless, cultureless life, centering round tinned food, *Picture Post*, the radio and the internal combustion engine', 'in which children grow up with an intimate knowledge of magnetoes and in complete ignorance of the Bible', it was in the 'vast new wildernesses of glass and brick', where 'the sharp distinctions of the older kind of town, with its slums and mansions, or of the country, with its manor-houses and squalid cottages, no longer exist', that listeners should 'look for the germs of the future England'.[72]

But even with such high hopes for the inhabitants of this utopian commuter-belt, Priestley and Orwell found it hard to shake off their hatred of the suburban aesthetic. Priestley berated its 'rather depressing monotony'. Inter-war suburbia was 'a large-scale, mass-production job', he claimed; 'Too much of this life is being stamped on from outside, probably by astute financial gentlemen, backed by the Press and their publicity services'.[73] And this was a key theme in Orwell's *Coming Up For Air*, in which the moneymen behind Metroland are typified by Sir Hubert Crum: a figure who cheats his tenants by building on land about their estate, thereby shutting them off from the countryside. The protagonist concludes that men like Crum have turned the 'inner-outer suburbs' into little more than a row of cells in a prison, a 'line of semi-detached torture-chambers where the poor little five-to-ten-pound-a-weekers quake and shiver, every one of them with the boss twisting his tail and the wife riding him like the nightmare and the kids sucking his blood like leeches'.[74] With bitter sarcasm he proposes that the Hesperides estate where he lives should be surmounted by an enormous statue to the god of building societies. 'The top half would be a managing director and the bottom half would be a wife in the family way. In one hand it would carry an enormous key – the key of the workhouse, of course – and in the other – what do they call those things like French horns with presents coming out of them? – a cornucopia, out of which would be pouring portable radios, life-insurance policies, false teeth, aspirins, French letters and concrete garden rollers'.[75] The statue could be a symbol for the indeterminacy and the inauthenticity that so infuriated Osbert Lancaster. Whatever the social merits of the emphasis placed on individuals over and above the collective in Metroland, it is clear that Priestley and Orwell found the resulting environment an oppressive and ugly non-place.

The turning point came with the publication of *The Castles on the Ground* in 1946, in which J.M. Richards, an architectural critic previously hostile to Metroland, consciously set out to re-evaluate the suburban aesthetic that the ordinary Englishman, 'when he is away at the war', had in his mind when he thought of home.[76] 'We well know the epithets used to revile the modern suburb', wrote Richards, 'and the scornful finger that gets pointed at spec-builder's Tudor with its half-inch boards nailed flat to the wall in imitation of oak timbering, though perhaps we should not criticize so fiercely the architectural idiom the suburb has adopted as its own if we understood the instincts and ideals it aims to satisfy, and how well, judged by its own standards, it often succeeds in doing so'.[77] Richards was the first to observe that conceptual history of Metroland could be traced 'back in time to the day when the city man's father set up in married life at Bedford Park in 1882', and the first to conclude that the 'suburban style – that style which is, we are told, the very citadel of debased and vulgar taste – is, [therefore], part of the background of the England we have all grown up in'.⁷⁸ Its enduring popularity could not be 'explained away as some strange instance of mass aberration'.⁷⁹ Instead, there was clearly something fundamentally wrong with the criteria with which the English intelligentsia had judged and condemned Metroland. Richards claimed that this was their emphasis upon functionality: 'the town evolves its shape from its function, from streets and squares and traffic intersections and the grouping of buildings, and the country from the adaptation of natural landscapes to human purposes', but 'the suburb is not primarily a mechanism, nor is it in any sense a modification of something previously existing; it is a world peculiar to itself and – as with a theatre's drop scene – before and behind it there is nothing'.⁸⁰ The 'leafy valleys of Metroland' worked more like scenery in a theatre, in that they were created not for functional purposes but to facilitate the play of fantasy. 'See the advertisements in which the earnest father, his pipe in his mouth, perhaps a fox terrier at his feet, his arm round the shoulders of his handsome son, gazes (with all the pride of the squire regarding his ancestral acres) at a cosy villa such as Metroland breeds by the thousand', remarked Richards; 'as though in direct answer to all such ambitions, there is the suburban style in the act of echoing the country-squire's own tradition-rooted architecture; there are the red roofs and chimneys – or a caricature of them, if you like – of manorial England, the smooth lawns and lattice windows belonging to the good old times when the world beyond the horizon could be ignored and a slump on the New York stock exchange did not result in the sudden dismissal of numberless bread-winners from their employment at Middlesbrough or Nottingham or West Drayton'.⁸¹ The eccentricities cited by Lancaster were therefore entirely functional. The clear boundaries the modernists had wished to establish between polarities such as town and country, house and garden, transit network and pastoral idyll had been fused into a single, intensely ambiguous artifice precisely because this provided the maximum scope for private fantasy: 'In the suburbs', wrote Richards, 'fantasy is functional'.⁸²

This same potential for fantasy had been recognised in the original garden suburb at Bedford Park by Wells and Chesterton, and in Metroland by Lancaster. It is something that Toni picks up on in Barnes's novel, when he criticises the flowers in Christopher's suburban garden for being 'escapist'. But these critical voices had failed to recognise that 'the very reasons for the suburb's existence demand that the suburban style contain an element of fantasy and make-believe'. By the time Richards came to write *The Castles on the Ground* the thought of a refuge from the scientific, collective world hailed by Wells, Chesterton and the modernists no longer seemed so utterly irrational. In a world that operates on 'a superhuman scale', argued Richards, in which 'people are imprisoned by the thousand and starve by the hundred thousand', a place which remained 'loyal to the significance of the individual' seemed at last a legitimate objective: 'The twentieth-century equivalent of the tasks of mechanical invention that so uplifted the nineteenth is the problem of social adjustment to the mechanical world'. Richards believed that it was time for 'a modern aesthetic that allows romance and fantasy to flourish, as distinct from one dictated solely by rational scientific planning'.[83]

Richards' book appears to have made little impact upon its first publication in 1946. Only following its republication, seventeen years later, were further architectural studies to appear that recognised the tremendous achievement the inter-war commuter-belt represented. The formerly exclusive suburban pastoral celebrated by E.M. Forster in *Howards End* (1910) had been miraculously mass-produced, multiplied to house at least four million Leonard Basts. Rusholme, Rustles, Rustlings, Rusty Tiles, Rose Hatch, Rose Hill, Rose Lea, Rose Mount, Rose Roof … Orwell once remarked that 'Not only the houses themselves, but even their names were the same over and over again. Reading the names on the gates as you came up Brough Road, you were conscious of being haunted by some half-remembered passage of poetry; and when you paused to identify it, you realized that it was the first two lines of Lycidas.'[84] Betjeman by contrast later perceived that 'Each one is slightly different from the next, / A bastion of individual taste / On fields that once were bright with buttercups'.[85] In his documentary film *Metro-land*, Betjeman celebrated the Metroland he had once despised: 'Lured by the lush brochure, down byways beckoned, / To build at last the cottage of our dreams, / A city clerk turned countryman again, / And linked to the Metropolis by train'.[86] The roses that disgusted Orwell were at last recognised for what they were: 'Roses are blooming in Metro-land just as they do in the brochures'.[87] The line is an allusion to the haunting war song 'Roses Are Blooming in Picardy' and indicate that Betjeman was conscious that Metroland was a necessary reaction to the worst aspects of modernity, 'Child of the First War, / Forgotten by the Second', and that it remained significant precisely because it asserted that the pastoral was still possible in the twentieth century. (In the time of the Great Plague, remarked the publicity brochure *Metro-land*, the war-weary Milton composed, in a cottage at Chalfont, *Paradise Regained*.)

'I wonder why happiness is despised nowadays', wonders Christopher Lloyd, 'dismissively confused with comfort or complacency, judged an enemy of social – even technological progress'.[88] The answer is contained in an earlier chapter, in which Christopher remembers how, as a child, he loathed Sunday, 'the day for which Metroland was created'.[89]

I loathed the Sunday papers, which tried to fill your dozing brain with thoughts you didn't want; I loathed the Sunday radio, spilling over with arid critics; I loathed the Sunday television, all Brains Trust and serious plays about grown-ups and emotional crises and nuclear war and that sort of stuff. I loathed staying in, while the sun crept furtively round the room and suddenly hit you smack in the eyes; and sitting out, when the same sun liquefied your brain and sent it slopping round your skull. I loathed Sunday tasks – swabbing down the car, with soapy water running upwards (how did it do that?) into your armpit; emptying the grass-cuttings and scraping your nails on the bottom of the metal barrow. I loathed working, and not working; going for walks over the golf course and meeting other people going for walks over the golf course; and doing what you did most, which was wait for Monday.[90]

The truth is, there is perhaps nothing as boring as other people's happiness, and poor Christopher is trapped in a previous generation's domestic idyll. But even boredom is a luxury, and one could argue that Metroland thereby provided a further spur to private fantasy. Christopher muses on the irony that he should be in Paris in '68 and not see a smudge of smoke on the sky, but by far the greater achievement are his two sojourns in Metroland, in 1963 and 1977: the former famous as the year in which sex began (between the end of the *Chatterley* ban and the Beatles' first LP) and the latter for the rise of the Sex Pistols. Neither event features even momentarily in the course of the book – and this is in striking contrast to the procedure in the film adaptation, starring Christian Bale and Emily Watson, in which Toni refers to the 'Sexy Sixties', and every imaginable period piece is shown in order to evoke the era of punk. In the novel, Christopher can successfully escape from the boredom of his boyhood into an elaborate French fantasy, and while the received wisdom is that, in the late 1970s, there *was* no future in 'England's dreaming', Christopher envelopes himself in a suburban pastoral, where houses have names like Ravenshoe and East Coker, 'carved in Gothic letters on slices of wood which are screwed to trees'.[91] Christopher's biography is a feat next to which Yeats's escape to the Lake Isle of Innisfree, while walking through Bedford Park, Chiswick, pales in comparison. Barnes suggests that Metroland is 'a concept in the mind' and by the end of the novel the nature of this concept is very clearly established. The Underground garden suburb is an imaginative elsewhere. To live in Metroland means to be to inhabit a psychic space that facilitates flights of fancy – not through the total plans intended to provoke the urban reverie advocated by the modernists – but through the creation of unplanned and open-ended spaces that seem to invite the creative intervention of the individual.

NOTES

1 Julian Barnes, *Metroland* (London: Picador, 1980), p. 31.
2 Oliver Green, ed., *Metro-Land* (1924), facsimile edition (London: Southbank Publishing, 2004), p. 27.
3 *Ibid.*, p. vi. See also Paul Oliver, Ian Davis and Ian Bentley, *Dunroamin: The Suburban Semi and Its Enemies* (London: Pimlico, 1994), p. 14.
4 Samuel Hynes, *The Edwardian Turn of Mind* (1968) (London: Pimlico, 1991), p. 63.
5 H.G. Wells, *The Time Machine* (1895), ed. John Lawton (London: J.M. Dent, 1995), p. 43.
6 Rosalind H. Williams, *Notes on the Underground: An Essay on Technology, Society and the Imagination* (Cambridge, MA, and London: MIT Press, 1990), p. 153.
7 David L. Pike, *Subterranean Cities: The World Beneath Paris and London, 1800–1945* (New York: Cornell University Press, 2005), p. 80.
8 Wells, p. 70.
9 *Ibid.*, p. 37.
10 Pike, p. 80.
11 *Ibid.*, p. 80.
12 Wells, p. 43.
13 H.G. Wells, 'The Time Machine' (1894), in *Early Writings in Science and Science-Fiction*, ed. Robert M. Philmus and David Y. Hughes (Berkeley, CA: University of California Press, 1975), p. 86. In subsequent notes this first version shall be called the '*National Observer* Time Machine'. A second published version was printed in the *New Review* in 1895. A third and final version was published as a book later that same year, *Time Machine*.
14 G.K. Chesterton, *The Annotated Thursday*, ed. Martin Gardner (San Francisco, CA: Ignatius Press, 1999), pp. 32–34.
15 Arthur M. Edwards, *The Design of Suburbia* (London: Pembridge, 1981), p. 63.
16 G.K. Chesterton, *Autobiography* (1936), ed. Anthony Burgess (London: Hutchinson, 1969), p. 139.
17 John Betjeman, 'Garden Suburbs', in *Coming Home: An Anthology of Prose*, ed. Candida Lycett Green (London: Vintage, 1998), p. 411.
18 *Ibid.*
19 W.B. Yeats, *John Sherman* (1891), *John Sherman and Dhoya*, ed. Richard Finneran (Detroit, MI: Wayne State University Press, 1969), p. 92.
20 Chesterton, *Autobiography*, pp. 140–141.
21 Chesterton, *Annotated Thursday*, pp. 35–36.
22 *Ibid.*, pp. 39–41.
23 Wells, '*National Observer* Time Machine', p. 81.
24 Wells, *Time Machine*, p. 19.
25 *Ibid.*, p. 19.
26 Wells, *National Observer* 'Time Machine', p. 90.

27 W.B. Yeats, *Memoirs: Autobiography*, ed. Denis Donoghue (London: Macmillan, 1972), pp. 124–126.
28 Elizabeth Robins Pennell, *The Life and Letters of Joseph Pennell* (London: Ernest Benn, 1930), Vol. 1, p. 247.
29 J.M. Barrie, *The Greenwood Hat: Being a Memoir of James Anon 1885–1887* (London: Peter Davies, 1937), p. 195.
30 Quoted by William Rothenstein, *Men and Memories: Recollections 1872–1938* (London: Faber, 1931), Vol. 1, p. 312.
31 H.G. Wells, 'Anticipations' (1901), W.L Courtney, ed., *Fortnightly Review*, Vol. 69, Jan-Jun 1901, p. 930, p. 931.
32 *Ibid.*, p. 1112.
33 *Ibid.*, p. 1113.
34 *Ibid.*, p. 176.
35 *Ibid.*, p. 177.
36 John Carey, *The Intellectuals and the Masses* (London: Faber, 1992), p. 47.
37 Graham Greene, *A Sort of Life* (London: Bodley Head, 1971), p. 35.
38 Carey, p. 48.
39 George Orwell, *Coming Up For Air* (1939), in *The Complete Novels* (London: Penguin, 2000), p. 189.
40 John Betjeman, 'Middlesex', in *Collected Poems* (London: John Murray, 2003), p. 163.
41 Betjeman, pp. 163–164.
42 J.B. Priestley, 'Houses', in *Saturday Review*, 11 June 1927, pp. 897–899. Ian Davis notes that of all the writers and critics of the suburbs between the wars, Priestley was perhaps unique in his sensitivity to the social context in which the new estates were being built. See *Dunroamin*, p. 34.
43 *Dunroamin*, p. 40.
44 Geoffrey Boumphrey, *Town and Country Tomorrow* (1940). Quoted in *Dunroamin*, p. 42.
45 Thomas Sharp, *Town Planning* (1940). Quoted in *Dunroamin*, p. 209.
46 *Ibid.*, p. 209.
47 Le Corbusier, *La Ville Radieuse* (1933). Quoted in *Dunroamin*, p. 41.
48 T.S. Eliot, *The Rock* (1934), in *The Collected Poems and Plays* (London: Faber, 1969), p. 152, p. 155.
49 George Orwell, *A Clergyman's Daughter* (1935), in *The Complete Novels*, p. 368.
50 *Ibid.*, p. 401.
51 Graham Greene, *The Lawless Roads* (1939) (London: Heinemann, 1955), p. 10.
52 Elizabeth Bowen, 'Recent Photograph' (1926), in *Collected Stories* (London: Vintage, 1999), p. 211.
53 *Ibid.*, pp. 212–213.
54 *Ibid.*, p. 218.
55 *Ibid.*
56 *Ibid.*
57 *Ibid.*, pp. 218–219.

58 Greene, pp. 7–8.
59 Evelyn Waugh, *Vile Bodies* (1930) (London: Eyre Methuen, 1978), p. 68.
60 Barnes, p. 37, p. 31.
61 Osbert Lancaster, *From Pillar to Post* (1938) (London: John Murray, 1979), p. 62.
62 *Ibid.*
63 Chesterton, *Annotated Thursday*, pp. 32–34.
64 John Betjeman, 'The Metropolitan Railway', in *Collected Poems*, pp. 169–170.
65 Barnes, pp. 6–8.
66 *Ibid.*, pp. 36–37.
67 *Ibid.*, p. 98, p. 170.
68 *Ibid.*, pp. 205–206. Like Osbert Lancaster before him, Christopher's fellow suburbanite Balldrop Leigh speculates that the modern tendency to make things look like things they aren't results from a 'profound escapism'; Christopher doesn't much care to follow up 'that pissy point, thank you very much.'
69 *Ibid.*, p. 214.
70 *Ibid.*, p. 163.
71 J.B. Priestley, *English Journey* (1934), ed. Margeret Drabble (London: Folio Society, 1997), p. 325.
72 George Orwell, *The Lion and the Unicorn: Socialism and the English Genius* (1941), ed. Bernard Crick (London: Penguin, 1982), p. 68.
73 Priestley, *English Journey*, p. 325, p. 326.
74 Orwell, *Coming Up For Air*, pp. 9–13.
75 *Ibid.*, p. 11.
76 J.M. Richards, *The Castles on the Ground* (1946) (London: John Murray, 1973), p. 14.
77 *Ibid.*, p. 16.
78 *Ibid.*, p. 17.
79 *Ibid.*
80 *Ibid.*, p. 23.
81 *Ibid.*, pp. 35–36.
82 *Ibid.*, p. 65, p. 35, p. 24.
83 *Ibid.*, p. 95.
84 Orwell, *A Clergyman's Daughter*, p. 368.
85 Betjeman, 'Metro-land', in *Coming Home*, p. 452.
86 *Ibid.*, p. 444.
87 *Ibid.*, p. 454.
88 Barnes, p. 212.
89 *Ibid.*, p. 44.
90 *Ibid.*, p. 45.
91 Barnes, p. 162.

5

CHRISTMAS IN HELL

The Tube-Shelter Children in Images by Bill Brandt and Henry Moore

> The pale children are asleep in the Underground,
> In the rabbit burrows, in the roots of goblin wood.
> (Naomi Mitchison, 'Siren Night'[1])

'The sleepers lie packed together making a continuous layer of bodies from one end of the platform to the other', wrote Louis MacNeice in his 'London Letter' to America on 1 January 1941. 'They sleep in a blaze of lights and their coloured blankets and patchwork quilts, their sandwiches and mouth-organs, give almost a Bank Holiday atmosphere.... Someone remarked to me that this was really Back to the Village, a revival of the archaic communal life in which the Tube station takes the place of the Village Hall.'[2]

This is undoubtedly the impression of the wartime Tube that continues to hold the public imagination. In 1940, as the metropolis became a terrain of blackout, ruins and inferno, the London Underground underwent an astonishing alteration. The transport system that had consistently been represented over the course of the previous century as a space of abstract circulation – as the archetypal non-place – became home to thousands of Londoners overnight. As Leonard Woolf recalled, when the bombs fell, the London Underground was where one might experience most fully 'the extraordinary blossoming of the sense of comradeship and good-will that settled upon us in London during the blitz'.[3] A showcase for the morale of civilians under fire. A crucible for a new collective spirit. The bombs of 1940 were to transform the Tube into the very centrepiece of what Angus Calder has labelled the myth of the Blitz. 'That civilian "morale" survived exposure to conditions often as frightful as those of battle', explains Calder, 'is what guarantees, mythically, that the British people, as a whole, deserved to save Europe and defeat Hitler'.[4] Quoting Roland Barthes, Calder defines *myth* as the abolition of complexity: 'it does away with all dialectics, with any going back beyond what is immediately visible, it organises a world which is ... without depth, a world wide open and wallowing in the evident, *it establishes a blissful clarity: things appear to mean something by themselves*'.[5] It does not matter if one later sees through the myth because 'its action is assumed to be stronger that the rational explanations which may later belie it'.[6] One could easily find facts that seem to contradict the sense of comradeship and good-will that is central to the myth of the wartime Tube. The subversive activities of the Communist Party, or the vicious anti-Semitism expressed by many East Enders, is inconsistent with the legendary stoicism and solidarity of the Tube dwellers. The 198 casualties incurred in station shelters as a result of enemy action during the Blitz sits uneasily with the popular conception of the wartime Tube as a place of security and peace. And the appalling sanitary conditions of the Underground shelters throughout the final months of 1940 cannot be reconciled logically with the folk memory of a 'home from home'.

Such a counterfactual exercise would probably leave the myth intact, as Calder and Barthes anticipated, but might leave you wondering whether this is necessarily because '*blissful clarity*' has proven impervious to fact. The first historical study entirely devoted to the topic, *The Shelter of the Tubes* (2001), contains all these facts and more, but they only serve to enrich what the author refers to with approval as 'the legend of the Tube dwellers'.[7] Its author, John Gregg, may well be playing down public support for the Communist Party (though he gives solid evidence for his views) but the racist attitudes of the shelterers are outlined in considerable detail and the horrific nature of life and death in the wartime Tube is vividly conveyed. If the 'legend of the Tube dwellers' has ultimately prevailed, this is surely because, far from being impervious to negative facts, the myth has proven capable of assimilating such facts to its fundamental narrative structure. Though the revolutionary agitation in the Tubes may be news to many, and the anti-Semitism news to anyone who possesses no great knowledge of the East End, both are symptomatic of the fear and misery of the Tube dwellers, and that is news to no one. If the background were not sufficiently darkened by such factors, the ultimate triumph of the Tube dwellers would not shine forth as brightly as it does. The happiness is significant precisely because it is hard won.

I would like to suggest that what we have here is a folk myth of regeneration driven by an underlying dualism and that it is high time this suggestive aspect of the overall myth of the Blitz received the critical attention it has hitherto failed to attract. There are historical accounts of the wartime Tube and some scholarly work on the shelter pictures of Bill Brandt and Henry Moore, but no one has yet considered the myth of the Blitz as it relates specifically to the Tube-shelters; nor has anyone looked at the shelter pictures of Bill Brandt and Henry Moore together in any detail, or placed these images within the wider context of pictures, photographs, novels and newspaper stories that went into the formation of the 'legend of the Tube dwellers'. This chapter will do that by focussing on the figure central to this legend, the figure of the child asleep in the Tube.

Children are prominent throughout this source material, and the association of children with the wartime Tube remains a popular one.[8] The child asleep in the Tube is a recurrent motif in photographs by Bill Brandt and in drawings by Edward Ardizzone, Edmond Kapp and Henry Moore. Children appear in a painting of the Southwark Tunnel by Anthony Gross and in a striking woodcut image of a Tube-shelter by the artist John Buckland Wright.[9] The Tube-shelter children feature frequently in the reports produced by Mass-Observation, in memoirs such as Bernard Kop's *The World Is a Wedding* (1963) and in contemporary magazines and newspapers. Of the thirteen Tube-shelter photographs to appear in the *Evening Standard*, for instance, all but three feature children. They cluster about the charwomen with their baskets of buns, wave cups at a watering-can full of tea or cocoa, or are shown asleep on the platforms or in hammocks slung between rails.[10] The children of the Tube are at the heart of this story. They are central to the Tube-shelter myth.

This is why it comes as rather a shock to discover that the children who receive so much attention in the written accounts of Mass-Observation were, in fact, consistently fewer than the number of men in a series of headcounts conducted by those same observers. In Piccadilly Circus, on 17 September 1940, only 19 per cent of the shelterers were children, while women and men each formed 40.5 per cent. In Holland Park, in a series of headcounts, only 23 per cent of the shelterers were children, while women formed 47 per cent and men 29 per cent. And in surveys conducted in five Underground stations on 21 and 23 of September 1940, the number of children exceeded that of men in only two instances, never exceeded the number of women, and averaged only 16 per cent of the total number of shelterers in all stations on both nights.[11]

The statistics are doubtless imperfect but the trend is clear. There were far fewer children sheltering in the Tube during the final terrible months of 1940 than we might expect from the attention they receive in reports, photographs and drawings produced at this time. Such an inconsistency might be easily explained when we consider sources such as the *Evening Standard*: the paper was furious at the lack of provision in the Tube-shelters and published stories and pictures that would sting the public to action. But to interpret the disproportionate space devoted to the figure of the child in Bill Brandt's images of the wartime Tube as mere propaganda would be crudely reductive.[12] That the photographs were used as such by the Ministry of Information is undeniable, but the photographer's genuine interest in the subject is evident, in that, of the three Tube-shelter images to appear in what Brandt intended to be the definitive collection of his work, *Shadow of Light* (1977), two are of children asleep in the Liverpool Street extension.[13] The compulsion to depict the children in the Tube, evident in the work of Brandt and Moore, clearly had its source in those emotions propaganda seeks to play upon rather than in any conscious need for propaganda itself. I hope to show that the Tube-shelter pictures of Brandt and Moore constitute a profound meditation upon the significance of the figure of the child in a time of total war, and that they form part of a wider preoccupation with childhood evident in the literature of the period.

FOUR TUBE-SHELTER IMAGES

Compare a photograph of three sleeping children taken by Bill Brandt in November 1940 (Figure 5) to a superficially similar photograph of four sleeping children that appeared in the *Evening Standard* on Friday 18 October of the same year (Figure 6). The former is one of three photographs that Brandt subsequently chose to modify and include in *Shadow of Light*. The latter is formally very unlike any of the other Tube-shelter photographs that appeared in the *Evening Standard* and entirely untypical of the 'Refreshments for Shelterers' series in which it also appears. One of these other photographs would doubtless have afforded more obvious contrasts. While Brandt often went to extraordinary lengths to capture his subjects asleep, the photographers whose work appeared in the *Evening Standard* chose to photograph children awake and trying hard to appear happy. This image has been chosen because the similarity of its composition to the photograph by Brandt should serve to highlight more subtle contrasts.

In the Brandt photograph, three children (two girls, one boy) lie under pale sheets on half-hammocks slung between the ribs of the curved tunnel wall. A woman, possibly the mother, reclines wrapped in a dark coat or blanket. She averts her face from the camera, towards the children, her right hand behind her head, her two knees raised. Her body from knee to elbow under the dark cloth forms a protective curve about the white faces of the nearest girl and boy, closing them off from the camera. But the pale fabrics worn by the children continue away up the tunnel with the second girl and with the bedclothes she seems to have cast aside, to form a crest which echoes the angle of the woman's knees. The head of an old lady, who sits upright wrapped in black, at the end of an arc described by the heads of the woman and the children and the two figures beyond them (their backs to the camera), provides a convergence for a series of lines which might frame the children; but the down-thrust of the great expanse of the wall is too great, and the children, who are situated at the outside of a bend in the tunnel, appear to be sliding down their pillows, out of the arc formed by the heads, out of the row of bodies lining the tunnel, and out over the curve formed by the mother. The blankets of the children trail away over the wide dirt of the tunnel floor.

In the photograph 'Tube Shelterers – Children Asleep' from the 'Refreshments for Shelterers' series, the faces of the four children form a row that curves away left up into the picture. As in the Brandt image, the lines formed by legs and by the folds and seams of blankets lead the eye up into this arc of faces; but while that other image forces the eye on and out, all the lines in this photograph bring you back to the faces. This is a close-up (you can see freckles and gaps between teeth): the photograph insists upon the pathos of the exhausted faces and holds them tightly in its frame. There is just no room here for the insecurity expressed in Brandt's image through slippage and space. The camera captures the varying textures of the nest formed by the woollen sheets, but excludes the terrain of concrete and cast-iron that dominates the photograph by Brandt. Even the casting aside of a coat that should cover a pair of scrawny white legs does not generate the sense of vulnerability suggested by the white sheets thrown away in the Brandt, for here the shins are covered with dense woollen socks and the feet are bound in bright buckled shoes. The general effect of this photograph was taken even further in the *Evening Standard*, where the photograph appears closely cropped about the faces of the first three children.[14] The image 'Tube Shelterers – Children Asleep' can thus be seen to guard itself against, and therefore to manifest, the very sense of child-related anxiety so skilfully expressed by Brandt.

Set a typical sketch of Tube-shelter children by the Hungarian artist

Joseph Bató beside a superficially similar image by Henry Moore and it soon becomes clear that such insidious anxiety was not confined to the newspapers but is also a feature of the cosy shelter sketches published in books such as Joseph Bató's *Defiant City* and Negley Farson's *Bomber's Moon*.[15] Julian Andrews has remarked that Henry Moore's *Women and Children in the Tube* (Figure 7) is a very curious drawing, being 'tentative and impressionistic'.[16] It is one of the earliest Tube-shelter images the artist produced, ostensibly after his first night in the Underground. In texture and colour, the paper resembles a slab of weathered concrete, smooth overall, in places bobbled and blotched. From this gloomy expanse figures emerge, in the distance mere scribbles of dark crayon, in mid-distance an indistinct mass of yellow and white wax, and in the foreground neat little portraits of three seated mothers, an infant in each lap, picked out from the grey soup with highlights of light wax and fine strokes of black pen. These latter figures are rendered in a traditional naturalistic style, at odds with the innovative, and highly idiosyncratic, medley of materials and techniques. In fact, the skinny girl seated towards the centre of the piece seems completely cut off from the rest of the work by a halo of fine vertical lines that suggest a wall. Through this abrupt discontinuity the picture achieves the same effect as that produced by the Brandt photograph. The viewer is struck by the incongruity of these figures in such a harsh and enormous environment. The skinny girl in her outsize slippers, clutching tightly her child, seems hopelessly out of her element here, exposed in this, the only shelter she has, an extent of spectral grey.

Joseph Bató's image of women and children in his book *Defiant City* (1942) is in pencil rather than paint; the full variety of effects exploited by Moore were thus not available to Bató.[17] But once this is taken into account it is quite remarkable how greatly an image so superficially similar to *Women and Children in the Tube* differs from it in meaning and tone. Again, women cradle their babies under the curve of a platform wall. But in this image, blankets, children and packing cases clutter the floor. And the space is neat, manageable, circumscribed; the tunnel extends for no very great distance before it is closed off with corrugated iron. Like the photograph 'Tube Shelterers – Children Asleep', this picture holds the women and their children tightly in frame. Bató will not permit this place of shelter to become a space of exposure. The woman feeding her baby smiles towards us. 'Their look was not tragic at all', he insists in a note on this picture; 'On the contrary, they looked cheerful, happy and even gay'.[18]

'THAT LOST POSSIBILITY OF EDEN'

This empathy for the figure of the child is a recurrent feature in much of the literature produced at this time, and its significance in the photographs and paintings by Brandt and Moore may be easier to understand if we take a moment to examine this material first. In *The Novel Since 1939*, an overview of the novels produced in England since the start of the War published in 1946, Henry Reed notes that 'almost every important English writer of the moment' has essayed to treat the theme of childhood. The reason, he argues, is perhaps to be sought in the growing acceptance of the importance attached to childhood and infancy by psychology.

> But this only accounts for a little, there are other things, more consciously apprehensible. In a world of darkness we learn to hug that memory of comparative light. A child may be unhappy, but it is never wholly so; its happiness is not the mere absence of pain, and it has an innocence which the happiness of adult life is too complex to have. It is natural to turn and attempt to recapture and understand and detail that lost possibility of Eden.[19]

In short, Reed hints that the contemporary interest in childhood 'may perhaps represent an honourable escape from present-day life'.[20] The four images considered above would constitute such an act of self-forgetting, an identification with a lost simplicity. Reed's suggestion is appealing both for its simplicity and for the wealth of material that would appear to support it. In 'Little Gidding', for instance, T.S. Eliot concludes that 'the end of all our exploring / Will be to arrive where we started / And know the place for the first time':

> Through the unknown, remembered gate
> When the last of earth left to discover
> Is that which was the beginning;
> At the source of the longest river
> The voice of the hidden waterfall
> And the children in the apple-tree
> Not known, because not looked for
> But heard, half-heard, in the stillness
> Between two waves of the sea.[21]

And the notion of an escape into the innocence and hope of childhood is central to Graham Greene's wartime 'entertainment' *The Ministry of Fear* (1943). 'In childhood we live under the brightness of immortality – heaven is as near and actual as the seaside', writes Greene. 'Behind the complicated details of the world stand the simplicities: God is good, the grown-up man or woman knows the answer to every question, there is such a thing as truth, and justice is as measured and faultless as a clock.' Greene's protagonist, an outcast racked by guilt for the mercy-killing of his wife, wanders London aching to regain this 'world of great simplicity', to 'mislay the events of twenty years'. He ultimately succeeds in doing so when a time-bomb (appropriately) wipes out every memory of his adult life: 'Now, with no memories nearer than his boyhood, he was entirely free'. When 'The Happy Man' has learned enough to participate again in the story, he will do so with renewed vigour and with far greater effectiveness. In ignorance of the world's true complexity, the nightmare of war will become 'a heroic back-cloth to his personal adventure'.[22]

However, most of the novels cited by Reed actually present problematic childhoods, and the critic himself seems to acknowledge that childhood is never simply 'a bed of roses'.[23] It is also the case that, of the *Four Quartets*, the one that makes the most extensive use of imagery derived from the poet's childhood is by far the bleakest: 'The Dry Salvages' is set on the Mississippi and on the coast of Cape Ann, Eliot's childhood homes. In the first movement, the river is represented as a pervasive and threatening presence in the poet's earliest memories:

> His rhythm was present in the nursery bedroom,
> In the rank ailanthus of the April dooryard,
> In the smell of grapes on the autumn table,
> And the evening circle in the winter gaslight.[24]

Even Greene's novel – with its fantasy of escape through regression the exemplary attempt to capture 'that lost possibility of Eden' – can be seen to raise serious questions about the interpretation posited by Reed. As the novel's childhood motif receives its most searching treatment in a chapter set entirely in the dormitory of an air-raid shelter, Greene's views on this hankering after childhood are particularly pertinent to this chapter, and merit close attention.

Greene's idealisation of the protagonist's childhood is in fact seriously compromised by events in the novel. The fête that draws Arthur Rowe into the action – which calls to him 'like innocence … entangled in childhood' – is soon shown to possess sinister undertones: 'It was as if the experience of childhood renewed had taken a strange turn, away from innocence'.[25] And as Rowe moves closer towards childhood through the course of the novel so events take ever-stranger turns into nightmare: Rowe's attempted poisoning by a dwarfish stranger, an apparent murder at a séance, the 'disappearance' of Rowe's private investigator, the explosion of the time-bomb that Rowe has been duped into carrying. The erasure of his adult life brought about by this explosion brings no peace either, but results in a spurious 'Arcady', in which Rowe is, in truth, at his most vulnerable, an amnesiac in a Nazi doctor's insane asylum.

This outcome is in keeping with Greene's curious use of images from childhood throughout Book 1 to indicate vulnerability and irrational terror as well as escape. The little light in Rowe's (as yet un-Blitzed) flat is compared to a 'nightlight in a child's nursery – a child who is afraid of the dark'. The engines of the German raiders are said to mutter 'like a witch in a child's dream, "Where are you? Where are you? Where are you?"' And Rowe's unease at the séance is likewise evoked with references to childhood terrors: 'In nightmares one knows the cupboard door will open: one knows that what will emerge is horrible: one doesn't know what it is....'[26]

Greene's childhood imagery is perhaps at its most negative, and certainly at its most complicated, in the chapter set in a Tube-shelter, 'Between Sleeping and Waking'.[27] Rowe, now homeless, seeks shelter from bombs and policemen in a 'dim lurid underground place' somewhere near Clapham, perhaps the very shelter in Elephant and Castle Underground that was photographed by Bill Brandt.

> All along the walls the bodies lay two deep, while outside the raid rumbled and receded.... An old man snored across the aisle and at the end of the shelter two lovers lay on a mattress with their hands and knees touching.

Here Rowe begins to dream of his childhood: 'tea on the lawn at home behind the red-brick wall and his mother was lying back in a garden chair eating a cucumber sandwich'. But what initially seems no more than 'honourable escape' from Rowe's present-day life soon turns into nightmare. His mother pays Rowe 'the half attention a parent pays a child', and in his child state Rowe can make nothing happen and make no one understand. This dream of childhood is in fact nothing more than an image of Rowe's waking life.

> It seemed terribly important to him to convince her; if she were convinced, she could do something about it, she could tell him it didn't matter and it would matter no longer, but he had to convince her first.... 'Mother, please listen to me,' but he suddenly realized that he was a child, so how could he make her believe? He was not yet eight years old, ... he only had childish words. 'I have. I have.'

Only after Rowe has woken and returned to the dream with the authority of an adult can he work the dream 'to suit himself': when the dream begins to regain control, Rowe finds himself again a child, trapped in a nightmare, rehearsing the very act which, throughout the novel, epitomises adult life in all its grim complexity – Rowe's mercy-killing of his wife.

> He was playing in a haystack with the vicar's son and a strange boy with a foreign accent and a dog called Spot. The dog caught a rat and tossed it, and the rat tried to crawl away with a broken back, and the dog made little playful excited rushes. Suddenly he couldn't bear the sight of the rat's pain any more; he picked up a cricket-bat and struck the rat on the head over and over again; he wouldn't stop for fear it was still alive....

Far from mislaying a compromised adulthood and regressing to a lost innocence, Rowe has merely exchanged one childlike state for another – a state of irrational terror and impotence, initiated by an act which has its roots in Rowe's boyhood, for a state of naivety and hope. Greene's novel thus present us with a radically contradictory vision of childhood – at once the symbol of a very adult crisis of selfhood, and of an escape into the fortitude associated with innocence. At one point the figure of the child even stands for both in the space of three lines: 'I've *escaped* for long enough', Rowe thinks, as he begins to regain his memory. 'It wasn't all fear that he felt; he felt also *the untired courage and the chivalry of adolescence*'; but then his head is racked with pain 'as other memories struggled to get out *like a child out of its mother's body*'.[28]

The ambivalent feelings toward childhoods manifest in Greene's novel, Reed's essay, *Four Quartets* and in the photographs and pictures that seem torn between fear and hope are touched upon by Elizabeth Bowen in the Postscript to her remarkable wartime collection *The Demon Lover and Other Stories*.[29] On the one hand, Bowen claims that childhood and adolescence provide the individual with 'saving illusory worlds'. But, as she herself admits, this hardly makes sense of the hallucinations in the stories, which, far from being escapist, often depict traumatic events in an individual's childhood or early adolescence. The explanation Bowen offers for this phenomenon is insightful: 'You may say that these resistance-fantasies are in themselves frightening. I can only say that one counteracts fear by fear, stress by stress.' A key crisis from a Victorian girlhood might provide the only means to comprehend a present 'out of all proportion to our faculties for knowing, thinking and checking up'. 'The hallucinations in the stories', she writes, 'are an unconscious, instinctive, saving resort on the part of the characters: life, mechanized and impoverished by changes, had to complete itself in some way'. A retrogressive interest in childhood within the confines of a cramped Tube-shelter, such as Rowe's in *The Ministry of Fear*, might then be interpreted as the retrieval of the 'I', the re-creation of private space in a total war.

> Sometimes I hardly knew where I stopped and somebody else began. The violent destruction of solid things, the explosion of the illusion that prestige, power and permanence attach to bulk and weight, left all of us, equally, heady and disembodied. Walls went down; and we felt, if not knew, each other. We all lived in a state of lucid abnormality.... The past, in all these cases, discharges its load of feeling into the anaesthetized and bewildered present. It is the 'I' that is sought – and retrieved at the cost of no little pain. And the ghosts ... hostile or not, they rally, they fill the vacuum for the uncertain 'I'.

But Bowen also perceives that it is because the 'general subconsciousness' saturates the *Demon Lover* that this collection possesses an authority that has nothing to do with the author. In wartime any such 'personal cry' must constitute a regression to a simpler, more universal, state of being.[30] In his critical overview of *Prose Literature Since 1939*, John Hayward elaborates upon this suggestion. 'In the struggle for survival', he writes, 'the individual, regimented, directed, and controlled at work and play, is forced to submerge his identity, and sacrifice, in the common interest, much of his freedom of action. There is some irony in the fact that as soon as war broke out every man, woman, and child in the British Isles was issued, for the first time, with an Identity Card – as if, without one, individuality might cease to exist.'[31] The country as a whole had been comprehensively mobilised. The dormitories of the Underground therefore represented an extreme version of conditions pertaining throughout the UK. 'For the first time in many hundreds of years civilised families conducted the whole of their leisure and domestic lives in full view of each other', a Mass-Observation file report notes: 'To anyone of a sociological turn of mind the situation was full of possibilities – for the first time sociologists could watch the living process of highly civilised individuals adjusting themselves to a pre-civilised, communal form of society'.[32] The national loss of privacy of which John Hayward wrote and which the conditions in the Tube re-enacted (in extreme and in miniature) was perceived as not merely a return to conditions endured in infancy but to conditions prevalent in an earlier phase of civilisation. The common language of the unconscious, of childhood and dream, was alone sufficient to express the extremities of fear and hope endured collectively by those sleepers in the Tube during the Blitz.

'A VISION OF CHRISTMAS IN HELL'

This interpretation resonates with Henry Moore's account of why he began to represent the Tube-shelters. Moore was an artist who worked in an extremely personal language, who hated anything in the nature of a commission, and yet the artist was able to produce an enormous body of comparatively public work in remarkably little time. The following passage suggests that the production of work had been facilitated by the increasing resemblance of the war-torn city to the artist's own inner world.

> I had never seen so many rows of reclining figures and even the holes out of which the trains were coming seemed to me to be like the holes in my sculpture. And there were intimate little touches. Children fast asleep, with trains roaring past only a couple of yards away. People who were obviously strangers to one another forming tight little intimate groups. They were cut off from what was happening above, but they were aware of it. There was tension in the air. They were a bit like the chorus in a Greek drama telling us about the violence we don't actually witness.[33]

Both Brandt and Moore worked hard to bring out the chorus in the crowd. Each utilised the language of the unconscious to assert the greater significance of the children in the Tube. In fact, it is possible to trace a common movement in each artist's Tube-shelter pictures from documentary to dream, from children to the figure of the child, from the scrupulous reportage of the particular to the intensity of myth and archetype.

This transition can be traced in Brandt's subsequent revision of the photograph referred to above, which is reproduced opposite another Tube-shelter photograph in his collection *Shadow of Light*.[34] The photographs meet in the middle and can be read as a single composite image, a variation upon the 'paired photographs' through which Brandt would create 'visual rhymes' to emphasise contrasts or to imply narratives and analogies.[35] In fact, some doctoring of the print would even appear to have taken place on either side of the joint – a bright tunnel support on the left-hand page seems to have been shaded in, while the shadowy tunnel support that sweeps down towards it from the right-hand page has been marked with a series of fine white scratches. Brandt has not blacked out the woman's head in the left-hand image or a child's head in the right, perhaps aware that these are easily missed in the joint between pages. There remain discontinuities of detail, perspective and scale but the viewer can very easily mistake this material, upon seeing it for the first time, for a single photograph. The knees of the reclining woman in the first photograph are now the feet of the woman in the second. The blankets bunched up over the torso, now the bulge of a hip. The two women have been conflated to form a single mother figure with a massive baby. And the three children, the farthest still slipping down the incline of the tunnel wall, nestle into the shelter provided by the mother's legs, forming part of a dynamic white curve across the two pages, culminating with the baby.

In his later years, Brandt would come to make increasing use of chiaroscuro: 'Before 1951, I liked my prints dark and muddy', he wrote in 1970. 'Now I prefer the very contrasting black-and white effect.'[36] The black shadow swallows up details, such as the clothes between tunnel supports, that previously undermined the isolation of the family, and the enlargement, recomposition and cropping required to offset the loss of detail that resulted from the heightened contrast enabled Brandt to remove the rest, such as the sleepers on the left. In this composite image the sense of exposure previously generated through excessive space has been replaced with a deep darkness, charged with menace, in which the three sleeping children seem smaller than before. But, since they are on a larger scale than the children on the left, the family group on the right seem able to meet this threat; the composite mother figure now seems to shelter the tiny sleeping children successfully; her figure has been invested with mythic scale, with archetypal significance. It has been said that the wartime photographs were taken at a pivotal point in Brandt's career, and it is possible to see, in this transition from the original composition to the final composite image, Brandt's own movement from the photo-journalism of the 1930s to the more poetic portraits, landscapes and nudes of his later years.[37] The official purpose of these photographs, to record the conditions in the Tube in the winter of 1940, has been replaced with a metaphysical imperative: to explore the larger implications of this situation, to express what one art critic has called 'a vision of Christmas in Hell'.[38]

Moore was slow to assimilate the children he saw in the wartime Tube to his sculptural style of drawing. Rather than imposing a ready-made aesthetic upon new material, and thus losing much of whatever makes it new, Moore chose to approach his material circumspectly, to let the material shape his style. In his early shelter pictures, women and children are represented in a highly naturalistic style. The plight of the Tube-shelter children is made tangible through a grinding disjunction of matter and medium.

In his shelter sketch books, Moore attempted to reconcile these conflicting elements. There is insufficient space to fully outline the evolution of the resulting synthetic style; instead, I will focus on the shelter painting singled out by the art critic Robert Ironside as an early example of what he called Neo-Romantic, a style of painting then beginning to emerge in British art.³⁹ A richly complex arrangement of colours and forms and textures, *Group of Draped Figures in a Shelter* represents an astonishing synthesis of the conflicting elements in Moore's early shelter pictures (Figure 8). The mother and child are heavily stylised, the humanism of these figures in the early shelter painting entirely reconciled to the modernist background. The child is blank, shaped like a ninepin. The mother has a broad face, turned away from the child, looking over her shoulder. Her bulky body with legs outstretched has weight like that of a harbour wall, and seems an exact equivalent to that of the enormously exaggerated maternal figure in the composite picture produced by Brandt. On the other hand, the nightmarish figures that lurk in the backdrop to previous shelter paintings are now humanised and brought into the society of the mother, their heads turned to face the child. The woman on the far right, for instance, is clearly related to the reclining figure immediately behind the mother in the picture *Mother and Child Among Underground Sleepers* – the same angular knees, the same yawning hole in the centre of the head, the body arranged upon the page at the same angle of forty-five degrees.⁴⁰ The two women in the middle, with their egg-like bodies and rudimentary heads, resemble the mummy-like sleepers who lined the walls in that earlier picture. The woman on the left has a face of sorts, with an elementary nose and an eye like a hole. The woman on the right has a face of concentric circles radiating from a hole at the centre. But the deathly quality of these three figures has been greatly reduced by their new proximity to the mother and child. The modernist medium itself has been transformed by the introduction of bright colours. The dark wash over the thin application of wax has produced blotches on the sheets, lending the figures an organic rather than mineral appearance.

Somewhat removed from the physical centre of this picture, the child is nevertheless at the heart of this composition. The infant emerges from a protective cavity in the mother's body and is poised above an empty space that curves between the mother's flank and the women behind her. Held in space, secure in exposure, the infant in Moore's painting possesses a profound and contradictory significance, which resonates with the conclusion of a short essay on the child motif produced by C.G. Jung in 1940. 'The "child" is all that is abandoned and exposed and at the same time divinely powerful', Jung wrote, 'the insignificant beginning, and the triumphal end'.⁴¹ The child may stand for our own past, as in Greene's story, and for our collective preconscious past, as in the wartime fiction by Bowen, but one of the essential features of the child motif is its futurity: 'The child is potential future'.⁴²

The recognition of this magical, transformative power is what sets the shelter pictures by Brandt and Moore apart from the work of their contemporaries. The massive baby in Brandt's composite image, held between the mother and the father, in this cavernous interior, recalls the reinvention of the Nativity by St Francis of Assisi, who placed actors representing the Holy Family at the mouth of a cave at the beginning of Advent. Once this initial connection has been made, the image of an old lady in a surface shelter, surrounded by sandbags, her brolly propped up behind her, might resemble a shepherd with his crook, surrounded by sheep. One picture has even been said to possess 'the exotic flavour of the Magi'.[43] The interplay of light and dark embodied by the child imposes a new significance upon such images and transforms documentary into something surreal. The winter city in moonlight. The sleepers piled up in the later, darker, perspective of the Elephant and Castle Tube station. These photographs suddenly become metaphysical statements, expressions of an unredeemed world waiting for a great light to come. In Moore's work, too, the women and children of the Tube acquire an explicitly Christian inflection, albeit not within the shelter pictures themselves. The Reverend Walter Hussey commissioned the Northampton *Madonna and Child* after being struck by the dignity and three-dimensional quality of the shelter drawings at a war artists' exhibition at the National Gallery in 1942.[44] As Geoffrey Hill has observed, the sculpture is closely modelled upon the representation of mother and child in the shelter pictures: 'an offering up of deep surfaces; chalk/sleepers from the underground | risen to this'.[45] There is the same 'load-bearing rt hipbone' as in *Mother and Child Among Underground Sleepers*, the same child's face, 'prím, sweetened, incúrious'. The ease of this move into religious art, at the first attempt, with so little change to an aesthetic so painstakingly developed in the shelter sketchbooks, serves to indicate the proximity of Moore's war art to the traditional iconography of Christmas. Confronted with children sleeping in a transport system, with the spectacle of their own problematic inhabitation of an inhuman modernity, Brandt and Moore capture the impossible combination of the monstrous and the miraculous by boldly exploiting religious iconography that remains potent and pervasive in Western culture – an infant compelled to sleep with beasts in a stable.

'A GREAT CHANGE'

Here we return to the problem of myth, as formulated by Barthes and Calder. In short, myth is false to life, imposing a pattern and a significance upon events that possess neither (these metaphysical images are surely far, far removed from the human actuality); and this mortification of life, in turn, mortifies – 'For the very end of myths is to immobilize the world', to 'stop its transformation, its flight towards other forms of existence'.[46] Both charges are levelled at the shelter pictures of Henry Moore by Adrian Lewis, in a provocative attack upon the 'ideological representation' of the shelter pictures by art historians.[47]

Lewis claims that Moore's shelter pictures lack the particularisation he finds in the photographs of Brandt: while we see 'various types and patterns of bedding, informal family groupings, suitcases and bags, occasional pets, and makeshift arrangements for hanging clothes' in the images by Brandt, we find no such evidence that 'Efforts were made to make things as home-like as possible' in the shelter pictures by Moore. 'What Moore sees, in his own words, is "hundreds of Henry Moore Reclining Figures stretched along the platform". In Moore's hands the scene in the Liverpool Street extension becomes a "formally monotonous double line of generalised recumbent figures, more dead than alive".' Lewis compares Moore's work unfavourably with that of other artists, such as Edmond Kapp, Feliks Topolski and Edward Ardizzone, who record 'many particularities'. He then contrasts Moore's sickly images of 'disease and fear' with the 'typical pattern of experience' to emerge from the records of Tom Harrisson's Mass-Observation.

This last procedure is a curious one, since the passage Lewis refers us to in Harrisson concludes that 'the subsequent picture has been distorted' by the erasure of 'normal human responses', such as 'fear and anxiety (and occasional exhilaration)', from images of the 'blitz "spirit" of courage and fortitude' – by which Harrisson must surely mean cheery images such as those produced by Ardizzone – 'whose figures', Lewis explains, 'all tend to an affectionate dumpiness and are contained in convenient boxed spaces'. As this chapter has shown, the 'convenient boxed' space is the very device employed by Bató and by the anonymous photographer working for the *Evening Standard*, an unconscious expression of the 'fear and anxiety' fully articulated by Brandt and Moore. Lewis has overlooked the fact that Brandt chose to eliminate bedding, bags, occasional pets and suitcases from his later prints. Like Moore's work, these late revised photographs serve to complicate rather than simplify not life, as Lewis would have us believe, but the popular conception of the wartime Tube that emerges from the upbeat newspaper stories, from pictures by Ardizzone, from the memories of those who, against all the odds, transformed the transport network into a home from home. Brandt and Moore enrich the folk myth that has ensured that these events are still remembered, and this is all that they could reasonably be expected to achieve. To speak of capturing a pre-existent visual/social reality without resort to myth is nonsensical. Structure and significance are imposed upon events whenever and however we make memory. Memory is myth.

Having recognised that Moore's 'alienating imagery of immemorial long-suffering and passive endurance' subsequently became 'the key image …

of a putative "people's war"', Lewis performs something of a volte-face and attacks Moore's Tube-shelter pictures for their participation in, rather than their opposition to, the popular 'myth of the blitz':

> Moore's images of passive suffering and active endurance by an anonymous collectivity might have its ideological roots in interwar British socialism but was reshaped as part of a blitz mythology of fundamental importance to both Labour and Conservative parties.... The shelter image performed a key function in the myth of the blitz, a period nostalgically reconstructed as a bedrock of 'British identity' when uncertainties prevailed later.

The Tories believed that the myth of the Blitz would preserve 'an illusion of great-power status', the socialists that the myth would serve to 'symbolise a time of trial for the British citizenry within the representation of the emergence of a new post-war consensus'. As Angus Calder says, the effect of the myth would thus be conservative: 'Because Blitz was held to have had near revolutionary consequences, to have somehow produced a "welfare state", the Myth would divert attention from the continuing need for radical change in British society'.[48] To this one can only respond that if the welfare state is now in decay, one can hardly blame the spirit of the Blitz, without which we might not have had a welfare state to begin with; and if the Tube-shelter myth is a force for reaction now, it was once a potent force for redemption, as the communist poet Randall Swingler observed:

> Deep down in the earth, a great change is happening to London's people, like the bursting of a seed buried in the earth. They are passing through the abyss of Purgatory. But the time will come when the people of the underground will rise again, breaking the surface of their winter. And they will change the world as radically as spring changes the winter earth.[49]

'In this station there are only a hundred and thirty children', wrote Louis MacNeice, 'but asleep you are all children'.[50] This insight was shared by Brandt and Moore and that is why their Tube-shelter images will remain much more than wartime documentary. Their haunting, radical and redemptive vision of the children asleep on the Underground must continue to resonate with our ongoing struggle to make a home in modernity. Brandt and Moore each recognised the miraculous element in the Tube-shelter myth, and the children in their work constitute its most memorable expression: 'a personification of vital forces quite outside the limited range of our conscious mind; of ways and possibilities of which our one-sided conscious mind knows nothing; a wholeness which embraces the very depths of Nature'.[51]

NOTES

1 Naomi Mitchison, 'Siren Night', in *A Girl Must Live: Stories and Poems* (Glasgow: Richard Drew, 1990), p. 130.
2 Louis MacNeice, 'London Letter [1]' (1941), in *Selected Prose*, ed. Alan Heuser (Oxford: Clarendon Press, 1990), p. 101.
3 Leonard Woolf, *The Journey Not the Arrival Matters* (London: Hogarth Press, 1969), pp. 59–60.
4 Angus Calder, *The Myth of the Blitz* (London: Jonathan Cape, 1991), p. 142.
5 Quoted by Calder, p. 3.
6 *Ibid.*, p. 4.
7 John Gregg, *The Shelter of the Tubes* (London: Capital Transport, 2001), p. 19.
8 See for example. Jill Paton Walsh's children's book *Fireweed* (London: Macmillan, 1969).
9 John Buckland Wright, *Tube Shelter No.2, 1940* (London Transport Museum).
10 *Evening Standard*, September 1940–January 1941.
11 From the Mass-Observation Archive at the University of Sussex: ref. no. TC23/5/E.
12 Infants and children feature prominently in seven of the eighteen photographs taken in the Tube. See 'Elephant & Castle Underground Station Shelter', 11 November 1940, and 'Liverpool Street Extension', 12 November 1940, D1566–D1572 and D1583, in the Imperial War Museum Photograph Archive, London.
13 See Bill Brandt, *Shadow of Light* (London: Gordon Fraser, 1977), Section 3.
14 *Evening Standard*, Friday 18 October 1940, p. 7.
15 See Joseph Bató's *Defiant City* (London: Victor Gollancz, 1942); and Negley Farson, *Bomber's Moon*, with illustrations by Tom Purvis (London: Victor Gollancz, 1941), p. 71 or p. 67.
16 Julian Andrews, *London's War* (Aldershot: Lund Humphries, 2002), p. 36.
17 See Joseph Bató's *Defiant City*. Introduction by J.B.Priestly (London: Victor Gollancz, 1942) p. 69.
18 *Ibid.*, p. 46.
19 Henry Reed, *The Novel Since 1939* (London: Longmans, Green and Co., 1946), p. 23.
20 *Ibid.*, p. 30.
21 T.S. Eliot, *Four Quartets* (London: Faber, 1944), p. 48.
22 Graham Greene, *The Ministry of Fear* (1943) (London: Penguin, 1963), p. 95, p. 13, p. 120, p. 113, p. 189.
23 Reed, p. 23.
24 Eliot, p. 31.
25 Greene, p. 11, p. 18.
26 *Ibid.*, p. 13, p. 59.
27 Unless otherwise indicated, all quotations in the following paragraph are derived from Book 1, Chapter 5, in *The Ministry of Fear*, pp. 67–72.
28 *Ibid.*, p. 157; emphasis added.

29 Unless otherwise indicated, all quotations in the following paragraph are derived from Elizabeth Bowen's 'Postscript' to *The Demon Lover and Other Stories* (London: Penguin, 1965), pp. 196–203.
30 *Ibid.*, p. 197.
31 John Hayward, *Prose Literature Since 1939* (London: Longmans, Green and Co., 1947), p. 22.
32 Angus Calder and Dorothy Sheridan, eds, *Speak for Yourself: A Mass-Observation Anthology, 1937–49* (London: Jonathan Cape, 1984), p. 102.
33 Henry Moore, *A Shelter Sketchbook*, ed. Francis Carey (London: British Museum, 1988), p. 9.
34 Brandt, Plate 5.3.
35 Nigel Warburton, ed., *Bill Brandt: Selected Texts and Bibliography* (Oxford: Clio Press, 1993), pp. 5–6.
36 Brandt, 'A Statement', in Warburton, p. 32.
37 Joanne Buggins, 'The Shelter Photographs', in Warburton, p. 51.
38 Ian Jeffrey, ed., *Bill Brandt* (London: Thames and Hudson, 1993), p. 91.
39 The painting is reproduced by Robin Ironside in *Since 1939* (London: Phoenix House, 1949) between pp. 156 and 157.
40 See Ann Garrould, ed., *Henry Moore. Volume 3: Complete Drawings, 1940–49* (Aldershot: Lund Humphries, 2001), p. 93.
41 C.G. Jung, 'The Psychology of the Child Archetype', first published as 'Zur Psychologie des Kind-Archetypus', in *Das göttliche Kind*, in 1940; trans. R.F.C. Hull, *The Archetypes and the Collective Unconscious* (London: Routledge and Kegan Paul, 1959), p. 179.
42 *Ibid.*, p. 164.
43 Mark Haworth-Booth, ed., Shadow Of Light (London: Gordon Fraser, 1977), p.19.
44 Roger Berthoud, *The Life of Henry Moore* (London: Giles de la Mare, 2003), p. 212.
45 Geoffrey Hill, *Speech! Speech!* (London: Penguin, 2001), p. 49.
46 Roland Barthes, *Mythologies* (1957), trans. Annette Lavers (London: Cape, 1972), p. 155.
47 Unless otherwise stated, quotations from the following paragraphs are from Adrian Lewis, 'Henry Moore's "Shelter Drawings" – Memory and Myth', in *War Culture*, ed. p. Kirkham and D. Thomas, *War Culture* (London: Lawrence and Wishart, 1995).
48 Calder, *The Myth of the Blitz*, p. 15.
49 Randall Swingler, 'Sheltering in London Tubes', *Daily Worker*, 14 September 1940, p. 7.
50 Louis MacNeice, 'Cook's Tour of the London Subways', *The Listener*, 17 April 1941, p. 554.
51 Jung, p. 170.

6

INSURRECTION IN ALPHABET-CITY

Counterculture in the London Underground

Wanda: Aristotle was not Belgian, the principle of Buddhism is not 'every man for himself', and the London Underground is not a political movement. Those are all mistakes, Otto. I looked them up.
(Jamie Lee Curtis in *A Fish Called Wanda*, 1988)[1]

'With the aid of old maps, aerial photographs and experimental drifts, one can draw up hitherto lacking maps of influences, maps whose inevitable imprecision at this early stage is no worse than that of the first navigational charts', wrote Guy Debord.[2] Among the many old maps that provided the raw material for this psychogeographical reappraisal of the urban landscape in Debord's *Mémoires* (1959) is an early map of the London railway network. *Mémoires* consists of text lifted from sources such as travel brochures, novels, political tracts and newspapers, juxtaposed with photographs, cartoons, maps and old book illustrations, and held together by the drips, dribbles and blotches of paint added by the artist Asger Jorn. The inclusion of the railway map recalls Debord's remark some years earlier, in the Belgian surrealist journal *Les Lévres Nues*, that he scarcely knew of anything that could rival in beauty the maps of the Paris Metro (which had not yet been remodelled on the pattern of Harry Beck's Tube Map): 'It will be understood that in speaking here of beauty I don't have in mind plastic beauty', he wrote, 'but simply the particularly moving presentation in both cases, of a *sum of possibilities*'.[3] As Simon Sadler observes, the inclusion of a map predating the one produced by Harry Beck points towards the new trends in art that were trying to break away from modernism's hard-edge geometry: Debord must have 'enjoyed the way the drifting nets of track reminded him of psycho-emotional meanderings generally – a little like those that guided Jackson Pollock's drips – and resembled the courses of the drift, which paid so little regard to the internal boundaries of the city'.[4] Where the modernist map imposed order upon the city's transport system, the image produced by Debord and Jorn encouraged uncircumscribed reverie: 'Rather than float above the city as some sort of omnipotent, instantaneous, disembodied, all-possessing eye, situationist cartography admitted that its overview of the city was reconstructed in the imagination, piecing together an experience of space that was actually terrestrial, fragmented, subjective, temporal, and cultural'.[5] The image is just one of Debord's 'host of proposals' for turning 'the whole of life into an exciting game'.[6] The reader is invited to negate the previous organisation of expression through *détournement* – misappropriation of the space for play.[7]

The radicalism of play in the infrastructure of a civilisation geared to production cannot be overstated. Debord believed that the pleasure the Situationist might take in drifting through the Tube was the first step towards the complete construction of architecture and urbanism that would someday be within the power of everyone: when the 'masses in action' awake to 'the conditions that are imposed on them in all the domains of life, and to the practical means of changing them'.[8] Writing at a time when the modernist space he rejected was approaching its zenith in the municipal and private housing schemes of tower and slab blocks thrown up in the 1960s, Debord believed psychogeography might reclaim the urban environment and thereby challenge the 'New Reality' brought into being by the state and the market. As photo-artist Stephen Willats has observed, the socially liberal concepts that had formed the basis for the post-war consensus were being embodied in buildings 'founded on parameters that reflect implicitly the ideology of an authoritative, deterministic society, where the occupants have been reduced to the level of objects'.[9] The Situationists sought to highlight this contradiction at the heart of post-war society by rendering its oppressive material structures the medium for a message of liberation. Their anti-establishment slogans were to be broadcast in 'leaflets, announcements over microphones, comic strips, songs, graffiti, balloons on paintings in the Sorbonne, announcements in theaters during films or while disrupting them, balloons on subway billboards, before making love, after making love, in elevators, each time you raise your glass in a bar'.[10] Their opportunity came with unrest at the recently built University of Nanterre, where students were kept in oppressive, overcrowded housing. 'The urbanism of isolation had grafted a university centre onto the high-rise flats and their complementary slums', claimed the *Situationist International*. 'It was a microcosm of the general conditions of oppression, the spirit of a world without spirit.'[11]

The uprising that followed in May '68 nearly brought down the French Republic. In a candid analysis on national television, President Charles de Gaulle blamed the 'explosion' on 'groups in revolt against modern consumer and technical society, whether it be the Communism of the East or capitalism in the West', 'which have no idea at all of what they would replace it with, but who delight in negation, destruction, violence, anarchy, and who brandish the black flag'.[12] The restoration of order in Paris heralded the end of the Situationist International, but it also marked the beginning of a new phase of pro-situ activity beyond France. As the 'microcosm' at Nanterre was reproduced throughout Britain, this widening fissure at the heart of the New Reality would spur a generation of artists and writers into similar efforts to reclaim the traumatised capital.

As Willats has noted, British youth in the New Reality had been made to feel remote from the dominant culture's idealisations that were constantly being projected onto them: 'the projections had become remote by reflecting a life with possessions that could never be obtained and this generated increasing alienation and hostility'.[13] The result was that people fought to reclaim their environment: 'What can be perceived as wanton vandalism by the authorities can also be seen as an expressed creativity, directed at the context that was most meaningful, the physical fabric of the building in which they lived'.[14] This chapter will trace attempts on the part of writers and artists to realise this objective over the course of the postwar era through the misappropriation of the transit system singled out by Debord as a space in which to begin revolution in London. It will be seen that such interventions have typically assumed a popular form (following Debord's prescription), and though none has (as yet) stimulated the political revolution promised by the Situationists, they can at least be shown to have provided the foundation for a new way of experiencing the urban landscape – which has been celebrated in work by Sam Selvon, Salman Rushdie, Hanif Kureishi and many more.

THE BIRTH OF BRITISH POP

As his mum never tires of telling him, the street-wise teenage narrator of the novel *Absolute Beginners* (1959) was born in a Tube-shelter with an air-raid warden acting as midwife – a 'Blitz baby'.[15] As the embodiment of the new youth culture, it is fitting that Colin MacInnes's nameless protagonist should have begun life in the London Underground. To begin with, the vibrant cultural scene depicted in the novel is predicated on the post-war multicultural society that London Transport had played an important part in bringing about: finding it hard to secure workers in the post-war boom, the company recruited 4,000 Barbadians between 1956 and 1965, and later established further recruitment offices in Jamaica and Trinidad.[16] In so doing, London Transport prepared the ground for a uniquely fruitful period of cross-cultural interaction that has been identified by theorists as the crucial factor in the emergence of British pop culture. In his groundbreaking study of subculture, for instance, Dick Hebdige demonstrates that 'the history of post-war British youth culture must be reinterpreted as a succession of differential responses to the black immigrant presence in Britain from the 1950s onwards'.[17] And the importance of cultural alliances between skinhead stomp and ska in the 1960s, and between reggae and punk in the 1970s, is stressed by Sukhdev Sandhu: 'It was these marriages encompassing fashion, music, sex and shared attitudes that helped to create the open-minded, pick'n'mix, urban British youth culture which flourishes to this day'.[18] But as well as creating the preconditions, London Underground provided a space that served as a crucible for British pop. Marc Bolan and Peregrine Took of T-Rex, Lene Lovich, inventor of the hippie plait, Steve Harley of Human Menagerie, Joe Strummer of the Clash, Ralph McTell, Gerry Rafferty and George Michael are just a few of the musicians who began their careers by defying the official ban on busking (in place till the late 1980s) to fill the tunnels with song. McTell first sang 'The Streets of London' as a busker there, and the unforgettable saxophone on Rafferty's 'Baker Street' was first heard in Baker Street Station. The miracle of occupation represented by the Blitz babies had been rendered habitual by the Absolute Beginners, who made their first home in the London Underground. The instrumental part played by the Tube-network in the evolution of British multicultural pop culture is a key theme in the fiction of Samuel Selvon, and the novelist's London-based writing will form the basis for this section. By far the most successful chronicler of the new Britain, I hope to show that Selvon also anticipates Britain's pop aesthetic.

Selvon's short story 'Working the Transport' is of particular interest in this respect.[19] On one level, the tale is an elegant act of revenge, ridiculing

London Transport's preference for the island of Barbados, where the company could expect to recruit personnel who were typically overqualified for the menial tasks they were allocated: 'you must be read in the papers about how London Transport send men down there in the West Indies to get fellars to work on the tube and bus, and it looks as if they like Barbadians, because they didn't go to any other island: they just get some of the boys from Little England'.[20] In this story the company is taken in by the big talk of a bold but inept boatman known as Small Change. The result is highly entertaining slapstick. Small Change slams a double-decker bus into a wall, fails to grasp the complexities of Britain's pre-decimal coinage and mistakenly evacuates a Tube-train, causing a dislocation of the schedules from West Ruislip to Ongar. Though untypical, the tale of Small Change nevertheless provides an extraordinary insight into the transformation of popular culture in the post-war period. It is revealed that the reason why Small Change cannot give more than perfunctory attention to his instructors at London Transport is that he is trying to think up an entirely new pop movement, to impress a girl he has started dating from the Elephant and Castle: 'So while the transport people trying to learn Change how to conduct, Change studying some kind of newfangled step, and when elevenses come he went to the other boys and tell them how he have to invent a new dance else the West Indies would be let down'.[21] The new dance is a kind of Gene Kelly mix-up with some mambo and samba and some carnival breakaway thrown in – an exotic combination that evokes the rich cultural cocktail then brewing in the capital – and which soon takes on a whole life of its own: 'It was a ruction when the teddies start up on this new dance that Change introduce, and pretty soon everybody forget about "rock'n'roll" and start to concentrate on "hip'n'hit", and the old Change figuring out if he can't make something on the side by giving lessons after work'. Small Change begins to teach the hip'n'hit to Teddy boys in the Elephant, until it becomes a real craze south of the river.

Selvon's tale is surprising because the potential for such mixing between the calypso musical tradition favoured by the black community in the 1950s and the white working-class youth movement behind the Notting Hill race riots of 1958 has (unsurprisingly) been overlooked by historians of pop culture. Hebdige, for instance, begins his attempt to reinterpret British subculture as a succession of reactions to the black immigrant presence somewhat belatedly with ska.[22] Yet calypso clearly possessed the potential for the surprising and intoxicating cross-cultural fusions and confusions with which it is credited in the fiction of Selvon. The two leading performers in the calypso style, Lord Kitchener and Lord Beginner, had forced themselves into Britain's collective consciousness when they stepped off the SS

Empire Windrush in 1948 and performed impromptu for a waiting Pathé newsreel. In that same year, the Trinidadian Edric Connor starred in a West End musical called *Calypso*, and the music very soon acquired a following that extended right up to the royal family: Princess Margaret reportedly purchased 100 copies of the single 'Ah, Berenice!', and Lord Kitchener was even invited to perform at the coronation of Queen Elizabeth II. Exposed to bebop and jazz, calypso artists residing in London soon began to incorporate elements from these related musical forms into their songs, and this new multicultural aesthetic was to find memorable expression in a classic track by Lord Beginner called 'Mix-Up Matrimony', which saluted Seretse Khama, chief of the Bamangwato people in Bechuanaland, who had been driven away into exile for marrying a white woman.

And the truth about the Teds is, in fact, far more complicated than they themselves later came to believe. Priding themselves on their racism and bigotry, the Teddy boys are usually portrayed as the one white working-class subculture that failed to take anything positive from the musical heritage of the West Indies.[23] Yet the music favoured by the Teddy boys before the onset of rock'n'roll was a form of folk jazz called skiffle, which was played on everyday objects like washboards and tea-chests, as in traditional calypso, and it would seem that Teds in many skiffle bands were prepared to take inspiration from this related musical form.[24] In 1957 Johnny Duncan released a skiffle version of the calypso song 'Last Train to San Fernando', while up in Liverpool a Ted called Ringo Starr developed his influential Mersey beat performing calypso hits in Butlin's Holiday Camp.[25] Calypso has played an important role, hitherto unrecognised, in the birth of British pop. Selvon's 'Working the Transport' therefore permits a rare glimpse into the formative stage of a phenomenon without which our contemporary culture would have been imported wholesale from the United States. As Hanif Kureishi has observed,

> Only Britain's cornucopia of music prevented the country from becoming a third-rate cultural outpost, the complete victim of US cultural power. Britain couldn't be entirely Americanized while it continued to generate its own identity through music and fashion and the political culture and activism of its youth.[26]

Significantly, procedures for the misappropriation of functional space for play theorised later by the Situationists are integral to Selvon's London-based writing. In 'Working the Transport', the Barbadians seize one of the buses that represent their official, limited role in the life of the capital and beat the soundtrack to their 'mix-up' on the bars and panels of the vehicle:

'Change sit down on the platform on a bus and start to beat the side, and Alipang finish drinking tea and hitting the empty cup with the spoon, while Jackfish keeping time on the bar it have what you does hold on to when you going in the bus'.[27] Small Change remarks that the bus they are playing on has a good tone, highlighting the fact that he has literally transformed public transport into a musical instrument. As Susheila Nasta notes, the trickster mode employed in Selvon's London fiction refuses the flat, functional roles Western tradition would impose on his characters, permitting them to emerge as natural agents of an alternative modern vision: 'This not only contests but transforms the white gaze, enabling the genesis of a new dialogue with the city to develop which can open out the reductive postures previously available to them in history'.[28] Over the course of 'Working the Transport', the trickster who meant short change for London Transport thus comes to signify a sudden and radical change in the use of public space. 'They does treat Piccadilly Circus like Green Corner', writes Selvon, 'and walked down Oxford Street is if they breezing down Frederick Street, and if they meet you in the road or in a bus or in the tube, is a big shout, "What happening there, papa?"'[29] In this respect, Selvon anticipates the playful subversion of a social space that has been integral to post-war pop culture in the capital. His work can be seen to herald the rebellious spirit expressed in this comment by David Benn, a long-time busker in Piccadilly Circus Station: 'I've been fined 2,000 times, marched out in handcuffs just for playing music. But music is good for the ghostly canyons below our streets.'[30]

The city's transport system is at the heart of Selvon's remarkable urban aesthetic and in this respect, too, his fiction can be seen to pre-empt international pop music. From the fast cars, motor-bikes and train journeys in American rock'n'roll, to the submarines, buses, rocket-ships and Tube-stations in its British equivalent, transport has remained a symbol for the power and speed that is an integral ingredient in the pop aesthetic. And, anticipating Guy Debord, Selvon recognises the metaphorical potential of the Tube in particular. In the short story 'My Girl and the City', the narrator observes that 'the creation goes on and on in my mind while I look at all the faces around me in the tube, the restless rustle of newspapers, the hiss of air as the doors close, the enaction of life in a variety of forms'.[31] The Tube is recognised as the only possible symbol for what he wishes to write about life in the capital. The narrator even persuades his stenographer girlfriend to ride about the Inner Circle with him, and to write down his thoughts as they occur to him so that they can 'make something of it'. This holds out the tantalising possibility that Selvon's London-based fiction, remarkable for velocity and sheer verve, was inspired by the London Underground.

But the representational history of the Underground is far from the uncomplicated proposition of the open road. In pop culture, the Tube-network would, in fact, come to embody the problems as well as the promise of mix and movement. In what is perhaps the most memorable reference to the Tube in a pop song, for instance, the Kinks sing of the exhaustion and alienation experienced by a man on the South Bank while watching millions of people swarming like flies about Waterloo Underground, his heart lifted only on seeing two lovers meet and cross over the river into the sunset.[32] And in a neglected motion picture by the figure in the film industry most closely associated with pop culture (through his film work for the Beatles) Richard Lester implies that the freedom of movement represented by the London Underground (which provided the initial impetus for societal metamorphosis) might even turn out to be a form of paralysis. *The Bed-Sitting Room* (1969) is a surreal black comedy written by Spike Milligan and John Antrobus that presents the spectacle of a Britain devastated by nuclear war. Following precedent, Arthur Lowe takes wife and child into the shelter provided by the London Underground, and they proceed to ride round and round the Circle Line, feeding on sweets from platform vending machines. In the course of this endless journey, the parents remain oblivious to the swelling belly of their sulky teenage daughter Rita Tushingham. The penny drops finally when Lowe pops out for a smoke one day to find his daughter asleep with a man in the next car claiming to be a commuter. The film suggests that the original act of *détournement* performed on the Home Front (perhaps indelibly associated with Arthur Lowe as Captain Mainwaring) made possible the liberties later enjoyed by a generation embodied by Rita Tushingham. But it soon emerges that Tushingham's character has been pregnant for seventeen months because she cannot bear to bring a baby into such a world. In Lester's bleak satire the Underground becomes the space between two worlds – one dead, one powerless to be born.

The metaphor of the Tube-network is used to express a similarly nuanced perspective on metropolitan movement in Selvon's fiction. In Selvon's radio play *Eldorado West One*, the first thing the newly arrived Galahad does upon arriving in the capital is to step carelessly on the escalator to the platform and slip: 'In London you have to keep on the move all the time', Moses remarks; 'Even the steps keep moving'.[33] The exhilarating fantasy of movement embodied by the Tube can often become a trap for the unwary: 'Under the kiff-kiff laughter, behind the ballad and episode, the what-happening, the summer-is-hearts, [Moses] could see a great aimlessness, a great restless, swaying movement that leaving you standing in same spot'.[34] Small Change is a case in point. His constant movement from position to position within London Transport could be read as paralysis, a failure to move up in the company. Bart in *The Lonely Londoners* is another example. When his English girlfriend abandons him he scours the public spaces of the capital, 'looking in the millions of white faces walking down Oxford Street, peering into buses, taking tube ride on the Inner Circle just in the hope that he might see she ... until he become haggard and hunted'.[35] In a cautionary tale told by Moses, a young man looking for freedom in the city is said to have ended his days trapped in the space that most embodied that freedom, crouching about in Tube-stations in an old coat picking cigarette butts from the pavement.[36] The narrator in 'My Girl and the City' is aware of the threat too: 'Motion mesmerises me into immobility'.[37]

This fear of being paralysed by perpetual motion was shared by other New Britons. In his famous song 'The Underground Train' Lord Kitchener attempts to travel from Piccadilly Circus to Lancaster Gate – and is on the cusp of striking up friendships with pretty young women on the way when he is frustrated by stairs that sweep him off his feet or by Tube-trains that take him far past his station.

> Ah-ha! My first misery
> Is when I embark at Piccadilly.
> I went down below
> I stand up in the crowd – don't know where to go!
> I decided to follow a young lady
> Well, I nearly met with my destiny
> That night was bad luck for Kitchener
> I fall down on the escalator.[38]

Similarly in Linton Kwesi Johnson's lyric 'Inglan Is a Bitch' (1980), the protagonist reflects that 'w'en mi jus' come to Landan toun / mi use to work pan di andahgroun / but workin' pan di andahgroun / y'u don't get fi know your way around'.[39]

In 'My Girl and the City', Selvon tries to understand why travel on the Underground holds such fascination for him. 'You could be lonely as hell in the city', he reflects, 'then one day you look around you and you realise everybody else is lonely too, withdrawn, locked, rushing home out of the chaos: blank faces, unseeing eyes, millions and millions of them, up the Strand, down the Strand, jostling in Charing Cross for the 5.20'. Following an exchange of looks with a pretty continental girl, he notes that he did not talk to her or look her way again or even think of her, that events in this place merely happen and are finished with forever. The public ways of the city are presented in this prose-poem as spaces of non-place. Here there are no relations, only solitude and silence. For those who came to make a home in Britain, the London Underground could therefore be nothing but a trap – open to everyone, it could be inhabited only by those prepared to remain outside mainstream society. Selvon had recognised the Tube as a heavily mediated environment that exists in the pattern assumed by its own signs, and took pleasure in reconstituting this space through language, even as he expresses a prescient awareness of the limitations to such *détournement*.

> At last I think I know what it is all about. I move around in a world of words. Everything that happens is words. But pure expression is nothing. One must build on the things that happen: it is insufficient to say I sat in the underground and the train hurtled through the darkness and someone isn't using Amplex. So what? So now I weave, I say there was an old man on whose face wrinkles rivered, whose hands were shapeful with arthritis but when he spoke, oddly enough, his voice was young and gay.
>
> But there was no old man, there was nothing, and there is never ever anything.[40]

In closing this section it seems fitting to recall the monument to pop culture in the Tube-station at Tottenham Court Road. The mosaics on the walls by Eduardo Paolozzi, pioneer of Pop Art, can be seen to have been informed by a similar insight into the potential and potential limitations of the post-war countercultural project. Commissioned by London Transport in 1979, Paolozzi's murals were conceived by the artist as a form of resistance to banal uniformity and a loss of the sense of place, restoring the right of citizens to a place in the city through landmarks created by art within the architecture.[41] Images of saxophones, fast food, music shops, satellites and Turkish art in resplendent mosaics capture the intoxicating cultural mix in the streets above: a public form that remains intimate, a large expanse that is brilliant and bold but richly encrusted and inviting to touch. Paolozzi was connecting passengers with the cultural topography of a district famous for its mix of ethnicities, its musical instruments and record boutiques, long considered to be the beating heart of London's multicultural pop aesthetic. But, as Richard Cork points out, although Paolozzi was one of the first British artists to immerse himself in pop culture, his enthusiasm for it was tempered by darker concerns: 'Far more conscious than most Pop artists of the destructive side of modern civilisation, he often returns to the vision of a world where the human presence has been overtaken by the forces of mechanisation'.[42] These perspectives are integrated in the Rotunda, the former lift shaft that now connects the Northern Line and the Central Line to the ticket hall overhead. Here circles hinting at wheels and cogs, pie charts and film reels float in convoluted patterns that suggest organisms and engines, architectural plans and the Mayan calendar, satellites and carnival masks, a bio-mechanical concatenation that entangles and penetrates a running man, a chicken and a cow, the more representational imagery that Paolozzi referred to as an 'Orwellian commuter, a fast-food chicken and hamburger'.[43] The rest of this chapter develops these concerns at greater length – in the course of recounting how, in the years immediately following the completion of Paolozzi's murals in 1985, young people across the metropolis took up the challenge themselves, transforming non-place into metaphor, through inscribing, in letters as hard and wild as the images in Tottenham Court Road, their secret names on rolling stock in the London Underground.

INVISIBLE INSURRECTION

The first writer to follow Debord's lead into the Tube was the Scottish novelist Alexander Trocchi, a founding member of the Situationist International, who achieved notoriety with his novels *Young Adam* (1954) and *Cain's Book* (1960). Trocchi planned to produce a 'poster magazine' called *The Moving Times* that would possess the format of a respectable broadsheet, and submitted a proposal to rent advertisement panels in four Tube-stations to the London Transport Authority in August 1964.[44] The only extant issue of the poster magazine contains surprisingly tame material by controversial countercultural figures such as William Burroughs, Robert Creeley, Kenneth White and Trocchi himself.[45] This was in fact entirely in keeping with Trocchi's stated intentions: 'We have already rejected any idea of a frontal attack', he had declared in an essay called 'Invisible Insurrection of a Million Minds' (1958). 'It is rather a question of perceiving clearly and without prejudice what are the forces that are at work in the world and out of whose interaction tomorrow *must* come to be; and then, calmly, without indignation, by a kind of mental ju-jitsu that is ours by virtue of intelligence, of modifying, correcting, polluting, deflecting, corrupting, eroding, outflanking ... inspiring what we might call *the invisible insurrection*.'[46] As James Riley observes, Trocchi intended to establish an intimate connection with the very structure that was the target of his subversion: and in this respect *The Moving Times* resembles earlier efforts on the part of the Vorticists, who wanted to transform the modern world by infiltrating and reordering its media, beginning with posters in the Underground: 'cultural revolt must seize the grids of expression and the power-house of the mind', wrote Trocchi.[47] This aspect of the project was so important to Trocchi that, following London Transport's refusal to display the broadsheet, he set about distributing it throughout the system himself. Trocchi was harnessing the Tube's power as a communications network to call for effective communications between participants in what he was to call Project Sigma: 'FROM NOW ON, you are invited to take part in a continuous international concordium concerning the future of things'.[48] *The Moving Times* was an open invitation to move with the times: 'we envisage a situation in which life is continually renewed by art, a situation imaginatively and passionately constructed to inspire each individual to respond creatively, to bring to whatever act a creative comportment'.[49] As the appearance of the word 'situation' in this passage suggests, Project Sigma was based upon a specifically Situationist critique of contemporary life. Consequently, it is rather ironic that it should have been *The Moving Times* that earned Trocchi exclusion from the Situationist International (SI): 'our friend Alexander Trocchi has since developed an activity of which we fully approve of several aspects', conceded Debord, but 'the SI could not involve itself in such a loose cultural venture'.[50] Debord was unable to stomach an organisation, like Project Sigma, from which 'No one is excluded'.[51]

Subsequent intervention in the physical fabric of the city would be more forthright. Economic turmoil exacerbated establishment neglect in regions like the East End and resulted in the withdrawal of services essential to the material and the social well-being of the New Reality.[52] Having been starved of cash while in the control of the British Transport Commission, the London Underground was in this respect some years ahead of more recent modernist developments. The space was undergoing systematic decay in the very period that saw the culmination of the New Reality that London Underground had pioneered. The extent of this neglect is reflected in the proliferation of horror-related movies and fiction set in the Tube from the late 1960s through to the 1980s. In *Quatermass and the Pit* (1967), construction workers excavating the Victoria Line unearth a mysterious space-ship that begins to stir up the hellish impulses planted in the human neural system millions of years ago by our infernal insect overlords, provoking a purge of non-Martian elements in the populace. In *Death Line* (1972), by the American horror master Gary Sherman, a lonely cannibal, trapped in the Tube-station his forefathers were building when a tunnel collapsed, returns to wreak vengeance upon the system, snatching solitary passengers from platforms and carrying them off to devour in the dark. In James Herbert's horror novel *The Rats* (1974), the lengthiest and bloodiest of the atrocities perpetrated by his mutant black rats takes place in a Tube-station called Shadwell: 'men and women were running, fighting, cowering as hundreds of black rats rampaged amongst them, leaping and tearing, their bloodlust stirring them to frenzy'.⁵³ And the Tube features in director John Landis's horror film *An American Werewolf in London* (1981): in a scene renowned for its terrifying velocity, a city banker hurtles through the station at Tottenham Court Road, past posters for Landis's fictional porn movie *See You Next Wednesday*, trapped in an ironic, self-referential product of pop culture; irrational, murderous and magical, the monster that pursues him is the embodiment of the aggressive countercultural activities then contesting the public authorities' capacity to police the London Underground.

Like New York artist Gordon Matta-Clark, who removed elliptical sections of wall (without permission) from a vast abandoned warehouse in an artwork called *Day's End* (1975), writers and artists in London would assert their right to combat neglect and abandonment – 'to improve the property, to transform the structure in the midst of its ugly criminal state into a place of interest, fascination and value'.⁵⁴ And in this respect the Tube-writers considered hereafter can perhaps be seen to depart from the Situationist project for the revolution of everyday life – with results that cast light upon the flawed nature of the dualism upon which it was premised. This new wave of insurrectionary art targeted a functionalist system – not for being functional – but for proving dysfunctional. Rather than discrediting the logic underpinning the system, Tube-writers were contesting that system's state of neglect, and though such weakness encouraged open confrontation, pure negations of the existing order that resulted in their being labelled vandals, named after the tribes that had overthrown the classical world, the very weakness that provided them with an opening can be shown to have exposed the representational space produced to the same fate that befell the Vorticist project. Like the ancient German tribes, these insurrectionaries seem doomed to be embraced as saviours of an order too weak to save itself.

THE GRAFFITI WAR

The story begins with Debord's expulsion of Christopher Gray, Timothy Clark and Donald Nicholson-Smith, the British contingent of the Situationist International, on 21 December 1967, 'just as they were getting ready to publish a journal in England and begin a group activity there'.⁵⁵ The action was taken following their fraternisation with an American called Ben Morea, publisher of the bulletin *Black Mask* and member of the Motherfuckers, a countercultural group sometimes referred to as Up Against the Wall Motherfucker. Together with brothers Dave and Stuart

Wise, the British-based members of the Motherfuckers, Gray proceeded with his programme for pro-situ activity in London. The group he formed was called King Mob, a name taken from the menacing graffito painted on the wall of Newgate Prison by the rioters who sacked the building during the Gordon Riots of 1780, 'His Majesty King Mob'. As Simon Ford notes, King Mob's main source of inspiration was not the intense theorising of the Situationist International but *Black Mask*, and the 'freak' scene of 1960s counterculture in general.[56] But, even so, King Mob can still be seen to owe much to the Situationists, not least their favoured means of expression. 'What sign should one recognise as our own?' asked Situationist Raoul Vaneigem: 'Certain graffiti, words of refusal or forbidden gestures inscribed with haste'.[57] As their name might suggest, King Mob chose to communicate primarily through graffiti, and in this respect they were following the example of the Situationists, who had daubed Paris with slogans in May '68. In fact, King Mob's most famous intervention in the urban landscape is an elaboration on a phrase first coined by the Situationist International:

SAME THING DAY AFTER DAY – TUBE – WORK – DINNER – WORK – TUBE – ARMCHAIR – T.V. – SLEEP – TUBE – WORK – HOW MUCH MORE CAN YOU TAKE ? ONE IN TEN GO MAD – ONE IN FIVE CRACKS UP.[58]

The impact of this slogan was heightened by its inspired location on a concrete wall surmounted by a wire fence between the Westway and the Hammersmith and City Line, where it could be read every day by passengers on their way to work. In pointing up the brutal utilitarianism of this space, King Mob triumphantly vindicated Vaneigem's claim that traffic circulation is the organisation of universal isolation: 'It is the opposite of encounter, it absorbs the energies that could otherwise be devoted to encounters or to any sort of participation'.[59]

Such interventions in a decaying urban environment remained an integral component in the punk movement that followed – as one might expect, given the pivotal role played in the creation of punk by Malcolm McLaren, a member of King Mob. Perhaps the most famous example figures in the Jam's hit record 'Down in the Tube Station at Midnight'. In this story of a man travelling home with takeaway curry, brutally attacked by neo-Nazi skinheads, the Tube is presented as an archetypal urban space threatened with apocalypse: 'toffee-wrappers and this morning's papers with their headlines of death and sorrow'. This is a non-place that the authorities can no longer maintain or control. Significantly, the last thing the protagonist sees – before losing the ability to see, hear, speak any longer – is what would seem to be an example of punk graffiti.

> The last thing that I saw
>   As I lay there on the floor
>   Was Jesus Saves painted by an atheist nutter
>   And a British Rail poster read have an away-day
> A cheap holiday
>   Do it today![60]

Presumably the graffiti is aggressively atheist because the phrase has been painted onto the poster – in which case it would imply that Jesus only saves money with British Rail. If so, the graffiti bears a startling resemblance to slogans sprayed onto advertisements in the Tube by the punk band Crass from 1977. Using stencils and aerosol spray-cans, Crass travelled throughout central London by Tube spraying one of up to six anti-sexist, anti-racist, anti-corporate, anti-imperial, anti-materialist, or pro-anarchist slogans onto posters they deemed offensive, or onto monuments immediately outside the station. The initial campaign was planned to avoid possible charges of vandalism: 'We decided we'd always be very neat and clean about it', explains band member Penny Rimbaud; 'we'd always put it on the appropriate poster, we wouldn't spray on property'.[61] The language used was thus as inoffensive as possible: 'We just wanted to help people think, to reconsider'. In fact, their objective was similar to Trocchi's, the subversion of the representational space of the metropolis, but on a hitherto unprecedented scale. 'It was like a military operation', recalls Mike Duffield, the band's film technician; 'we'd divide up the mechanics of doing it: one person would be responsible for the stencils, one for the spray paint, another person masking what we were doing'.[62]

The band's success with the spray-can inspired a movement committed to political sloganeering and subverting advertisements with stencil graffiti, making them pioneers of what political theorist Naomi Klein has since termed 'culture jamming', the practice of hijacking advertisements in order to drastically alter their messages. Klein shows the activity to stem from mounting anger at the extent to which aggressive marketing is penetrating our mental and physical environment, and from an increasing awareness that so much that makes it powerful is in fact virtual and therefore open to semiotic warfare. 'The process forces the company to foot the bill for its own subversion, either literally, because the company is the one that paid for the billboard, or figuratively, because anytime people mess with a logo, they are tapping into the vast resources spent to make that logo meaningful'.[63]

Banksy (who has made stencil graffiti internationally famous) has called it Brandalism: 'Any advertisement in public space that gives you no choice whether you see it or not is yours. It belongs to you. It's yours to take, re-arrange and re-use. Asking for permission is like asking to keep a rock someone just threw at your head.'[64] There is some irony in the fact that the network that pioneered the mediated spaces of late capitalism should have seen the earliest concerted attempt to subvert them. And curiously enough, the first recorded instance of the co-option of such culture jamming by reactionary forces seems to have happened there too. Three months into its campaign, Crass found that they were being imitated by a group of Christian fundamentalists. 'It was almost like the Christians were appropriating what we were doing – you could have seen it as being all one programme.'[65] In a further twist, Crass responded by branding their work: 'that was the point at which we started putting the Crass symbol on it', explains Penny Rimbaud, 'and slightly beefing up what we were saying'.[66] Graffiti from this later stage in the campaign is featured on the cover of their album *Stations of the Crass*: phrases such as 'FIGHT WAR NOT WARS', 'DESTROY POWER NOT PEOPLE' and 'STUFF YOUR SEXIST SHIT' are shown on a badly maintained wall in the Tube, next to symbols of anarchy, the mysterious numerals 621984 and 521984, and the cross/snake logo for Crass.

This political stencil graffiti was swiftly eclipsed by the new 'tag' graffiti derived from New York. In the band's view this new form of graffiti was the work of 'hip-hop artists who have done little but confirm the insidious nature of American culture'.[67] And, though the band's historian, George Berger, is prepared to concede that, in some cases, the result is beautiful, talented and colourful art, he believes that it more often resembles a coloured snail trail: 'Either way, the short-lived political anarcho-graffiti ideas had been usurped by a culture that said little more than "I woz ere"'.[68]

I would like to suggest that there is in fact a remarkable continuity between the two. To begin with, the practice of 'tagging' a locale with name or symbol was from the start an important element in punk graffiti. The Sex Pistols and the Clash tagged up around the clubs where they played and, as we have seen, tagging was then taken up by Crass. Secondly, it was the Clash who introduced New York-style graffiti to London when they brought legendary subway artist Futura 2000 to the capital in 1981. Futura 2000 designed the cover for their single 'Radio Clash' and liner-notes for the album *Combat Rock*, and was even guest vocalist on track 7, 'Overpowered by Funk'. In return, the band provided the music for the street artist's own unfortunate venture into the music industry, *The Escapades of Futura 2000*. It is no coincidence that Futura 2000 chose to create the first 'piece' in the capital at Ladbroke Grove, the district haunted by King Mob and the Clash. Thirdly, it is agreed that American-style graffiti received its first real impetus in Britain with the Malcolm McLaren hit record 'Buffalo Gals' (1983).[69] The video for this seminal hip-hop track brought break dancing, scratching and spray-can art to an American and international audience for the first time. The subway artist known as Dondi is shown outlining the name of the song in enormous letters on a rooftop in New York. Both punks and former members of King Mob intuitively recognised that the vibrant subway art emerging in New York shared similar objectives to their own graffiti, fulfilling in some respects the reclamation of the urban landscape that had been envisaged by the Situationists.

New York's subway art came about when a teenager known as Taki 183 started tagging the inside and outside of subway trains, ensuring that his name would be seen throughout the city.[70] It must have been immediately obvious to a member of King Mob that the thriving subculture which subsequently developed was the mirror image of the advertising industry. New York's subway writers were circulating their names through a communications network that had been monopolised by the market – and were making their signs bigger, brighter and more stylish to ensure that their personal brand stood out from the rest. 'It is like a logo', observes Norman Mailer in 'The Faith of Graffiti' (1974): 'Moxie or Socono, Tang Whirlpool, Duz. The kids bear a not quite definable relation to their product. It is not MY NAME but THE NAME.'[71] As Jean Baudrillard points out, in his landmark essay on the graffiti subculture in New York, 'Kool Killer, or The Insurrection of Signs' (1976), the graffiti writers had gone further than mere identitarian revolt, in that they had opposed pseudonyms rather than names to anonymity. 'Retaliation, reversion of the code according to its own logic, on its own terrain, gaining victory over it because it exceeds semiocracy's own non-referentiality.'[72] Attacking those who argued that tag graffiti, devoid of overt political content, represented a retreat from the graffiti produced in May '68, Baudrillard argues that its very emptiness gives it strength. 'There is no need for organised masses, nor for a political consciousness to do this – a thousand youths armed with marker pens and cans of spray-paint are enough to scramble the signals of urbania and dismantle the order of signs.'[73] SUPERBEE, SPIX, COLA 139 are names taken straight from comics and mass advertising. These empty signifiers resist the principle of signification and erupt into a city of signs claiming only the radical exclusivity of the clan – of the group identities that the social structure of the modern metropolis tears apart, imposing proper names, private individualities and shattering all solidarity in the name of an urban abstract. But graffiti writers are of an older, territorial order: 'They territorialise decoded urban spaces – a particular street, wall or district comes to life through them, becoming a collective territory again'.[74] The super-hero personas that constituted and were constituted by the collective identity were being circulated through the system of tunnels under the city in a way that anticipates the reconfiguration of social identities now taking place within cyberspace. The practice of subway writing represents the appropriation of industrial systems of circulation to produce a mechanical site for social networking: prototype for 'A biocybernetic self-fulfilling prophecy world orgy I'.[75] As Norman Mailer perceived, the graffiti subculture was part of a wider shift. 'As we lose our senses in the static of the oncoming universal machine, so does our need to exercise the ego take on elephantiasistical proportions', he concluded.[76] If the future promised by graffiti were ever realised, the look of New York, and then the world, would be transformed: 'the interlapping of names and colors, those wavelets of ego forever reverberating upon one another, could have risen like a flood to cover the monstrosities of abstract empty techno-architectural twentieth-century walls where no design ever predominated over the most profitable (and ergo most monotonous) construction ratio implicit in a twenty-million-dollar bill.'[77]

The insurrectionary element in this new graffiti art was slow to emerge in London. The first writers in this country, such as the Chrome Angelz and the Incredible Grove Artists, were permitted to realise its utopian promise entirely legally, through farsighted policies introduced by Ken Livingstone's Greater London Council (GLC), which commissioned established writers to paint murals, and even ran classes on the art of aerosol painting in order to strengthen its links with disaffected young people.[78] In their seminal book on graffiti, *Spraycan Art* (1987), Henry Chalfont and James Prigoff cite Tabernacle Community Centre in Ladbroke Grove as an example of how a mere £2,000 could transform an entire urban community for the better: 'We found the centre bustling with activity and kids full of plans for painting murals and preparing for an up-coming break-dancing battle'.[79] In such a hospitable environment it seems that there was no incentive for writers to re-enact the subterranean exploits of their American counterparts in the London Underground. In fact, one writer based in London known as Shame 181 is even reported to have said that 'Our style over here, I couldn't see any of that stuff being put on a train 'cause I don't think it would rock'.[80]

This would change following Margaret Thatcher's abolition of the GLC in 1986. Curiously, this action has often been interpreted as a reprisal for the government's humiliation in a high-profile row with the GLC over the role public subsidies should play in maintaining the London Underground. London Transport had been transferred to local control in 1970 – and this release from the iron grip of the Treasury had brought some immediate benefits, such as the refurbishment of the station at Tottenham Court Road by Eduardo Paolozzi. But the leader of the GLC, Ken Livingstone, soon found his efforts to cut fares and raise standards hampered by a series of legal and political fights. The Conservative-run Borough of Bromley claimed that, since it was not on the Tube-network, it was being unfairly penalised by the rise in rates. 'Judges, not noted for the frequency with which they use public transport, ruled against the GLC both at the Court of Appeal and in the House of Lords.'[81] The only way to comply with this ruling was to double fares, and the resulting public outrage forced the government into a humiliating U-turn, compelling it to accept the 'Balanced Plan' proposed by the GLC. In revenge, Thatcher introduced a Parliamentary Bill to seize London Transport and in an act of 'astonishing vindictiveness' abolished the GLC.[82] The writers who began to work on Tube-cars from the mid-1980s, as funding for the legal outlets previously available to them began to dry up, were thus engaged, whether they knew it or not, in a peculiarly apt form of revenge.

Even as Thatcher stamped out political dissent throughout the rest of the country, these Tube-writers were striking back in a space that held tremendous political resonance in the fierce struggle taking place over the future of Britain. The military terminology imported from New York took on new significance as the spray-can became a symbolic weapon in a form of urban warfare: 'It's almost exchanging a gun for a spray can', remarked Tube-writer Proud 2.[83] As Nancy MacDonald explains, although writers do not and will never literally control the Tube-network, they use their art as a symbol of domination: 'The authorities' failure to keep their trains free of graffiti is taken to signify the subculture's supremacy'.[84] Nor is this perception limited to the subculture. The British Transport Police take graffiti so seriously because they really believe that 'Stations and trains covered in graffiti make users of the railway think that the vandals are in control, not railway management or the police'.[85] In choosing to assert their own personalities in the Tube-network, writers were taking on the state – and it would seem that, for a while at least, they won. The tube-writer called Prime asserts: 'Early '87, the underground system nearly got completely taken over'.[86] And veteran tube-writer Drax remembers the late 1980s as a golden age in the graffiti subculture's history:

> The Hammersmith Shed, full of burners, Christmas '88. A whole train in Moorgate, Christmas '89. Another at Fulham, Christmas '91, the deaths of Rase, Evil, Bliss and Zone, the disappearance of Cast and the WD Tube parties of 87–88 on the circle line with as many as 250 people jamming on a tube train and then going on mass bombing rampages never since seen ('Graffiti gang in $10,000 orgy of vandalism' was one headline) 100 or so

artists bombing the same few carriages or the same station cheered on by 100 to 150 assorted clubbers, girls, opportunists, hangers on or bystanders who had been swept along by the party travelling rapidly beneath the city, think about the sheer power of it.[87]

Unfortunately, little of the Tube-writing produced in this period has been recorded. As Drax points out that, no one had thought to photograph the material they produced. 'Only the Chrome Angelz period was in any way documented, all the other styles and stories became private London issues not really known by those who didn't venture here.'[88] Only 200 photographs of the Tube-writing produced in this brief period have been collated in online archives, and though these necessarily provide a partial and limited insight into the subculture, they still manage to convey the astonishing range and talent of those involved. The surviving photographs suggest that Tube-writers favoured the Brooklyn style, with its flourishes and arrows, over the cheery bubble letters from the Bronx. The use of the 'herald' (a cartoon directing viewers to the name) is rare and when it does appear in Tube-writing of the late 1980s it is typically anything but cute. In fact, the London art soon developed a distinct visual style that was more angular and harder-edged than the big-hearted original from New York. As Shame 181 had remarked months before writers moved into the Tube, the London style looked as though it was being torn apart.[89] The Tube-writers' intense and conflicted perception of the urban experience is conveyed through jagged swooping arrows, in a maelstrom of clashing, hard-edged, geometrical forms. The London style bears a curious resemblance, in fact, to the aggressive abstraction practised by the Vorticists and to the famous psychogeographical maps of Paris created by Asger Jorn and Guy Debord, in which the lines of force at work in the city are marked with military-style arrows. The Tube-writers tapped that same ecstasy of being caught up in a fast-moving metropolis, and expressed it more effectively than any other previous group of artists. Marinetti would have been delighted to see that these belligerent images had been painted onto the trains themselves, to crash briefly through the Underground like a lurid fair-ground ride before rushing to meet their erasure at the depot. Achieving maximum exposure while remaining instantly ephemeral, Tube-writing is the ultimate urban art form, and in the late 1980s it threatened to make real the fantasy harboured for so long by the English avant-gardes, in what was, at that time, one of the most politically fraught spaces in Britain. Tube-writers recognised the radical potential of their writing in this pivotal moment in the country's history, and their art possesses a political urgency that is entirely absent in the subway writing of New York. The subway writers might paint a 'whole-car' to express love for a mother or girlfriend, but in London the surviving photographs seem to indicate that whole-cars were reserved for the most important political messages. Fuel's whole-car expresses the artist's fury at 'MUSHROOM MADNESS', the new phase in the Cold War initiated by the Allied powers: 'welcome to the new age of nuclear war!!!' Prime's whole-car of 1990 revels in the fact that Tube-writing was insurrection: a militia-man with roses sprouting from his gun is presented next to a fire burning about the revolutionary slogan '100 SACRIFICES 2 REVOLT'.

But like the whole-trains themselves, this triumph of graffiti would prove ephemeral. 'Unfortunately, it would be true to say that '92 was probably London's worst year yet', Drax complained. 'Since the days when Kosh, Haze, Krash 151, Robbo, and the others like them first started bombing the streets of Europe's biggest city and artists like Shades, Rom, Snake, and The Trailblazers started developing styles which were to inspire and influence the rest of Europe, there hasn't been a year with such a level of police created paranoia, such a breaking down of our channels of information, such a lack of promise and disappointingly, such grayness on the underground system'.[90] A huge onslaught by the British Transport Police in the course of 1991 had finally resulted in what proved to be a permanent, near-comprehensive reconquest of the Tube-network by the establishment.

> Will all the sacrifices of those imprisoned, fined, or thrown out of their homes be forgotten, will it all be stuck in a big book title 'That was aerosol art'.... Will we have to look under the section titled 'trains' to see how 'strange warped individuals' used to go into yards and spray on the trains and will the final edit of the book be done by the British transport police? Is that how it will be?[91]

This turning-point in the history of the graffiti subculture in the network is captured by John Healy in the novel *Streets Above Us* (1990). In this book the British Transport Police focus their efforts on catching Tube-writers while larger, more terrible crimes remain uninvestigated. 'Graffiti, murals, spray-can art, tagging, bossing, painting, whatever the name, to the rest of the coppers they seem in the light, artificial as it is, a minor problem.... But to the sergeant they are a personal affront, a real threat, never far from his mind.'[92] Confronted one day with a voluptuous blonde nymph semi-draped in fibreglass armour, her long muscular legs firmly gripped about a rocket, an arrogant smile playing on her lips, as though showing contempt for those who still travel by train, painted six feet high and three feet wide across the wall of the eastern tunnel, Sergeant Cuffam becomes obsessed with eliminating the incomparable graffiti artist Narcissus One.[93] The Transport Police conduct an elaborate raid on the depot in which the School of Narcissus paint their murals – and successfully hound the maestro onto the live rail. 'Well, so much for art', says Sergeant Cuffam, looking down at the lifeless body.[94]

But Tube-writing remains extremely resilient. Though the amount of work produced by the graffiti subculture in the 1990s was diminished, Tube-writers still developed flamboyant and vibrant new styles that were responsive to the new brightly coloured Tube-cars introduced to prevent graffiti. And the subculture reconquered the network in devastating style on Christmas Day 2006, when stations on the Northern Line were invaded and painted with belligerent messages proclaiming a new phase in the graffiti war. The signs, maps and messages that render the network functional, impressing upon passengers the belief that the system is under control, were systematically effaced. The photogenic faces pouting and frowning on posters were made over with slavering insane pig men and blue-toothed freaks. And, in the margins of an official line diagram, opposite a newly painted six-foot mural to Babs and Buster Bunny of the Tiny Toons, the following manifesto was scribbled:

THE DIRTY TUNNEL BUNNYS WERE A LUVLY RACE OF BUNNIES WHO LIKED TO PAINT PICTURES ON TUBE TRAINS ... BUT NOW THE EVIL RULERS TRY TO DESTROY THEIR PASSION ... LITTLE DID THEY KNOW THAT BUNNY'S ARE READY 4 WAR ... !

GRAFFITI WAR ...

THE DEATH OF NARCISSUS

Viewing Manhattan from the 110th floor of the World Trade Center, Michel de Certeau reflects upon the imaginary totalisation effected by the solar eye, and the practices that are foreign to the geometrical or geographical space of visual, panoptic or theoretical constructions. 'If ... an illustration were required, we could mention the fleeting image, yellowish-green and metallic blue calligraphies that howl without raising their voices and emblazon themselves on the subterranean passages of the city, "embroideries" composed of letters and numbers, perfect gestures of violence painted with a pistol, Shivas made of written characters, dancing graphics whose fleeting apparitions are accompanied by the rumble of subway trains: New York graffiti.'[95] The countercultural history, traced in this chapter, of the London Underground in the post-war era, offers a no less exemplary case-study of what Certeau terms the *tactics* practised by those who operate within and against the strategic plans that constitute the concept city. Tube-writers in particular had recognised in the London Underground a semiological system peculiarly open to practices that disrupt the official significance of the network. Though all users produce representational spaces that reflect their sum total of passages through the system (the space as *lived*) Tube-writers were engaged in activity that fused sign making and social networking on a scale that can be seen to have had a material impact upon the space as *perceived*. The London Underground had been transformed into a space for a radical form of play – and this is reflected in the role the Tube-network plays in a variety of fictive material produced in this period. Following Sam Selvon, writers such as Alan Moore, Hanif Kureishi, Salman Rushdie and Barbara Vine have all represented the Tube as a symbol for the new, urban aesthetic celebrated in their work.

In the graphic novel *V for Vendetta* (1981–88), written by Alan Moore and illustrated by David Lloyd, for instance, it is a Tube-train (entirely covered in graffiti) that delivers the *coup de grace* to the fascist regime ruling England.[96] The premise is that, having narrowly averted extinction in a nuclear conflict, England has been transformed into the sort of totalitarian, corporate state advocated by Thomas Hobbes. The Eye and Ear monitor the populace, the Mouth broadcasts propaganda and Fingermen patrol the streets. The story follows the vendetta of a character known only as V – an anarchist who seeks to overthrow this totalitarian body politic. Like Subcomandante Marcos, the Zapatista who conceals his identity and wears a mask, V is not a leader in the conventional sense, but a representative figure: 'Marcos is gay in San Francisco, black in South Africa, an Asian in Europe, a Chicano in San Ysidro, an anarchist in Spain, a Palestinian in Israel, a Mayan Indian in the streets of San Christobal, a Jew in Germany, a Gypsy in Poland, a Mohawk in Quebec, a pacifist in Bosnia, a single woman on the Metro at 10pm, a gang member in the slums, an unemployed worker, an unhappy student and, of course, a Zapatista in the mountains'.[97] The regime is thus overthrown by the cumulative effect of the actions of numerous minor characters. The Tube-train packed with explosives that destroys Whitehall is sent through the tunnel not by the hero, but by former damsel-in-distress, Evey Hammond. The graffitied train sets off from a space that has served in the graphic novel as a refuge for culture as well as anarchy, a repository for music, books, films and paintings that the fascist organisation Norsefire has tried to eradicate. Initially referred to as the Shadow Gallery, it is eventually revealed to be the station at Victoria, reflecting the powerful symbolic resonance the Tube-network had come to possess in the public mind as the one place in which resistance was still possible in Thatcher's England – through a primitive, pre-electronic form of hacking and anonymous social networking.

If *V for Vendetta* has influenced the tactics of online activists in the twenty-first century, Hanif Kureishi's remarkable fantasy screenplay of life in the 1980s, *Sammy and Rosie Get Laid* (1988, directed by Stephen Frears), can be seen to engage with procedures that have since become central to the Occupy movement. The hero (who has named himself after his favourite Tube-line, Victoria) lives in a caravan parked somewhere near Ladbroke Grove: 'The fat concrete curve of the motorway hangs above a dusty stretch of waste ground which itself is skirted by a mainline railway line and a tube track'.[98] Having been compelled through poverty and neglect to inhabit a no-man's land, Victoria formally declares his intention to carve out a home here. This reclamation project produces some extraordinary set-pieces. Victoria is shown having breakfast at a long table set out in the open, the motorway thundering overhead, while a woman walks about with a watering-can cobbled together from bucket and dildo, watering the vegetables planted in the waste; there are sculptures in the vegetable patch and a bookshop has been set up in a shack selling volumes that are manufactured on site with an old printing press; the kids even play on a swing that hangs down from under the motorway.[99] But by far the most important means by which the 'straggly kids' from the wasteland have reclaimed the space of non-place is music: the kids are first seen making music in a Tube-station at the start and are next seen playing trumpet, drum and violin while crossing the motorway.[100] According to Kureishi, most of the actors playing the itinerant musicians were in fact buskers from the London Underground: 'Few of them have a regular place to live, and when Debbie wants to inform them of a day's shooting, she has to send her assistants round the tube stations of central London to find them'.[101] The musicians in the film present a powerful vision of the city as a place that is somehow utopian in spite of everything. In one memorable scene, trumpeters, saxophonists, a hurdy-gurdy player, bassoonists and rappers perform the theme song of the movie in the Tube: 'If we could film them from the front for a moment', suggests Kureishi, 'we could easily see for a second, the whole tube tunnel dancing, like in a Cliff Richard film'. This irrepressible euphoria clearly stems from his belief that the capital is a place of unlimited creative potential: 'As an expert, I suggest the tunnel that connects the Piccadilly with the Victoria Line at Green Park', remarks Kureishi, 'a superb sensation you get here of endless walking in both directions'.[102]

As Sukhdev Sandhu observes, this passion for the city is probably intensified by the fact that Kureishi did not grow up there, but was brought up in Bromley: 'Neither truly urban nor rural, it is for its critics, marooned somewhere in-between, a lingering and painful half-life'.[103] It is interesting that Kureishi should hail from the suburb that, in refusing to pay for the Tube-network, indirectly brought about Thatcher's elimination of the GLC. Perhaps Kureishi's rejection of his suburb and everything it stood for accounts for the writer's love and fascination for the network in *Sammy and Rosie Get Laid*. 'My father has a small furniture store and used to be the Mayor of Bromley!' sniggers Rosie as she prepares to make love to the personification of the Victoria Line in a caravan parked by the Hammersmith and City.[104] Rosie fell in love with Sammy because their open relationship seemed to promise freedom from the family, from the narrow-minded suburbs.[105] As their relationship starts to fail, Rosie tries to recapture that original moment of freedom with Victoria, in a space where the city's potential for magic and movement are at their most intense and surreal.

But this utopia beneath the motorway is a fragile thing and it is eventually destroyed by the official vision of urban regeneration that began to be implemented in the capital from the late 1980s. In the diary he kept at this time, Kureishi states that the West London streets by the railway line had somehow gone wrong: 'In 1978 most of the five-storey houses with their crumbling pillars, peeling façades and busted windows were derelict, inhabited by itinerants, immigrants, drug-heads and people not ashamed of being seen drunk on the street.... Now the centre of the city is inhabited by the young rich and serviced by everyone else; now there is the re-establishment of firm class divisions; now the sixties and the ideals of that time seem like an impossible dream or naivety'.[106] As Sandhu observes, even as gentrification led to moneyed professionals moving into previously unfashionable areas such as Clapham and Notting Hill, the under-investment in new buildings and a decline in private rented accommodation 'led to a huge rise in the number of people sleeping rough under the Embankment, in the doorways of Covent Garden restaurants, and huddled amidst the dustbins behind Irish pubs in Camden'.[107] This societal change is reflected in the powerful final scenes in *Sammy and Rosie Get Laid*, when the impoverished but vibrant community under the motorway is bulldozed while a property developer announces through a loudspeaker that he is proud to be 'making London a cleaner and safer place'.[108] As Sandhu points out, what the property developer is saying, of course, is a cleaner and safer place for people like us – 'This is the totalitarian language of social hygiene' – and the movie establishes a clear parallel between the property developer's attitude and the Islamism fostered by Sammy's father Rafi back home in Pakistan.[109] The former wants to clean up London in order to facilitate the flow and accumulation of capital by multinational corporations. The latter contrasts the capital unfavourably with Pakistan, where 'There is identity through religion and a strict way of life', and expresses his warm approval for Thatcher's 'strong hand on this country'.[110] Each project promises utopian renewal, but the means both use to achieve it are brutal and inhumane: 'they hold scant regard for human individuality, for the lives of the six million people who pour through the streets of London each day'.[111] A right-wing form of urban renewal was triumphing over that alternative version fostered by the GLC – and this was soon the case even in the space that had for so long been a bastion for countercultural expression. The 1990s would see the construction of a Tube-extension built entirely for the benefit of the capital's political and financial elite, linking Portcullis House in Westminster to the bleak corporate citadel at Canary Wharf – via miles upon miles of warehouses that were soon to be refitted as luxurious river-side apartments. The often immense stations built along the Jubilee Line are among the most spectacular non-places produced by a resurgent capitalism.

This monomaniacal urban regeneration is an important theme in Salman Rushdie's *The Satanic Verses* (1988), a book that looks set to be remembered only as satire on the Prophet Mohammed, but which is primarily a celebration of London as vortex for the migrations, metamorphoses and multiplicities that fascinate Kureishi. Rushdie suggests that the city is under attack from a variety of extremists, ranging from the Thatcherite Hal Valance to a mullah clearly modelled upon the Ayatollah Khomeini. These reactionary forces find their champion in Gibreel Farishta, formerly a Bollywood star, now the Archangel of the Lord, who plans to redeem the city in his street atlas square by square, from Hockley Farm in the far north-west of the chart to Chance Wood in the south-east: 'Geographers' London, all the way from A to Z'.[112] However, he soon learns that the city, in its corruption, refuses to submit to the dominion of cartographers, 'changing shape at will and without warning, making it impossible for Gibreel to approach his quest in the systematic manner he would have preferred'.[113] Significantly, the insanities of the city that frustrate this project of urban renewal are at their most pronounced in the London Underground.

> And even though he did not have any idea of the true shape of that most protean and chameleon of cities he grew convinced that it kept changing shape as he ran around beneath it, so that the stations on the Underground changed lines and followed one another in apparently random sequence. More than once he emerged, suffocating, from that subterranean world in which the laws of space and time had ceased to operate, and tried to hail a taxi; not one was willing to stop, however, so he was obliged to plunge back into that hellish maze, that labyrinth without a solution, and continue his epic flight.[114]

Curiously, Gibreel's ordeal begins in the same Tube-line featured in *Sammy and Rosie Get Laid* and in *V for Vendetta*. Perhaps this reflects the fact that the Victoria is the one line in the entire network built to benefit poorer regions in the capital, connecting Brixton and Walthamstow to the West End. Or perhaps Rushdie is remembering *Quatermass and the Pit*, in which the excavation of the Victoria unleashed the end of civilisation as we know it (at a station with a name that might suggest the end of Hobbesian government or anarchy's last stand – Hobbs End). Gibreel's enemy certainly bears a peculiar resemblance to the hallucinatory devil that hovers over the city in the movie, 'rising up in the Street like Apocalypse and burning the town like toast'.[115] In the novel, this devil becomes symbol for political dissent: 'While non-tint neo-Georgians dreamed of a sulphurous enemy crushing their perfectly restored residences beneath his smoking heel, nocturnal browns-and-blacks found themselves cheering, in their sleep, this what-else-after-all-but-black-man, maybe a little twisted up by fate class race history, all that, but getting off his behind, bad and mad, to kick a little ass'. The kids in the street start wearing rubber devil horns on their heads, and the symbol of the Goatman begins to crop up on button-badges, sweatshirts, posters and banners at political demonstrations. 'It's an image white society has rejected for so long that we can really take it, you know, occupy it, inhabit it, reclaim it and make it our own'.[116]

But the fiction considered in this chapter is perhaps less interesting for the antithetical forces thus depicted than for a synthesis this fiction itself represents. These mass-media products offer romanticised fantasies of urban life that cater to Sammy and Rosie and their circle. The latter are highly trained professionals who choose to live in the most impoverished parts of the city – and are therefore part of the creeping gentrification that they profess to despise. Their fascination for and attempt to participate in the communal life represented by Victoria transforms the 'urban' into a highly valued commodity and paves the way for the extension of more formal schemes for 'regeneration'. The bourgeois bohemians of Shoreditch and Brixton, together with the fiction that defined this urban aesthetic, are no alternative to neoliberal regeneration – because the spatial duality they assert is self-sustaining, the relationship symbiotic. Once this is understood the futility of the controversy that rages over the commercial success of Banksy's stencil graffiti must become clear. The street artist might well have developed his distinctive technique in response to the major clamp-down on spray-can art by the British Transport Police in the 1990s – but its subsequent mass appeal does not mean the street artist has succeed in realising a utopian city that feels like a party to which everyone is invited, 'not just the estate agents and barons of big business', as he claims.[117] Nor does its status as highly sought after commodity mean that the street artist has sold out or been co-opted. Consider: In April 2007 Transport for London painted over an image of John Travolta and Samuel L. Jackson from *Pulp Fiction* sprayed onto the external wall of an electricity sub-station in Shoreditch. 'Transport for London takes a tough line on removing graffiti because it creates a general atmosphere of neglect and social decay which in turn encourages crime', Transport for London explained. 'We recognize that there are those who view Banksy's work as legitimate art, but sadly our graffiti removal teams are staffed by professional cleaners not professional art critics.'[118] The image is estimated to have been worth £300,000 and had become a tourist attraction – attributes entirely inconsistent with its characterisation as a sign of social decay. The urban aesthetic that Banksy's art participates in represents the subsumption of antithetical energies in the dominant spatial concept, in order to produce a new synthesis that is structured about a binary opposition. The insights of punk and hip-hop are now part of the contemporary spectacle. In 2012 'London's Burning' by the Clash was the soundtrack of the Olympic Games; the jagged fame-train graffiti of the 1980s was almost certainly an inspiration for the official logo.

In a sense, this is a great triumph. The history of countercultural activities considered in this chapter has resulted (and is resulting) in a significant modification in the concept city that underpins the projects of the urban planners. That phase of thought crystallised by Situationist International has won a victory at once as comprehensive and as partial as that of the socialists and modernists earlier in the century: what the latter achieved in the sphere of work, the former have achieved in the sphere of leisure. This qualified victory is cause for neither congratulation nor despondency, but should be seen to have propelled revolutionary activity into a new phase. New contradictions must arise that present the potential for the production of spatial practices that differ from and contest the dominant concept. But there can be no pretending that those practices that now form an integral part of the concept city remain in antithetical relation to it. In fact, in the current struggle, much that protestors seek to preserve from the zealots of Neo-Liberalism can be shown to be a legacy of the Modernist movement – that New Reality which sustained such unforgiving attack from those theorists who remain the inspiration for so much contemporary protest. It is time that the *tactics* of protest were reconsidered. In any case, the air of gloom that pervades the psychogeographical material produced from the early 1990s (some of which is considered in the following chapter) is quite clearly misplaced.

NOTES

1 *A Fish Called Wanda*, dir. Charles Crichton (United Kingdom: Metro-Goldwyn-Mayer, 1988).
2 Guy Debord, 'Theory of the Dérive' *Les Lèvres Nues #9* (November 1956) reprinted in *Internationale Situationniste #2* (December 1958), and *Situationist International: Anthology*, trans. Ken Knabb (Berkeley, CA: Bureau of Public Secrets, 1981), p. 53.
3 *Ibid.*, p. 7.
4 Simon Sadler, *The Situationist City* (London and Cambridge, MA: MIT Press, 1998), pp. 86.
5 *Ibid.*, p. 82.
6 Debord, 'Introduction to a Critique of Urban Geography', *Les Lèvres Nues #6* (1955) reprinted in Knabb, p. 55.
7 *Ibid.*, p. 6.
8 *Ibid.*, p. 8.
9 Stephen Willats, 'Intervention and Audience' (1986), in *Panic Attack: Art in the Punk Years*, ed. Mark Sladen and Ariella Yedgar (London and New York: Merrell, 2007), p. 193.
10 Occupation Committee of the People's Free Sorbonne University, 'Slogans to be Spread by Every Means' (16 May 1968). Reprinted with other 'May 1968 Documents', in Knabb, p. 344.
11 Quoted in Simon Ford, *The Situationist International: A User's Guide* (London: Black Dog, 2005), p. 117.
12 Charles de Gaulle, 30 May 1968. Quoted in Ford, p. 128.
13 Willats, p. 197.
14 *Ibid.*
15 Colin MacInnes, *Absolute Beginners* (1959) (London: Allison and Busby, 1993), p. 30.
16 Christian Wolmar, *The Subterranean Railway* (London: Atlantic Books, 2004), p. 296.
17 Dick Hebdige, *Subculture: The Meaning of Style* (London and New York: Methuen, 1979), p. 29.
18 Sukhdev Sandhu, *London Calling: How Black and Asian Writers Imagined a City* (London: HarperCollins, 2003), p. 228.
19 Samuel Selvon, 'Working the Transport', in *Ways of Sunlight* (1957) (Harlow: Longman, 1987), p. 120.
20 *Ibid.*
21 *Ibid.*, p. 122.
22 See Hebdige, p. 29 and p. 49.
23 *Ibid.*, pp. 50–51. See also Don McCullin, *Unreasonable Behaviour: An Autobiography* (1990). Quoted in Hanif Kureishi and Jon Savage, eds, *The Faber Book of Pop* (London: Faber, 1995), p. 25.
24 'The practice of using everyday objects [in Calypso] is similar to the using of

washboards and tea chests like those used in the '50s for Skiffle music'. Stephen Nye, liner notes to *Trojan Calypso Box Set* (London: Trojan Records, 2002).
25 See Pete Pointon, <http://www.skiffle50.co.uk/skiffle.html> (6 June 2008).
26 Hanif Kureishi, Introduction to *Outskirts and Other Plays* (London: Faber, 1991), p. xiii.
27 Selvon, 'Working the Transport', p. 123.
28 Samuel Selvon, *The Lonely Londoners* (1956), ed. Susheila Nasta (London: Penguin, 2006), p. xiv.
29 Samuel Selvon, 'Come Back to Granada', in *Foreday Morning: Selected Prose 1946–1986*, ed. Kenneth Ramchand and Susheila Nasta (Harlow: Longman, 1989), p. 168.
30 Ex-musical clown David Benn in a comment on 'My Busking Tips for Badly Drawn Boy', BBC News, Thursday 27 February 2003, <http://news.bbc.co.uk/1/hi/uk/2798281.stm>.
31 Selvon, 'My Girl and the City', in *Ways of Sunlight*, p. 176.
32 The Kinks, 'Waterloo Sunset', on *Something Else by the Kinks* (London: Pye Records, 1967).
33 Samuel Selvon, *Eldorado West One* (Leeds: Peepal Tree, 1988), p. 25.
34 Selvon, *The Lonely Londoners*, pp. 138–139.
35 *Ibid.*, pp. 51–52.
36 *Ibid.*, p. 128.
37 Selvon, 'My Girl and the City', in *Ways of Sunlight*, p. 176.
38 Lord Kitchener, 'The Underground Train' (1950), in *London Is the Place For Me: Trinidadian Calypso in London, 1950–1956* (London: Honest Jon's Records, 2002).
39 Linton Kwesi Johnson, *Inglan Is a Bitch* (London: Race Today, 1980), p. 26.
40 Selvon, 'My Girl and the City', in *Ways of Sunlight*, p. 176.
41 Richard Cork, ed., *Eduardo Paolozzi Underground* (London: Royal Academy of Arts, 1986) p. 8.
42 *Ibid.*, p. 40.
43 *Ibid.*, p. 8.
44 Alexander Trocchi, *Invisible Insurrection of a Million Minds*, ed. Andrew Murray Scott (Edinburgh: Polygon, 1991), p. 195.
45 Alexander Trocchi, ed., *The Moving Times* (London: Stanhope Press, 1960).
46 Trocchi, *Invisible Insurrection*, p. 179.
47 Trocchi, *The Moving Times*. I am indebted to James Riley for much of the information on Project Sigma, which has as yet received little critical attention. See James Riley, 'Avant-Garde Literature and the Recording Process' (Doctoral Dissertation, University of Cambridge, 2008).
48 Trocchi, *The Moving Times*.
49 *Ibid.*
50 *Internationale Situationniste #10* (March 1966). Quoted by Knabb, note 136, p. 373.
51 Trocchi, *The Moving Times*.
52 For more information on the East End see Jon Savage, *Teenage: The Creation*

of Youth Culture (New York: Viking, 2007), p. 19. For the deterioration of the new estates see Willats, p. 193.
53 James Herbert, *The Rats* (1974) (Basingstoke: Pan Macmillan, 1999), p. 125.
54 Gordon Matta-Clark, 'My Understanding of Art' (1975), in *Gordon Matta-Clark*, ed. C. Disrerens (London: Phaidon, 2003), p. 204.
55 Guy Debord. Quoted in Knabb, p. 293.
56 Ford, p. 148.
57 Raoul Vaneigem, 'Commentaires contre l'urbanisme', *Internationale Situationniste*, August 1961. Quoted by Ford, p. 125.
58 King Mob. The slogan is reproduced in photographs by Roger Perry – reproduced over several pages in *The Writing on the Wall*, ed. George Melly (London: Hamish Hamilton, 1976).
59 Raoul Vaneigem and Attila Kotányi. Quoted in Knabb, p. 66.
60 The Jam, 'Down in the Tube Station at Midnight' (1978), on *The Jam Story* (UK: Polydor, 2006).
61 Quoted in George Berger, *The Story of CRASS* (London: Omnibus Press, 2006), p. 110.
62 *Ibid.*
63 Naomi Klein, *No Logo* (London: HarperCollins, 2005), p. 281.
64 Banksy, *Wall and Piece* (London: Century, 2006), p. 196.
65 Penny Rimbaud. Quoted in Berger, p. 110.
66 *Ibid.*, p. 110.
67 CRASS, liner-notes, *Best Before 1984* (London: Crass Albums, 1986).
68 Berger, p. 110.
69 Henry Chalfont and James Prigoff, *Spraycan Art* (London: Thames and Hudson, 1987), p. 58.
70 Martha Cooper and Henry Chalfont, *Subway Art* (London: Thames and Hudson, 1984), p. 14.
71 Norman Mailer, 'The Faith of Graffiti' (1974), in *Pieces and Pontifications* (Sevenoaks: New English Library, 1983), p. 136.
72 Jean Baudrillard, 'Kool Killer, or The Insurrection of Signs' (1976), in *Symbolic Exchange and Death*, trans. Iain Hamilton Grant (London: Sage, 1993), p. 78.
73 *Ibid.*, p. 80.
74 *Ibid.*, p. 79.
75 Quoted by Baudrillard, p. 82. See Gilles Deleuze and Felix Guattari, *Anti-Oedipus: Capitalism and Schizophrenia I*, trans. R. Hurley, M. Seem and H.R. Lane (London: Athlone, 1984), and *A Thousand Plateaux: Capitalism and Schizophrenia II*, trans. Brian Massumi (London: Athlone, 1988).
76 Mailer, p. 157.
77 *Ibid.*, p. 143.
78 Chalfont and Prigoff, p. 11.
79 *Ibid.*
80 *Ibid.*, p. 9.
81 Christian Wolmar, *Down the Tube: The Battle for London's Underground* (London: Aurum, 2002), p. 43.

82 Christian Wolmar, *The Subterranean Railway* (London: Atlantic Books, 2005), p. 303.
83 Quoted in Nancy MacDonald, *The Graffiti Subculture* (Basingstoke: Palgrave, 2001), p. 109.
84 *Ibid.*
85 The British Transport Police website: <http://www.btp.police.uk/issues/graffiti.htm>.
86 Quoted in MacDonald, p. 109.
87 Drax, 'Maybe It's Because I'm a Londoner' (1993), *Graphotism*, Number 3, p.7
88 *Ibid.*
89 Quoted in Chalfont and Prigoff, p. 9.
90 Drax, p.7
91 *Ibid.*
92 John Healy, *Streets Above Us* (1990) (London: HarperCollins, 1991), p. 184.
93 *Ibid.*, p. 171.
94 *Ibid.*, p. 176.
95 Michel de Certeau, *The Practice of Everyday Life*, trans. Steven Rendall (London: University of California Press, 1988), p. 102.
96 Alan Moore and David Lloyd, *V for Vendetta* (New York: Vertigo, 1988), ch. 7, pp.1-2.
97 Quoted in Klein, p. 455.
98 Hanif Kureishi, *Sammy and Rosie Get Laid: the script and the diary*, (London: Faber, 1988), p. 72.
99 *Ibid.*, p. 44, p. 40, pp. 53–54.
100 *Ibid.*, p. 1, p. 9.
101 *Ibid.*, p. 100.
102 *Ibid.*, p. 19.
103 Suhkdev Sandhu, *London Calling: How Black and Asian Writers Imagined a City* (London: HarperCollins, 2003), p. 233.
104 Kureishi, p. 39.
105 *Ibid.*, p. 35, p. 48.
106 *Ibid.*, p. 77.
107 Sandhu, pp. 240–241.
108 *Ibid.*, p. 245.
109 *Ibid.*, p. 246.
110 Kureishi, p. 42, p. 10.
111 Sandhu, p. 247.
112 Salman Rushdie, *The Satanic Verses* (1988) (London: Vintage, 1998), p. 322.
113 *Ibid.*, p. 327.
114 *Ibid.*, pp. 200–201.
115 *Ibid.*, p. 285.
116 *Ibid.*, pp. 286–287.
117 Banksy, p. 13 and p. 97.
118 Quoted in the *Daily Telegraph*, 24 April 2007.

7

THE GHOST IN THE MACHINE

Psychogeography in the London Underground

> At every Underground stop, people climb to the surface, emerge into the light of day, but the train goes on, the circulation continues, the Circle Line providing a visual and conceptual magnet for the way the city stays alive by pumping flows of energy around the system. At the end of the line this fiction dissolves; it is not only people but the place itself that releases its grip on the idea of the city as a closed system.
>
> (Rod Mengham, 'End of the Line', 2003)[1]

Turning away from the rationalisation of time and space represented by the Tube Map, Rod Mengham and photographer Marc Atkins set out to chart the region where this pattern most obviously unravels. In their photo-essay 'The End of the Line', termini on the Central, District, Metropolitan and Jubilee are shown to burrow into other organisations of space, or even into entirely different times, 'portals into something other than the idea of the city we automatically link them with'.[2] At the western extremity, Uxbridge is entombed in a future remembered by all who were teenagers in the 1960s.[3] Stanmore is paralysed at a fixed point in the history of the Underground's development: 'Passengers climbing up and down the hill traverse the strata of transport archaeology, with the prehistory of railway heritage'.[4] And in Richmond, there is a peculiar overgrown patch of ground between the buffers and the end of the track: 'This small deposit of neglect, with its little pockets of chalk and the different-sized gravels, has accumulated indifference at specific moments of alteration and redefinition: it is a transport midden, a municipal burnt mound; by-product of energies that were focused elsewhere'.[5] Mengham concludes that this overlapping of materials, constantly revised by the superimposing of new layers, provides an even better insight into the historical process than the more striking anachronisms at Uxbridge and Morden: 'the evidence of powerplay is not enshrined in the canonical details of a metal-framed clerestory, or an abstracted Egyptian façade; it is preserved in a pile of detritus'.[6]

This emphasis on the marginal aspects of a place is a feature of psychogeography. The term was invented by the Lettrists, forerunners of the Situationist International, to describe the study of the precise laws and specific effects of the geographical environment on the emotions and behaviour of individuals, and gained currency in the early 1990s through work by London-based writers Iain Sinclair and Peter Ackroyd. Originally a reaction to the renovation of Paris in the post-war period, it is no coincidence that the psychogeographical project should have resurfaced in London in the wake of the urban regeneration initiated in the Thatcher era.[7] As Phil Baker observes, psychogeography represents a last-ditch attempt to resist the erasure of place by space: 'It accompanied an alienation of an almost unprecedented kind from the built environment, responding to anxieties perhaps definitively expressed in Marc Augé's book *Non-places*'.[8] This is why psychogeography takes refuge in interstitial zones of private meaning and esoteric knowledge, privileging aspects of place that are not reducible to economics: to maintain a psychic investment in the street. 'Its overlap with histories and myths of place is a further way of gaining a purchase on the inhospitable environment of the metropolis. People want to inscribe marks and find traces in the city, like the stories they used to tell about the stars and constellations, in order to feel more at home in an indifferent universe.'[9]

In practice, this means that writers must have recourse to the trope of the *uncanny*. 'Only ghosts, after all, can walk through walls, breach the boundaries of the increasingly privatized zones of the city, and shimmer impossibly between past and present Londons', writes Roger Luckhurst.[10] According to architecture historian Anthony Vidler, the more ruthless the modern speculative transformation of the city, the more likely it is that suppressed history will return as the uncanny in the wasted margins and surfaces of post-industrial culture: 'in contemporary architecture, the incessant reference to avant-garde techniques devoid of their originating ideological impulse, the appearance of a fulfilled aesthetic revolution stripped of its promise of social redemption, at least approximates the conditions that, in Freud's estimation, are ripe for uncanny sensations'.[11] Recent interest in the uncanny as a metaphor for our fundamentally unliveable urban condition may therefore result from the fact that 'within many of the projects that pretend to a radical disruption of cultural modes of expression, there still lurks the ghost of avant-garde politics, one that is proving difficult to exorcise entirely'.[12]

Perhaps this is why the Tube-network often features in psychogeographical material. As one of the earliest modernist spaces, the London Underground is a prominent symbol of urban alienation – but a space peculiarly open to forgotten places with tremendous myth-making potential. As Mengham points out, there are forty ghost stations in the city centre alone: 'repositories of gloom, amplifying the distant vibrations, allaying the slight breezes that pulse through the labyrinth, to decelerate as they get further and further away from the rushing air of tunnels where the trains still run'.[13] Resisting the panoptic rational pattern embodied by the Underground Map, these abandoned stations excite our imagination because we see in them the working of forces hitherto unsuspected in the modern city, but which we are aware of in some remote corner of our own being: they speak to our condition as ghosts in the machine, our sense that we *haunt* rather than *inhabit* the modern city.[14] This final chapter will show this to be a recurring theme in millennial film and fiction set on the London Underground, part of a theoretical reengagement in recent years with the question of the *Unheimlich*.

The possibility that other times and places might exist somewhere in the darkness between stations is the premise of the fantasy television series *Neverwhere* (1996). Based on an idea by comedian Lenny Henry, with a script by novelist Neil Gaiman, music by Brian Eno, opening titles by artist Dave McKean and performances from Laura Fraser, Hywel Bennett and Paterson Joseph, the series is surely one of the most unusual ever produced by the BBC.[15] 'There are little bubbles of old time in London, where things and places stay the same, like bubbles in amber', explains one character. 'There's a lot of time in London, and it has to go somewhere – it doesn't all get used up at once.'[16] Astonishingly, most of these bubbles of old time in the city are entirely real. According to Gaiman, the producers were simply making the most of a low budget. Unable to build large sets, they were compelled to film in striking subterranean locations never seen before on screen. Serpentine's dinner party, for instance, takes place on the platform of the ghost station at Down Street; and the miniature Tube-train in which Mr Croup and Mr Vandemar hunt down the unfortunate Varney is on the former Post Office Railway. The series itself is an object lesson in how easily such forgotten places in the capital can be taken over by the *Unheimlich*.

Having fallen through the cracks over millennia, these fragments of time have entered the subterranean realm of the lost and forgotten, called

London Below. Invisible to the surface folk, its citizens are divided into rival baronies and fiefdoms, haunted by rat-speakers, vampires and a solitary angel. Significantly, these mythical creatures are, for the most part, inspired by names taken from that pre-eminently rational space, the Tube Map: there is an order of black friars, and there is an earl's court (which moves about in a Tube-train, feasting on Coke and chocolate snatched from vending machines whenever his baronial hall happens to stop at a station). Gaiman has exploited the fact that these richly resonant names, cut loose from whatever they once signified, have been rendered potentially uncanny by the clinical whiteness in which they float: 'an uncanny effect is often and easily produced when the distinction between imagination and reality is effaced', Freud observed, 'as when something that we have hitherto regarded as imaginary appears before us in reality, or when a symbol takes over the full functions of the thing it symbolizes'.[17]

Significantly, the protagonist enters this uncanny realm by becoming homeless. Richard Mayhew lives a boring but comfortable existence with his fiancée Jessica until the night he sees a young homeless girl bleeding to death on the street and stops to help her. This act of charity costs Richard his life. He wakes up on Monday morning to find that no one can see him – his friends cannot remember him, his credit cards do not work, his flat is repossessed. Richard seeks help from the homeless girl he saved, but learns that she is in trouble herself, hunted by an engaging pair of psychopaths, called Mr Croup and Mr Vandemar. Richard is now a non-person, one of the 'people who fell through the cracks in the world'.[18] In order to win his life back he must obtain a magical key for an angel called Islington, reputed to live at the heart of the labyrinth of alleys and roads and corridors and sewers that have fallen into the world of the lost and forgotten over millennia: and the key can only be taken by one who passes through an Ordeal.[19]

Having fallen this far into wonderland, it is a tremendous shock to find that the Ordeal is nothing other than reality. Richard sees his reflection in the window of a Tube-train in Blackfriars Station: 'He looked crazy; he had a week's growth of beard; food was crusted around his mouth and in his beard; one eye had recently been blackened, and a boil, an angry red carbuncle, was coming up on the side of his nose; he was filthy, covered in black, encrusted dirt which filled his pores and lived under his fingernails; his eyes were bleary, his hair was matted and snarled. He was a crazy homeless person, standing on a platform of a busy Underground station, in the heart of the rush hour.'[20] In a savage sequence of jump-cuts, freeze-frames, fast-forwards and flash-backs, Richard is told by a doppelganger who claims to represent whatever is left of his mind that this is the closest to sanity he has been in a week, pointing out just how ludicrous the story-line has become by this point. Undercutting the suspension of disbelief slowly engineered over the course of the previous episodes, Gaiman breaks the one rule of the fantasy genre: and the result is devastating. 'I wandered, alone and crazy, through the streets of London, sleeping under bridges, eating food from bins and skips', intones the *doppelgänger* 'Shivering and lost and alone. Muttering to myself, talking to people who weren't there....'[21] Kicked and buffeted by commuters in the London Underground, Richard's profound alienation, his status as a non-person, is forcibly impressed upon him by the space itself.

Then the Underground tempts him with the promise that he can once again belong. His former fiancée calls to him from a poster over the track; his former best friend throws one of the plastic trolls Richard used to collect onto the third rail; 'if he could only get the troll back, perhaps he could get everything back'.[22] The viewer is suddenly aware that all the posters in the Tube-station are telling Richard to commit suicide: 'HAVE A FATAL ACCIDENT TODAY'. Crawling to the platform's edge, Richard realises he wants to belong again, even if that means becoming 'an incident at Blackfriars station'.[23] 'The train was coming towards him, its headlights shining out of the tunnel like the eyes of a monstrous dragon in a childhood nightmare. And he understood then just how little effort it would take to make the pain stop – to take all the pain he ever had had, all the pain he ever would have, and make it all go away for ever and ever.'[24] Richard is ultimately saved by the memory of the heroism displayed by a homeless girl. Refusing to accept the logic of a consumer society that says he has no right to exist, Richard holds fast to his condition of alienation: and thereby wins 'the key to all reality'.[25]

This is a recurring theme in subsequent material set in the London Underground. Homelessness is invariably the key to the uncanny realm. For instance, in the movie *Creep* (2004), Franka Potente is pursued through the uncanny spaces beneath the capital by a mutant raised in a long-forgotten government institution (perhaps the vengeful ghost of the botched welfare state, or an aborted Blitz baby?) soon after encountering a homeless couple in the Tube-station at Charing Cross. In the final shot of the movie, Potente is herself mistaken for a homeless girl by a commuter, as she slumps exhausted on the platform, next to a stray dog.[26] According to Julian Wolfreys, 'the Freudian uncanny relies on the literal meaning and the slippage of, and within, the German unheimlich, meaning literally "unhomely"'.[27] Perhaps the homeless represent, in its most extreme form, the *unhomely* condition of the modern capital. As Marc Augé said of beggars in the Paris Metro, 'All moorings broken and with their only link to the world the scribbled text at their feet (sometimes written directly on the ground), they symbolize by way of negation and to the point of dizziness the whole social order, terribly concrete and terribly complete – black holes in our daily galaxy'.[28] The homeless are the human resources that the state and market cannot use. They are the end of the line. They are the point from which we can survey our society in its entirety and the gap within the structures we mistakenly believe to be unities, complete, whole and undifferentiated.[29] They are the representatives of 'the gods and the dead'.[30] In offering alms we simultaneously acknowledge our kinship with them and reinforce our sense of separation, paying off the powers that rule this space so that life can continue. Thus, in Seamus Heaney's *District and Circle* (2006), the poet offers alms to secure safe passage through earth scarred by recent terrorist atrocities:

> I'd trigger and untrigger a hot coin
> Held at the ready, but now my gaze was lowered
> For was our traffic not in recognition?
> Accorded passage, I would re-pocket and nod,
> And he, still eyeing me, would also nod.[31]

Perhaps the most skilful portrayal of the homeless as a portal to the urban uncanny is Tobias Hill's *Underground* (1999). The protagonist, Ariel Casimir, is a Polish immigrant who works in the London Underground because he believes that there is a feeling of control in the tunnels and halls, 'their light and air and even life rationed out', which enables him to feel that the darkness in his own history is under control – 'It is something he needs, the control'.[32]

> The Underground starts out perfect. At first it isn't like the city above it because it is conceived all at once. Everything must be created, heat and passage of air. For the engineers and architects it begins as a perfect technical form. Then years go by – decades. Cross-tunnels are found to be unnecessary, so they are bricked up. Deeper tunnels are added by the government, then closed down. Limestone comes through the concrete as if it were muslin. Up above, communications die out. Stations are abandoned.... The Underground becomes a reflection of the city above – organic, not perfect. Full of small animals and weak plants. Good hiding places, and places that are dangerous.[33]

These hiding places are soon occupied by those sheltering from the cold or the police. Their graffiti and posters cover the walls, their music echoes in the empty tunnels. Casimir can sympathise with them: 'he knows homelessness in himself, years old, still felt as if the bones are indelibly stained inside him'.[34] But he knows only too well that the tunnels can be an unsafe hiding place: 'There is always the way the Underground can contain things, trapping them in its corners, hiding them, making them stronger'.³⁵ Against his better judgement, Casimir is drawn to this souterrain, 'all snickets and pope-holes'.³⁶ Fascinated by a beautiful white-haired homeless girl, Casimir tracks her through neglected cross-passages to the abandoned station at South Kentish Town, where rows of tiny stalactites hang from the platform's lip: 'Now it feels more like a great natural cave than a place dug and built'.³⁷ The girl is called Alice, and she sleeps here underground, 'Like something from a children's story or folk tale'.³⁸ Casimir thinks of the mythical Ohyn, 'babies stillborn with cauls and teeth, who come back at night to eat their grieving parents', and in her parting words Alice herself seems to echo the folk tale of Eurydice: 'Don't look back'.³⁹

As in *Neverwhere*, the homeless girl is being hunted down by a monster in the dark. There is a serial killer in the tunnels who pushes young, white-haired women onto the third rail, and his true target is Alice. Hill builds on this trope in an inventive manner, eventually revealing that the serial killer is Alice's former foster carer and that Casimir's confrontation with this perverse father figure is the symbolic resolution of the character's own long-standing conflict with his monstrous father in Poland. In chapters that alternate with those set in the present, it is revealed that Casimir's mother is Jewish, his father a vicious anti-Semite, and that this secret has cast its shadow over Casimir's earliest memories, filling them with images of subterranean darkness. It is in an underground den that Casimir imagines making love to a Jewish girl called Hanna, and it is here that he hurls a squirrel in a cage down a shaft into water in what amounts to an act of violence against her: like Hanna, the squirrel 'is a beautiful thing, but it scares us too'.⁴⁰ The crisis takes place underground. Hanna gives Casimir an amber lion as a gift, symbol of the secret name given to him by his mother – 'Ariel', which, Hanna tells him, means 'lion' in Hebrew. Angry and upset, Casimir throws her gift down the shaft into water, to join the drowned squirrel.⁴¹ Hanna's revelations raise awkward questions that Casimir long refuses to confront. And when he finally can bring himself to ask, the facts are even worse than he might have expected. Casimir's father participated in a pogrom that killed forty-two members of the Jewish community returning from Buchenwald, in spite of the fact that the wife he loves is Jewish.

> 'You see how it is now? Your father hated the Jews, and married a Jew.... Myself, I always thought he hated Anna too. Hated loving her. And now there's you. I wonder if he hates you too.'⁴²

Casimir's outrage is compounded by the revelation that his father earns money selling nerve gas to terrorists. Significantly, the moment he turns against his father is marked with images of submersion and eclipse:

> A shadow is coming across the sea towards us, racing across the flat water. It is the shadow of the moon. It is as big as Poland. It makes no sound as it swallows us, a cold mouth without language. I look up, head right back on my shoulders. Straight up into the sun's black death mask.
>
> 'Casimir? Casimir?'
>
> I look back down for my father, but my father has gone. Behind me stands nothing but an evil man.[43]

This is why Casimir has taken to places where darkness seems to be under control. 'He is here because the dark is here, because he will not run away from it. He has never turned away from what scares him. Because the fear is too great for him to ever turn his back.'[44] But as his belief in the ordered nature of the Tube-network begins to fade, the space starts to facilitate the return of the family history he has repressed. In his nightmares Casimir imagines the rattle of the squirrel's cage coming at him in the Underground, and when he at last confronts the killer, the latter's moon-like face recalls the eclipse that marked the beginning of Casimir's homelessness. 'It reminds Casimir of his father, and he tries to picture him. A weak man, twisted by amorality and a brutal, simple nationalism.'[45] In this novel, homelessness is related to the psychological as well as the architectural *Unheimlich*. The father comes back to insist upon a relationship that Casimir and Alice have both sought to suppress, and proceeds to haunt them with violence until he is acknowledged.

Hill also imparts this pattern with political significance. The protagonist's struggle to forgive his father echoes the problematic relationship of citizens across Eastern Europe to communism, for which so many atrocities were committed by the USSR. At one point Hill even likens the Underground to 'Joe Stalin's railway, where one bloody worker died for each sleeper'.[46] In order to rescue the homeless Alice, Casimir must first break with the crimes of the past, and this means acknowledging that he is his father's son: 'He remembers Anna's voice: *There is good in you that comes from him*'. In the final act of the novel, Casimir remembers how strong his father was, and wonders whether he would have used his strength for this: 'Casimir thinks that perhaps he would'.[47]

In thus aligning communism with the uncanny, Hill is building on an important theme in China Miéville's fantasy novel *King Rat* (1998). In this story the protagonist, Saul, is compelled to flee his home after the murder of his foster-father, an old-fashioned Marxist, by an unknown assassin. Saul finds that he is in truth the son of the Rat King, and that he is being hunted by an Enemy who represents the consumer capitalism his foster-father warned him against: the supernatural piper of Hamelin, who can summon Tube-trains with his flute to crush opponents.[48] Sleeping rough in the sewer system, Saul opens himself to an urban voodoo that enables him to defeat the piper and the financial Gormenghast of the City: 'He had defeated the conspiracy of architecture, the tyranny by which the buildings that women and men had built had taken control of them, circumscribed their relations, confined their movements'.[49] In the last chapter, Saul is said to inhabit an abandoned Tube-station, where he incites his army of rats to revolution: 'let's put the "rat" back into "Fraternity"'.[50]

This curious insistence on the uncanny power of Marxist theory in the renovated, overly determined cityscapes produced by international consumer capitalism may reflect the enormous impact that Jacques Derrida's historic lecture on *Specters of Marx* (1993) has had on psychogeographical fiction set on the London Underground. It is interesting to note that Nicholas Royle, the novelist hailed as a doppelganger by his namesake, the theorist who has (quite literally) written the book on the Derridean uncanny, decided to set much of his novel *The Director's Cut* (2000) in the forgotten spaces of the London Underground. His avant-garde film director Frank Munro is said to haunt the ghost station at Wood Lane and rides the Hammersmith and City Line, roaming from carriage to carriage with a cut-throat razor in his pocket, killing those passengers who fail to make the 'final cut'. In the course of the novel it emerges that he is the double of another Frank Munro (whom he has killed), and has assumed another alter-ego in order to conceal his crimes, reflecting the emphasis Derrida placed upon the *iterability* of the spectral.[51] Speaking in that period when the West first started to implement capitalism in what had recently been the Eastern bloc, Derrida insisted that the end of history declared by the American political theorist Francis Fukuyama was yet another, inevitably unsuccessful, attempt to exorcise the spectre of Marx: 'Hegemony still organizes the repression and thus the confirmation of a haunting'.[52] Derrida observed that Marxism had in fact never been anything other than a spectre – a *revenant* – a memory that comes back. 'A spectre is haunting Europe – the spectre of communism', wrote Karl Marx in the *Manifesto* of 1848.[53] Contrary to what good sense might lead us to believe, the spectre therefore signals towards the future. It is a legacy that can only come through that which has not yet arrived. 'Repetition *and* first time, but also repetition *and* last time, since the singularity of any *first time* makes of it also a *last time*'.[54] The *revenant* is a staging of the end of history and calls for a *hauntology*, or logic of haunting, larger and more powerful than an ontology, or a thinking of being, which would harbour within itself the discourse of the end, and the opposition between *to be* and *not to be*.[55]

'Hamlet already began with the expected return of the dead King. After the end of history, the spirit comes by *coming back* [revenant], it figures both a dead man who comes back and a ghost whose expected return repeats itself, again and again.'[56]

The logic of haunting is a key theme in Conrad Williams's *London Revenant* (2004). In this novel the protagonist, Adam Buckley, is propelled into lost pockets of magic in the rotten heart of the city, where he becomes increasingly aware that his own past is honeycombed with the forgotten. He seems to recognise people he has never met, at parties to which he cannot remember being invited. He cannot help thinking that he somehow knows the person who is pushing people under Tube-trains in the rush hour. He slowly begins to understand that all his haunts in London are governed by the 'dirty magic' of the Underground.[57]

> There were thirty or forty of these limbo stations beneath the city. Lonely platforms, dead staircases, gutted lift shafts. Places that had once known thousands of feet a day now knew none, none that were human at least, beyond the plod of staff, or the occasional guided tour. This is how it used to be. This is how we were. How many more souterrains were there? How many more secrets could a city keep before it collapsed under the weight of them all? How strong could a city built on a honeycomb be?[58]

Eventually it is revealed that Adam was once one of the 'Missing' in the *Big Issue*.[59] Some years earlier, Adam had been captured by a community of troglodytes inhabiting the forgotten Fleet Tube, and made to work on the excavation of a portal into the mythical subterranean city of Beneothan.[60] He has now been returned to his previous life to track down the serial killer in the Tube-network – a renegade from the world below.

> Here we know him as Blore. We need to stop him, and the handful he has recruited, bent to his will, or he will reveal us. And that must not happen.... There are religions down here, philosophies born of the earth. If knowledge is observation, we have all the wisdom we'll ever need to survive here. Up Top, we'd be dust.[61]

As the Queen of the Underworld speaks, thick furry coats of grime move against each other like wads of iron filings in the field of a magnet, and it occurs to the protagonist that she is dust already.[62] The serial killer, on the contrary, is a vital incarnation of the capital's repressed history, willing to tap the potential of the *Unheimlich*. It is revealed that he is the descendant of a workman killed in a particularly gruesome accident while excavating the earliest Tube-railway in 1887.⁶³ As the protagonist observes, he is the Tube's history, all its energy and desperation, its blood and sweat, its disease, its tears: 'Blore was somehow a link, the connective tissue between topside and Underground. He was London made flesh, a cipher between the living and the dead.'⁶⁴ And this *revenant* is entirely aware of his role as a force that can shock people out of themselves and into new selves:

> I never intended to kill anyone. Death isn't the point to all this. Life is. One I pushed, she lost an arm. I read about her. She was a data inputter for a law firm in the City. She was suffering from RSI, she was paying through the nose for a tiny flat in Holborn. Now she's looking after sheep on an island in the Hebrides. She's happier now than she ever was.⁶⁵

It emerges that the killings are a rehearsal for the catastrophe that will herald the end of history – the violent earthquake about to hit London.⁶⁶ This catastrophe is followed by the combat between Adam and Blore. Blore is caught in an explosion, and the project of building a modernist utopia begins anew, but this time renovation will leave no possible space for the *Unheimlich*. 'The Underground had been damaged beyond repair. It was decided that it should be completely sealed off and tenders sought for a new overland transportation system.'⁶⁷ The earthquake is even said to have been a blessing in disguise: 'The designs that had already begun to be considered for the centre would see the streets completely pedestrianised, with plenty of green spaces instead of road choked by taxis and buses. Shuttles that clung to tracks on terraced buildings would provide transport around the heart of the capital. The government pushed for people to get their bikes out. Adverts for cheap microlite aircraft began cropping up.'⁶⁸ But as in a horror movie, every time Adam thinks he has slain the monster, Blore comes back, and comes back. The outcome of their last combat, in which it looks as though Adam might achieve victory, remains beyond the scope of the novel. It would seem that, while the uncanny must return after the end of history, the human imagination cannot pass beyond the extirpation of the *Unheimlich*.

This may suggest that the uncanny is in fact part of the viral onslaught on rationalised time and space examined by Jean Baudrillard in *The Transparency of Evil* (1990). *London Revenant* cannot pass beyond the elimination of the uncanny because it is precisely this uncontrollable, unknowable component in the machine that constitutes the essence of what it means to be human. According to Baudrillard, it is thanks to the 'vital resistance' offered by the viral that we shall not be going straight to the culminating point of the development of information and communication, 'which is to say: death'.⁶⁹ As cultural geographer Lewis Mumford once observed, the processing that has become the chief form of metropolitan control cannot stop with production, prices and movement, but must finally make over the human personality: 'So complicated, so elaborate, so costly are the processing mechanisms that they cannot be employed except on a mass scale: hence they eliminate all activities of a fitful, inconsecutive, or humanly subtle nature – just as "yes" or "no" answers eliminate those more delicate and accurate discriminations that often lie at one point or another in between the spuriously "correct" answer.'[70] The final result, Mumford predicted, would be the triumph of the dehumanised homunculus he called 'Post-Historic Man'.[71]

> He will look remarkably like a man accoutred in a 'space-suit': outwardly a huge scaly insect. But the face inside will be incapable of expression, as incapable as that of a corpse. And who will know the difference?[72]

According to Baudrillard, the extreme phenomena which periodically afflict the closed system of our society may be an attempt on the part of the human to survive such a culture of total transparency: 'the actual catastrophe may turn out to be a carefully modulated strategy of our species – or, more precisely, our viruses, our extreme phenomena, which are most definitively real, albeit localised, may be what allows us to preserve the energy of that *virtual* catastrophe which is the motor of all our processes, whether economic or political, artistic or historical'.[73]

These themes are central to Geoff Ryman's remarkable internet novel *253* (1998). Set in a Tube-train heading south on the Bakerloo Line from Embankment Station on 11 January 1995, the novel has 253 characters and takes place in the seven and a half minutes it takes for the Tube-train to travel to the Elephant and Castle. Ryman provides each character with one page of exactly 253 words. The characters are numbered and their personal information is divided into the following 'helpful' sections, 'So that the illusion of an orderly universe can be maintained'.[74]

> **Outward appearance**: does this seem to be someone you would like to read about?
>
> **Inside information**: sadly, people are not always what they seem.
>
> **What they are doing or thinking**: many passengers are doing or thinking interesting things. Many are not.[75]

The passengers are categorised, numbered and monitored in the grid of the train in a manner which serves to recall Michel de Certeau's claim that the railway car is a perfect actualisation of the rational utopia: 'A bubble of panoptic and classifying power, a module of imprisonment that makes possible the production of an order, a closed an autonomous insularity'.[76] In a spoof online advertisement, Ryman promises the reader powers of surveillance that he terms 'Godlike'. He promises that the '253 description code' will enable the reader to 'categorise people' more effectively, so that we can spot the criminals in our midst with 'professional' acumen. This theme is important in a work in which most characters are observing other passengers or are being observed. No. 145, for instance, works for a company that offers image enhancement to video-surveillance systems. A visit to Scotland Yard is said to have left him exhausted. He has watched cameras follow a man the operators didn't like around a department store, warn the other stores by radio after he leaves, follow him down the street with further cameras, watch him board a bus and then video the interior of the bus to make sure the man does not get off. 'The whole country is wired', he reflects; 'The English live in 1984 and don't know it.'[77] The internet novel replicates this situation, presenting the reader with a database composed of passengers, their personal information structured by the numerical grid. In fact, the process of reading *253* is an experience that resembles nothing so much as the use of later web-based data-retrieval systems, such as Wikipedia. In his choice of form, content and medium, Ryman has come as close as possible to presenting the reader with the spectacle of that total transparency of data feared by Mumford.

But, as Baudrillard predicted, totalitarian surveillance produces its own opposition. Seeking to eliminate external aggression, integrated and hyper-integrated systems secrete their own internal virulence, their own malignant reversibility: when a certain saturation point is reached such systems undergo this alteration willy-nilly and tend to self-destruct: 'A world purged of the old forms of infection … offers a perfect field of operations for the impalpable and implacable pathology which arises from the sterilisation itself'.[78] According to Baudrillard, *virulence* takes hold when a network rejects its negative components and resolves itself into a system of simple elements: 'It is because a circuit or a network has thus become a *virtual* being, a non-body, that viruses can run riot within it'.[79] The triumph of transparency must render the machine itself immaterial and thus peculiarly open to the vengeance of the ghosts it has created along the way. As Baudrillard concludes, virtual and viral go hand in hand.[80]

Passenger 83, for instance, works at the NHS Tabulation and Processing Agency.[81] She wants the institution to have an ISO standard quality accreditation: a process that involves plying 'ambulance customers' with a questionnaire intended to ascertain whether they think the vehicle comfortable, the driving of a safe but speedy quality, the staff polite and informative. She overlooks the fact that someone in need of an ambulance is not very likely to want to provide feedback. The form intended to improve the customer's experience can only frustrate its own end. Effective surveillance must fail to take the human into account – and must thereby eliminate its very reason for being. Traces of this terrible omission assume an uncanny significance. Within the restrictive numerical and structural grid imposed on each character sketch, humanity resurfaces, a *revenant*, beyond the panopticon's comprehension or control. To read Ryman's internet novel is like watching a brilliant escape artist emerge, without apparent effort, from 253 seemingly inescapable cages. The story of the first passenger, Valerie Tuck, perfectly illustrates the procedure of the novel as a whole.[82] After a theft of computer chips from her office Valerie, with the rest of the workforce, has been compelled to wear a photo-pass with an unflattering blue photograph, on a badge held by a clip or chain. We learn that she is writing an article on how to wear the photo-pass stylishly. 'Try hanging it down your back from its chain. This is simple, elegant, and less nerdish than clipping it to your front pocket.' She recommends spraying the badges lightly with gold nail polish, 'to neutralise the ice-blue, just-arrested look', and suggests that 'Younger staff members into punk may wish to clip badges to ears or run the chains through nasal piercings'.[83]

However, this inherent unpredictability in the machine comes at a huge cost. Consider the fate of Steven Workman, inventor of a satellite navigation system that can provide every driver in the country with instant information on where they are, the best way to reach a destination and the traffic problems en route, by tapping into Scotland Yard's traffic monitoring unit. On exiting the Tube-car Steven catches his watch in the frazzled hair of Angie Strachan and is carried on to the Elephant – where the Tube-train smashes into the barriers in a catastrophe that wipes out all but three of the thirty-eight passengers still on board. In the space of just seven pages, each little community formed in the previous seven and a half minutes is annihilated. It's like watching a society vanish. And though the carnage in each Tube-car is dealt with in exactly 253 words, the effect is not to impose order but rather to undermine the idea that numerical systems can maintain the illusion of a controlled universe. In line with the theories of Baudrillard, the catastrophe is brought about by the human component at the heart of the machine. The driver, Tahsin Celikbilekli, has hung his jacket on the dead man's handle (the device which should automatically stop a Tube-train in the event of a driver being incapacitated) and fallen asleep. As the Tube-train is flattened, Tahsin dreams of golden letters in the ancient language of his homeland: *Love, Freedom, Peace*.[84]

Significantly, this final section in Ryman's novel is called 'The End of the Line'. As in the essay of the same title by Mengham, this is a place where our belief in the power of rationality to order and control our lives, our belief in the closed system, breaks down. The terminus is literally the portal into another order of time and space. The passengers in car 6, for instance, shoot forward to the New York Metro, to the shimmering towers and bullet holes of Lebanon, to a limbo of vengeful cabbies, to the monkey-god Hanuman, and 'away from the illusory which exfoliates like stone, towards the airy real'.[85] The perspective imposed by 'The End of the Line' imparts every passenger's tiniest thought and action with a significance the various surveillance systems featured in the text have failed to comprehend. Harold Pottluck, the market researcher, for instance, is invited to dance with an elderly lady moments before he is killed. Though he is moved by her appeal, he chooses to finish his report. The old lady pleads that they have so little time – 'This is a matter of life and death'.[86] In the light of the coming crash, Harold's refusal to embrace this utopian moment becomes nothing less than a tragedy. In this text, humanity haunts the margin between total control and catastrophe, an immortal ghost that is compelled to return after the end that each should impose. Rising up from the mangled carriage, passenger 253 takes the list Harold has compiled of people who do not travel on the Underground: the unemployed, the sick, the retired and elderly, the mentally subnormal, prisoners, pre-school infants, nuns, children driven to school, housewives: 'It is the list of useful people who will survive'. Murmuring the kaddish for the dead, passenger 253, the now immortal diarist Anne Frank, walks up the tunnel into the light: 'She wanders and bears witness. She cannot forget them, nor can she die.'[87]

'Beneath the discourses that ideologize the city, the ruses and combinations of powers that have no readable identity proliferate', observes Certeau; 'without points where one can take hold of them, without rational transparency, they are impossible to administer'.[88] This is the line taken by much of the theoretical material produced in the aftermath of the historic failure, in France, of Situationist International. The fictional material that followed the UK's own phase of pro-Situ activity takes much the same position. 'Except for a few cultural details and a few technological adjustments, every society has its subway', remarks Augé, 'and imposes on each and every individual itineraries in which the person uniquely experiences how he or she relates to others'.[89] The material reviewed in this chapter reiterates this rhetoric; the salient fact is neither alienation nor its negation but the negotiation each of us constructs every day – the construction of the sense of the individual life from the limited number of routes possible in the mediated spaces of the modern world. The time may now have come to reconsider the terms of this settlement; to explore the ways in which this space remains open to forms of tactical reinvention that might have a *material impact* upon our "market-prison-metropolis", to begin to imagine how we might *inhabit* rather than *haunt* the Machine.

NOTES

1. Rod Mengham and Marc Atkins, 'End of the Line', in *London: From Punk to Blair*, ed. Joe Kerr and Andrew Gibson (London: Reaktion Books, 2003), p. 199.
2. *Ibid.*, p. 199.
3. *Ibid.*, p. 201.
4. *Ibid.*, p. 204.
5. *Ibid.*, p. 208–209.
6. *Ibid.*, p. 209.
7. Guy Debord, *Situationist International: Anthology*, trans. Ken Knabb (Berkeley, CA: Bureau of Public Secrets, 1981), p. 5.
8. Phil Baker, 'Secret City', in Kerr and Gibson, p. 332.
9. *Ibid.*, p. 326.
10. Roger Luckhurst, 'Occult London', in Kerr and Gibson, p. 337.
11. Anthony Vidler, *The Architectural Uncanny: Essays in the Modern Unhomely* (Cambridge, MA: MIT Press, 1992), p. x, p. 14.
12. *Ibid.*, p. 3, p. 14.
13. Mengham, p. 199.
14. This is how Freud explains the uncanny effect of epilepsy and madness: 'The layman sees in them the working of forces hitherto unsuspected in his fellow-men, but at the same time he is dimly aware of them in remote corners of his own being'. Sigmund Freud, 'The "Uncanny"', in *The Standard Edition of the Complete Psychological Works of Sigmund Freud*, trans. James Strachey, Vol. 17, 1917–19 (London: Hogarth Press, 1955), p. 243.
15. *Neverwhere*, dir. Dewi Humphreys (London: BBC, 1996).
16. Neil Gaiman, *Neverwhere* (London: Hodder Headline, 1996), pp. 235–236. All subsequent references are to the novelisation.
17. Freud, p. 244.
18. Gaiman, p. 128.
19. *Ibid.*, p. 318.
20. *Ibid.*, p. 318.
21. *Ibid.*, p. 254.
22. *Ibid.*, p. 256.
23. *Ibid.*, p. 255.
24. *Ibid.*, p. 258.
25. *Ibid.*, p. 357.
26. *Creep*, dir. Christopher Smith (UK Film Council, 2004).
27. Julian Wolfreys, *Victorian Hauntings: Spectrality, Gothic, the Uncanny and Literature* (Basingstoke: Palgrave, 2002), p. 5.
28. Marc Augé, *In the Metro*, trans. Tom Conley (Minneapolis, MN: University of Minnesota Press, 2002), pp. 47–49.
29. This is how Wolfreys, p. 6, defines the *Unheimlich*.
30. Augé, pp. 47–49, p. 65.

31 Seamus Heaney, *District and Circle* (London: Faber, 2006), p. 17.
32 Tobias Hill, *Underground* (London: Faber, 1999), p. 8.
33 Ibid., p. 136.
34 Ibid., p. 6.
35 Ibid., p. 45.
36 Ibid., p. 8.
37 Ibid., p. 67.
38 Ibid., p. 164.
39 Ibid., p. 62, p. 149.
40 Ibid., p. 111.
41 Ibid., p. 120.
42 Ibid., p. 199.
43 Ibid., p. 215.
44 Ibid., p. 62.
45 Ibid., p. 239, p. 246.
46 Ibid., p. 87.
47 Ibid., p. 247.
48 China Miéville, *King Rat* (Basingstoke and Oxford: Macmillan, 1998), pp. 170–180.
49 Ibid., p. 288.
50 Ibid., p. 420.
51 Nicholas Royle, *The Director's Cut* (London: Abacus, Little, Brown, 2000).
52 Jacques Derrida, *Specters of Marx*, trans. Peggy Kamuf, ed. Bernd Magnus and Stephen Cullenberg (London and New York: Routledge, 1994), p. 37.
53 Ibid., p. 50.
54 Ibid., p. 196, p. 10.
55 Ibid., p. 10.
56 Ibid., p. 196, p. 10.
57 Conrad Williams, *London Revenant* (London: The Do-Not Press, 2004), p. 113, p. 46.
58 Ibid., p. 184.
59 Ibid., p. 274.
60 Ibid., p. 299.
61 Ibid., p. 83.
62 Ibid., p. 83.
63 Ibid., p. 327.
64 Ibid., p. 239.
65 Ibid., p. 288.
66 Ibid., p. 286.
67 Ibid., p. 307.
68 Ibid., p. 308.
69 Jean Baudrillard, 'Prophylaxis and Virulence', in *Posthumanism*, ed. Neil Badmington (Basingstoke: Palgrave, 2000), p. 39.
70 Lewis Mumford, *The City in History* (1961) (New York: MJF Books, 1989), p. 542.

71 *Ibid.*, p. 4.
72 *Ibid.*, p. 542.
73 Baudrillard, p. 40.
74 Geoff Ryman, *253* (London: HarperCollins, 1998), p. 2. Unless otherwise specified subsequent references are to the print version. The original internet version of the novel is still available at <http://www.ryman-novel.com> (18 January 2008).
75 Ryman, the website.
76 Michel de Certeau, *The Practice of Everyday Life*, trans. Steven Rendall (London: University of California Press, 1988), p. 111.
77 Ryman, p. 202.
78 Baudrillard, p. 35.
79 *Ibid.*, p. 36.
80 *Ibid.*
81 Ryman, p. 121.
82 *Ibid.*, p. 12.
83 *Ibid.*
84 *Ibid.*, p. 10.
85 *Ibid.*, p. 350.
86 *Ibid.*, p. 351.
87 *Ibid.*, p. 340.
88 Certeau, p. 95.
89 Augé, pp. 69–70.

SELECT BIBLIOGRAPHY

ARCHIVES

British Council, East Acton
British Film Institute
British Library
Cecil Higgins Art Gallery, Bedford
Fitzwilliam Museum, Cambridge
Guildhall Library, London
Henry Moore Foundation
Imperial War Museum, London
London Transport Museum
Mass-Observation Archive at the University of Sussex
Museum of London
Tate Gallery
Tate Storage Facility
V&A

NEWSPAPERS & PERIODICALS

The Daily Mail
The Daily Mirror
The Daily News
The Daily Telegraph
The Daily Worker
The Dial
The Egoist
The Evening News
The Evening Standard

Fortnightly Review
Graphotism
The Guardian
Harper's New Monthly Magazine
The Idler Magazine
The Illustrated London News
The Listener
Manchester Guardian
The National Observer
The New Review
The New York Times Magazine
The Observer
Parliamentary Debates
Parliamentary Papers
The Penny Illustrated Paper
Picture Post
Punch, or The London Charivari
The Railway Times
The Royal Magazine
The Times
To-Day
The Tribune
The Westminster Gazette

BOOKS & ARTICLES

Ackroyd, Peter. *The House of Doctor Dee*. London: Penguin, 1994.

Adams, Henry. 'The Dynamo and the Virgin' in *The Education of Henry Adams* [1918]. New York: OUP, 1999.

Aldington, Richard. *Collected Poems*. New York: Covici/Friede, 1981.

Aldington, Richard. 'In the Tube'. *The Egoist*, 1 May 1915.

Aldington, Richard. 'The Poetry of F.S. Flint'. *The Egoist*, 1 May 1915.

Allen, Rick. *The Moving Pageant: A Literary Sourcebook on London Street life, 1700–1914*. London: Routledge, 1998.

Altick. Richard D. *The Presence of the Present: Topics of the Day in the Victorian Novel*. Columbus: Ohio State University, 1991.

Amicis, Edmondo de. *Jottings About London*, trans. Robert S. Minot. First published as *Ricordi di Londra* in 1874. Boston: Alfred Mudge and Son, 1883.

Amis, Martin. *Success* [1978]. London: Penguin, 1985.

Andrews, Julian. *London's War.* Aldershot: Lund Humphries, 2002.
Anscombe, R. 'The Hour of Darkness' in *Penguin New Writing*, No.25, 1945.
Apollonio, Umbro, ed. *Futurist Manifestos.* London: Thames and Hudson, 1973.
Arnold, Matthew. *Culture and Anarchy* [1869]. Cambridge: CUP, 1971.
Ashplant, T.G. and Gerry Smyth, eds. *Explorations in Cultural History.* London: Pluto Press, 2001.
Asimov, Isaac, M.H. Greenberg and C. Waugh, eds. *Isaac Asimov Presents the Best Science Fiction of the 19th Century.* New York, Knightsbridge, 1991.
Asquith, Anthony, dir. *Underground.* United Kingdom: British Film Institute, 1928.
Auden, W.H. 'Letter to Lord Byron' [1937]. *The Collected Longer Poems.* London: Faber and Faber, 2002.
Augé, Marc. *In the Metro*, trans. Tom Conley. Minneapolis and London: University of Minnesota Press, 2002.
Augé, Marc. *Non-Places: Introduction to an Anthropology of Supermodernity*, trans. John Howe. London and New York: Verso, 1995.
Bachelard, Gaston. *The Poetics of Space*, trans. Maria Jolas [1964]. Boston, Massachusetts: Beacon Press, 1969, 1994.
Bailey, Paul, ed. *The Oxford Book of London.* Oxford: OUP, 1995.
Baker, Phil. 'Secret City' in *London: From Punk to Blair*, ed. Joe Kerr and Andrew Gibson. London: Reaktion Books, 2003.
Baker, Roy Ward, dir. *Quatermass and the Pit.* United Kingdom: Hammer Film, 1967.
Balchin, Nigel Marlin. *Darkness Falls from the Air* [1943]. London: Pan Books, 1969.
Banksy. *Wall and Piece.* London: Century, Random House, 2006.
Banton, Eric. 'Underground Travelling London'. George R. Sims, ed. *Living London: Its work and its play. Its humour and its pathos. Its sights and its scenes.* First published 1901–03. Reprinted as *Edwardian London*, 4 vols. London: Village Press, 1990.
Barker, T.C. and Michael Robbins. *A History of London Transport.* London: George Allen and Unwin, 1974.
Barman, Christian. *The Man Who Built London Transport.* North Pomfret, Virginia: David and Charles, 1979.
Barnes, Julian. *Metroland* [1980]. London: Picador, 1990.
Barr, Robert. 'The Doom of London', *The Idler Magazine: An Illustrated Monthly*, eds. Jerome, Jerome K. and Barr, Robert. Vol.II, August 1892 to January 1893. London: Chatto and Windus, 1893.

Barrie, J.M. *The Greenwood Hat: Being a Memoir of James Anon 1885–1887.* London: Peter Davies, 1937.

Barthes, Roland. *Camera Lucida: Reflections on Photography,* trans. Richard Howard London: Random House, 2000.

Barthes, Roland. *Mythologies* [1957], trans. Annette Lavers. London: Cape, 1972.

Bató, Joseph. *Defiant City,* intro. J.B. Priestly. London: Victor Gollancz, 1942.

Baudrillard, Jean. 'Prophylaxis and Virulence' [1990]. *Posthumanism,* ed. Neil Badmington. Basingstoke: Palgrave, 2000.

Bayliss, Derek A. *The Post Office Railway.* Sheffield: Turntable Publications, 1978.

Benjamin, Walter. *The Arcades Project,* trans. Howard Eiland and Kevin McLaughlin London and Cambridge, Massachusetts: The Belknap Press of Harvard University Press, 2002.

Bennett, Arnold. *Buried Alive: A Tale of These Days.* London: Eyre Methuen, 1912.

Bennett, Arnold. *Riceyman Steps.* London: Cassell and Company, 1923.

Bennett, Michael and David W. Teague, eds. *The Nature of Cities: Ecocriticism and Urban Environments.* Tucson: The University of Arizona Press, 1999.

Benson, Gerard, Judith Chernaik and Cicely Herbert, eds. *Poems on the Underground.* Tenth Edition. London: Cassell and Co., 2001.

Berger, George. *The Story of CRASS.* London: Omnibus Press, 2006.

Berman, Marshall. *All That Is Solid Melts Into Air: The Experience of Modernity.* London: Verso, 1982.

Berthoud, Roger. *The Life of Henry Moore.* London: Giles de la Mare, 2003.

Betjeman, John. *Collected Poems.* London: John Murray, 2003.

Betjeman, John. *Coming Home: An Anthology of Prose,* ed. Candida Lycett Green. London: Random House, 1998.

Betjeman, John. *Metroland,* dir. Edward Mirzoeff. UK: BBC, 1973.

Binchy, Maeve. *London Transports.* London: Century Publications, 1983.

Blum, Cinzia Sartini. *The Other Modernism: F.T. Marinetti's Futurist Fiction of Power.* Berkeley: University of California Press, 1996.

Blumenfeld, R.D. *R.D.B's Diary 1887–1914.* London: Heinemann, 1930.

Blumenfeld, R.D. *All In A Lifetime.* London: Ernest Benn, 1931.

Blythe, Ronald George. *Components of the Scene: Stories, Poems and Essays of the Second World War.* Harmondsworth: Penguin, 1966.

Bobrick, Benson. *Labyrinths of Iron.* New York: Newsweek Books, 1982.

Booth, Michael R. *Theatre in the Victorian Age.* Cambridge: CUP, 1991.

Bosterli, Margaret Jones. *The Early Community at Bedford Park.* London: Routledge and Kegan, 1977.

Boucicault, Dion. *After Dark: A Tale of London* [1868] in *British Plays of the 19th Century*, ed. J.O. Bailey. New York: Odyssey, 1966.
Bowen, Elizabeth. *Collected Stories*, ed. Angus Wilson. London: Random House, 1999.
Bowen, Elizabeth. *The Demon Lover & Other Stories*. London: Penguin, 1965.
Bowen, Elizabeth. *The Mulberry Tree*, ed. Hermione Lee. London: Virago, 1986.
Bowlby, Rachel. *Just Looking: Consumer Culture in Dreiser, Gissing and Zola*. New York: Methuen, 1985.
Bowman, Rob, dir. *Reign of Fire*. United Kingdom: Touchstone Pictures, 2002.
Brandt, Bill. *Behind The Camera*, intro. Mark Haworth-Booth. Oxford: Phaidon, 1985.
Brandt, Bill. *Shadow Of Light*, ed. Cyril Connolly and Mark Haworth-Booth. London: Gordon Fraser, 1977.
Briggs, Asa. *Victorian Cities*. London: The Folio Society, 1996.
Brooker, Peter. *Bohemia in London: The Social Scene of Early Modernism*. Basingstoke: Palgrave, 2004.
Brooker, Peter and Andrew Thacker, eds. *Geographies of Modernism: Literature, cultures, spaces*. London and New York: Routledge, 2005.
Brooker, Peter. *Modernity and Metropolis: Community Experiments, 1900–1945*. Basingstoke: Palgrave, 2002.
Bruno, Giuliana. *Atlas of Emotion: Journeys in Art, Architecture, and Film*. New York: Verso, 2002.
Buchan, John. *The Complete Richard Hannay*. London: Penguin, 1992.
Buckley, Jerome Hamilton. *William Ernest Henley: A Study in the 'Counter-Decadence' of the 'Nineties*. Princeton University Press, 1945.
Burke, Peter. *Varieties of Cultural History*. Cambridge: Polity Press, 1997.
Calder, Angus. *The Myth of the Blitz*. London: Jonathan Cape, 1991.
Calder, Angus. *The People's War*. London: Jonathan Cape, 1969.
Calder, Angus and Dorothy Sheridan, eds. *Speak for Yourself: A Mass-Observation Anthology, 1937–49*. London: Jonathan Cape, 1984.
Campbell, Alan and Tim Neil. *A Life in Pieces: Reflections on Alexander Trocchi*. London: Rebel Inc., Canongate Books, 1997.
Čapek, Karel. *Letters from England*, trans. Geoffrey Newsome. Brinksworth, Wiltshire: Claridge Press, 2001.
Carey, John. *The Intellectuals and the Masses*. London: Faber, 1992.
Carter, Ian. *Railways and Culture in Britain: the Epitome of Modernity*. Manchester: MUP, 2001.
Casson, Stanley. 'Modern Sculpture'. *The Listener*, 26 February 1930.

Céline, Louis-Ferdinand. *Guignol's Band*, trans. Bernard Frechtman and Hack T. Nile. New York: New Directions, 1969.

Certeau, Michel de. *The Practice of Everyday Life*, trans. Steven Rendall. London: University of California Press, 1988.

Chalfont, Henry and James Prigoff. *Spraycan Art*. London: Thames and Hudson, 1987.

Chalfont, Henry and Martha Cooper. *Subway Art*. London: Thames and Hudson, 1984.

Chesterton, G.K. *Autobiography* [1936], ed. Anthony Burgess. London: Hutchinson, 1969.

Chesterton, G.K. *The Annotated Thursday*, ed. Martin Gardner. San Francisco: Ignatius, 1999.

Chesterton, G.K. *What's Wrong With The World*. London: Cassell & Company, 1910.

Christie, Agatha. *The Man in the Brown Suit* [1924]. London: HarperCollins, 1997.

Clark, Kenneth. *Henry Moore Drawings*. London: Thames and Hudson, 1974.

Clayton, Anthony. *Subterranean City*. London: Historical Publications, 2000.

Colomina, Beatriz. *Privacy and Publicity: Modern Architecture as Mass Media*. London: The MIT Press, 1994.

Core Design. *Tomb Raider III*. UK: Eidos Interactive, 1998.

Cork, Richard, ed. *Eduardo Paolozzi Underground*. London: Royal Academy of Arts, 1986.

Cork, Richard. *Jacob Epstein*. London: Tate Publishing, 1999.

Cork, Richard. *Vorticism and Abstract Art in the First Machine Age*. London: Gordon Fraser, 1976.

Cork, Richard. *Vorticism and its Allies*. London: Arts Council of Great Britain, 1974.

Coverley, Merlin. *Psychogeography*. Harpenden, Hertfordshire: Pocket Essentials, 2006.

CRASS. *Best Before 1984*. London: Crass Albums, 1986.

Crichton, Charles, dir. *A Fish Called Wanda*. United Kingdom: Metro-Goldwyn-Mayer, 1988.

Croome, Desmond F. and Alan A. Jackson. *Rails Through Clay*. Harrow Weald, Middlesex: Capital Transport, 1993.

Crosland, T.W.H. *The Suburbans* [1905]. London: John Long, 1905.

Crouch, Christopher. *Modernism in Art, Design and Architecture*. New York: St. Martin's Press, 1999.

Daly, Nicholas. *Literature, Technology and Modernity, 1860–2000*. Cambridge: CUP, 2004.

Davidson, John. 'Thirty Bob A Week' [1894] in *Poems and Ballads*, ed. R.D. Macleod. London: The Unicorn Press, 1959.

Day, John R. and John Reed. *The Story of London's Underground*. London: Capital Transport publications, 2001.

Debord, Guy. *Society of the Spectacle*, trans. Ken Knabb. London: Rebel Press, 1992.

De Larrabeiti, Michael. *The Borribles Trilogy*: *The Borribles: The Great Rumble Hunt* [1978], *The Borribles Go For Broke* [1981], *The Borribles: Across the Dark Metropolis* [1986]. London: Macmillan, 2002.

DeLillo, Don. *Underworld*. London: Picador, 1998.

Derrida, Jacques. *Specters of Marx*, trans. Peggy Kamuf, eds. Bernd Magnus and Stephen Cullenberg. New York, London: Routledge, 1994.

Dickens, Charles. *Dombey & Son* [1848]. London: Penguin, 1964.

Dixon, Ella Hepworth. *The Story of a Modern Woman*. London: Heinemann, 1894.

Doré, Gustave and Blanchard Jerrold. *London* [1886]. Newton Abbott, Devon: David and Charles Reprints, 1971.

Douglas, Hugh. *The Underground Story*. London: Robert Hale, 1963.

Doyle, Arthur Conan. 'The Bruce-Partington Plans' [1908] in *His Last Bow: Some Reminiscences of Sherlock Holmes*, ed. Owen Dudley Edwards. Oxford: OUP, 1993.

Doyle, Arthur Conan. 'A Study in Scarlet' [1887] in *The Original Illustrated 'STRAND' Sherlock Holmes: The Complete Facsimile Edition*. Hertfordshire: Wordsworth Editions, 1989.

Dreiser, Theodore. *Letters of Theodore Dreiser*, ed. Robert H. Elias. Philadelphia: Pennsylvania Press, 1959.

Dreiser, Theodore. *The Stoic* [1947]. New York: Apollo Edition, Thomas Y. Crowell, 1974.

Dreiser, Theodore. *A Traveler at Forty*. New York: The Century Co., 1913.

Dreiser, Theodore. *A Traveler at Forty*, ed Renate von Bardeleben. Urbana and Chicago: University of Illinois Press, 2004.

Duffy, Carol Ann. 'Woman Seated in the Underground, 1941: after the drawing by Henry Moore' in *Standing Female Nude*. London: Anvil Press Poetry, 1998.

Eagleton, Terry. *The Idea of Culture*. Oxford: Blackwell, 2000.

Edwards, Arthur M. *The Design of Suburbia*. London: Pembridge, 1981.

Edwards, Denis and Ron Pigram. *London's Underground Suburbs*. London: Baton Transport, 1986.

Edwards, Denis and Ron Pigram. *Metro Memories: A Pictorial History of Metro-Land*. London: Bloomsbury, 1977.

Eliot, George. *Felix Holt, the Radical* [1866], ed. William Barker and Kenneth Womack. Ontario: Broadview, 2000.

Eliot, T.S. *The Complete Poems and Plays*. London: Faber and Faber, 1969.

Eliot, T.S. 'London Letters: September 1921' in *The Dial*, Vol.71.

Epstein, Jacob. *Epstein: An Autobiography*. London: Vista Books, 1963.

Falconer, Rachel. *Hell in Contemporary Literature: Western Descent Narratives since 1945*. Edinburgh: EUP, 2006.

Farleigh, John. *It Never Dies*. London: Sylvan Press, 1946.

Farson, Negley. *Bomber's Moon*, illustrated by Tom Purvis. London: Victor Gollancz, 1941.

Ferney-Hough, Frank. *The History of Railways in Britain*. Reading: Osprey Publishing, 1975.

Ferns, C.S. *Narrating Utopia*. Liverpool: Liverpool University Press, 1999.

Fitzgibbon, Constantine. *The Blitz* [1957]. London: McDonald, 1970.

Flint, F.S. 'Contemporary French Poetry' in *Poetry Review*, No.VIII, Aug 1912.

Flint, F.S. 'Poems'. *The Egoist*, 1 January 1914.

Ford, Ford Madox. *The Soul of London: A Survey of a Modern City* [1905], ed. Alan G. Hill. London: Dent, 1995.

Ford, Simon. *The Situationist International: A User's Guide*. London: Black Dog, 2005.

Forster, E.M. *Howard's End* [1910]. London: Everyman's Library, 1992.

Forster, E.M. 'The Machine Stops' [1909] in *The New Collected Short Stories*, ed. P.N. Furbank. London: Sidgwick & Jackson, 1987.

Freeman, Michael. *Railways and the Victorian Imagination*. New Haven: Yale University Press, 1999.

Freud, Anna and Dorothy Burlington. *Infants Without Families: Reports on the Hampstead Nurseries, 1939–1945, The Writings of Anna Freud, Volume III*. New York: International Universities Press, 1973.

Freud, Sigmund. 'The "Uncanny"', *The Standard Edition of the Complete Psychological Works of Sigmund Freud, Vol.XVII, 1917–1919*, trans. James Strachey. London: Hogarth Press, 1955.

Friswell, J. Hain. 'A Journey Underground', *Once A Week*, Vol.VII, 20 Sept 1862.

Fry, Roger. *Art and Commerce*. London: Hogarth Press, 1926.

Gaiman, Neil. *Neverwhere* [1996]. London: Hodder Headline, 2000.

Galsworthy, John. *The Forsyte Saga, Volume 1*. London: Penguin, 1978.

Gardiner, Juliet. *The People's War*. London: Collins and Brown, 1991.

Gardiner, Stephen. *Epstein: Artist Against the Establishment*. London: Flamingo, 1993.

Garland, Ken. *Mr Beck's Underground Map*. Harrow Weald: Capital, 2003.

Garrould, Ann. *Henry Moore: Volume Three: Complete Drawings: 1940–49*. Aldershot: Lund Humphries, 2001.

Gasiorek, Andrzej. '"Architecture or revolution"? Le Corbusier and Wyndham Lewis', in *Geographies of Modernism: Literature, cultures, spaces*, eds. Peter Brooker and Andrew Thacker. London and New York: Routledge, 2005.

Gerber, Richard. *Utopian Fantasy: A Study of English Utopian Fantasy since the End of the 19th Century*. London: Routledge and Kegan Paul, 1995.

Gibson, Andrew and Joe Kerr, eds. *London: From Punk to Blair*. London: Reaktion Books, 2003.

Gilbert, Michael. 'Mr Duckworth's Night Out' [1959]. *Circle On The Lines: A Anthology of Mystery Short Stories with a Railway Setting*, ed. Bryan Morgan. London: Routledge and Kegan Paul, 1975.

Gissing, George. *Collected Letters*, eds. Paul F. Matthiesen, Arthur C. Young and Pierre Coustillas. Athens, Ohio: Ohio University Press, 1991.

Gissing, George. *Demos: A Story of English Socialism* [1886], ed. Pierre Coustillas. Brighton: Harvester Press, 1972.

Gissing, George. *London and the Life of Literature: The Diary of George Gissing*, ed. Pierre Coustillas. Hassocks, Sussex: The Harvester Press, 1978.

Gissing, George. *The Nether World* [1889], ed. Stephen Gill. Oxford: OUP, 1992.

Gissing, George. *New Grub Street* [1891], ed. Irving Howe. Boston: Houghton Mifflin, 1962.

Gissing, George. *Thyrza* [1887], ed. Jacob Korg. Brighton: The Harvester Press, 1984.

Gissing, George. *The Whirlpool* [1897], ed. Patrick Parrinder. Sussex: The Harvester Press, 1977.

Gissing, George. *In the Year of Jubilee* [1894], ed. John Halperin. London: The Hogarth Press, 1987.

Grahame, Kenneth. *The Wind in the Willows* [1908]. London: J.M. Dent, 1993.

Graves, Charles. *London Transport At War, 1939–1945*. Surrey: Almark, 1974.

Green, Oliver and Alan Powers, eds. *Away We Go! Advertising London Transport: Edward Bawden and Eric Ravilious*. Norwich: The Mainstone Press, 2006.

Green, Oliver, ed. *Metro-Land: British Empire Exhibition Number: facsimile edition*. First published 1924. London: Southbank Publishing, 2004.

Green, Oliver. *Underground Art: London Transport Posters, 1908 to the Present*. London: Laurence King, 1999.

Greene, Graham. *It's a Battlefield* [1934]. London: William Heinemann, 1962.
Greene, Graham. *The Lawless Roads* [1939]. London: Heinemann, 1955.
Greene, Graham. *The Ministry of Fear* [1943]. Harmondsworth: Heinemann, 1963.
Greene, Graham. *A Sort of Life*. London: Bodley Head, 1971.
Gregg, John. *The Shelter of the Tubes*. London: Capital Transport, 2001.
Haining, Peter, ed. *Murder on the Railways*. London: Orion, 1996.
Halliday, Stephen. *Underground to Everywhere*. Gloucestershire: Sutton Publishing, 2001.
Hardy, Dennis. *Utopian England: Community Experiments, 1900–1945*. London: E. and F.N. Spon, 2000.
Hardy, Thomas. *Selected Letters*, ed. M. Millgate. Oxford: Clarendon, 1990.
Harris, Meiron and Susan. *The War Artists*. London: Michael Joseph, 1983.
Harrison, Michael. *London Beneath the Pavements*. London: Peter Davies, 1961.
Harrison, Tom. *Living Through the Blitz*. London: Collins, 1976.
Hassall, Christopher. 'Tube Shelter Leicester Square, 1941' in *The Slow Night and Other Poems, 1940–1948*. London: Arthur Baker, 1969.
Haworth-Booth, Mark. *E. McKnight Kauffer*. London: V&A Publications, 2005.
Hay, M. Doriel. *Murder Underground*. London: Skeffington and Son, 1934.
Hayward, John. *Prose Literature Since 1939*. London: Longmans Green and Co., 1947.
Head, Dominic. *The Cambridge Introduction to Modern British Fiction, 1950–2000*. Cambridge Unversity Press, 2002.
Healy, John. *Streets Above Us*. London: HarperCollins, 1991.
Heaney, Seamus. *District and Circle*. London: Faber and Faber, 2006.
Heaney, Seamus. 'The Underground' [1984] in *Opened Ground: Poems 1966–1996*. London: Faber and Faber, 1998.
Hebdige, Dick. *Subculture: The Meaning of Style*. New York, London: Methuen, 1979.
Henley, W.E. *The Selected Letters of W.E. Henley*, ed. Damian Atkinson. Aldershot, Hampshire: Ashgate Publishing, 2000.
Hepburn, James G. 'Some Curious Realism in *Riceyman Steps*', *Modern Fiction Studies*, Volume 8, Summer 1962.
Herbert, James. *The Rats* [1979]. London: Pan Books, 1999.
Hern, A. 'The People of the Tubes' in *Tribune*, 27 September 1940.
Hill, Geoffrey. *Speech! Speech!* London: Penguin, 2001.
Hill, Tobias. *Underground*. London: Faber and Faber, 1999.
Hoban, R. *Kleinzeit* [1976]. London: Picador, 1979.

Hobsbawm, Eric. *Behind the Times: The Decline and Fall of the Twentieth-Century Avant-Gardes*. London: Thames & Hudson, 1999.

Hobson, J. *Imperialism*. London: George Allen and Unwin, 1902, 1905.

Hollingshead, John. *Ragged London in 1861*, ed. Anthony S. Wohl. London: J.M. Dent, 1986.

Hollingshead, John. *Underground London*. London: Groombridge and Sons, 1862.

Honnef, Klaus. *Pop Art*. Köln: Taschen, 2006.

Household, Geoffrey. *Rogue Male* [1939]. London: Phoenix, 1999.

Hulme. T.E. *Collected Writings*, ed. K. Csengari. Oxford: OUP, 1994.

Humphreys, Dewi, dir. *Neverwhere*. UK: BBC, 1996.

Huxley, Aldous. *Brave New World* [1932]. London: Hogarth Press, 1987.

Huxley, Aldous. *Crome Yellow* [1921]. London: Chatto & Windus, 1974.

Huxley, Aldous. *Point Counter Point* [1928]. London: Chatto & Windus, 1963.

Hylton, Stuart. *Their Darkest Hour: The Hidden History of the Home Front 1939–1945*. Stroud: Sutton, 2001.

Hynes, Samuel. *The Edwardian Turn of Mind* [1968]. London: Pimlico, 1991.

Ibrahim, Mecca. *One Stop Short of Barking: Uncovering the London Underground*. London: New Holland, 2004.

Ironside, Robin. *Painting Since 1939*. London: British Council, 1947.

Jackson, Alan A. *London Metropolitan Railway*. London: David and Charles, 1986.

Jackson, Alan A. and Desmond F. Croome, *Rails Through the Clay*. London: George Allen & Unwin, 1962.

Jackson, Lee. *A Metropolitan Murder*. London: Arrow Books, 2004.

Jam, The. 'Down In the Tube Station at Midnight' [1978] on the album *The Jam Story*. UK: Polydor, 2006.

James, Henry. *A London Life and The Reverberator* [1888], ed. Philip Horne. Oxford University Press, 1989.

James, Henry. *The Wings of the Dove* [1902], ed. Cheryl B. Torsney. London: J.M. Dent, 1997.

James, Norah C. *Strap-Hangers: A Novel*. London: Duckworth, 1934.

Jameson, Frederic. *Postmodernism, or the Cultural Logic of Late Capitalism*. London: Verso, 1991.

Jane, Fred T. 'Romance of Modern London', *The English Illustrated Magazine*, Vol.X, 1892–1893.

Jefferies, Richard. *After London: or Wild England* [1885]. Oxford: OUP, 1980.

Jeffrey, Ian. *Bill Brandt: Photographs, 1928–1983*. London: Thames & Hudson, 1993.

Johnson, Linton Kwesi. *Inglan Is A Bitch*. London: Race Today, 1980.

Jung, C.G. *The Archetypes and the Collective Unconscious*, trans. R.F.C. Hull. London: Routledge and Kegan Paul, 1959.

Kellett, John R. *The Impact of Railways on Victorian Cities*. London: Routledge and Kegan Paul, 1969.

Kenner, Hugh. *The Mechanic Muse*. Oxford: OUP, 1987.

Kern, Stephen. *The Culture of Time and Space, 1880–1918*. London: Weidenfield and Nicholson, 1983.

Kerr, Joe and Andrew Gibson, eds. *London: From Punk to Blair*. London: Reaktion Books, 2003.

Kinks, The. 'Waterloo Sunset' on the album *Something Else by the Kinks*. London: Pye Records, 1967.

Kirby, Lynne. *Parallel Tracks: The Railroad and Silent Cinema*. Exeter University Press, 1997.

Kitchener, Lord and Vincent Street Six. 'Sweet Jamaica' [1952]. *London Is The Place For Me*. London: Honest Jon's Records, 2002.

Kitchener, Lord. 'The Underground Train' [1950] on *London Is The Place For Me: Trinidadian Calypso in London, 1950–1956*. London: Honest Jon's Records, 2002.

Klein, Naomi. *No Logo*. London: Harper Perennial, 2005.

Knadd, Ken, trans. *Situationist International: Anthology*. Berkeley, California: Bureau of Public Secrets, 1981.

Knowles, S.D.G. *A Purgatorial Flame*. Philadelphia: University of Pennsylvania Press, 1990.

Kops, Bernard. *The World is a Wedding* [1963]. London: Mayflower, 1970.

Kumar, Krishan. *Utopia and Anti-Utopia in Modern Times*. Oxford: Basil Blackwood, 1997.

Kureishi, Hanif and Jon Savage, eds. *The Faber Book of Pop*. London: Faber and Faber, 1995.

Kureishi, Hanif. *Outskirts and Other Plays*. London: Faber and Faber, 1998.

Kureishi, Hanif. *Sammy and Rosie Get Laid: The Script and The Diary*. London: Faber and Faber, 1988.

Labour Research Department. *The London Traffic Combine*. London: L.R.D., 1932.

Lacan, Jacques. *Ecrits: A Selection*, trans. Alan Sheridan. London: Tavistock, 1977.

Lancaster, Osbert. *From Pillar to Post* [1938]. London: John Murray, 1979.

Landis, John, dir. *An American Werewolf in London*. United Kingdom: Universal, 1981.

Lawrence, David. *Underground Architecture*. Middlesex: Capital, 1994.

Le Corbusier. *The City of To-morrow and its Planning* [1929], trans. Frederick Etchells. New York: Dover, 1987.

Le Corbusier. *Towards A New Architecture* [1927], trans. Frederick Etchells. London: The Architectural Press, 1982.

Leboff, David and Tim Demuth. *No Need To Ask! Early Maps of London's Underground Railways*. Harrow Weald, Middlesex: Capital Transport, 1999.

Lee, Vernon. *Vanitas*. London: Heinemann, 1892.

Lefebvre, Henri. *The Production of Space* [1974], trans. Donald Nicholson-Smith. Oxford: Blackwell, 2000.

Lester, Richard, dir. *The Bed-Sitting Room*. UK: Oscar Lewenstein, 1969.

Lethaby, W.R. *Form in Civilisation*. London: OUP, 1927.

Levy, Amy. *The Romance of a Shop* [1888]. Gainsville: University of California Press, 1993.

Lewis, Adrian. 'Henry Moore's "Shelter Drawings": Memory and Myth' in *War Culture*, ed. P. Kirkham and D. Thomas. London: Lawrence and Wishart, 1995.

Lewis, Wyndham, ed. *BLAST* [1914–1915]. Santa Rosa: Black Sparrow Press, 2002.

Lewis, Wyndham. *Blasting and Bombardiering* [1937]. London: John Calder, 1982.

Lewis, Wyndham. *The Caliph's Design: Architects! Where is Your Vortex?* [1921], ed. Paul Edwards. Santa Barbara: Black Sparrow Press, 1986.

Lewis, Wyndham. 'Plain Homebuilder: Where is Your Vorticist?' [1934], *Creatures of Habit and Creatures of Change: Essays on Art, Literature and Society, 1914–1956*, ed. Paul Edwards. Black Sparrow Press, 1989.

Lewis, Wyndham. *Rude Assignment* [1950], ed. Toby Foshay. Santa Barbara: Black Sparrow Press, 1984.

Lewis, Wyndham. *The Tyro: A Review of the Arts of Painting, Sculpture and Design*. London: The Egoist Press, 1922.

Lewis, Wyndham. *The Wild Body*. London: Chatto and Windus, 1927.

Lewis, Wyndham. 'A Young Soldier'. *The Egoist*, 1 March 1916.

Loving, Jerome. *The Last Titan: A Life of Theodore Dreiser*. Berkeley, Los Angeles and London: University of California Press, 2005.

Lowe, Keith. *Tunnel Vision*. London: Arrow Books, 2001.

Luckhurst, Roger. 'Occult London' in *London: From Punk to Blair*, ed. Joe Kerr and Andrew Gibson. London: Reaktion Books, 2003.

Macauley, Rose. *Told by an Idiot* [1923]. New York: Doubleday, 1983.

MacDonald, Nancy. *The Graffiti Subculture*. Basingstoke, Hampshire: Palgrave, 2001.

Machen, Arthur. *The London Adventures or The Art of Wandering*. London: Martin Secker, 1924.

MacInnes, Colin. *Absolute Beginners* [1959]. London: Allison and Busby, 1992.

MacInnes, Colin. *City of Spades* [1958]. London: Allison and Busby, 1993.

MacNeice, Louis. *Collected Poems*. London: Faber and Faber, 1966.

MacNeice, Louis. 'Cook's Tour of the London Subways' in *The Listener*, 17 April 1941.

MacNeice, Louis. *Selected Prose*, ed. Alan Heuser. Oxford: Clarendon Press, 1990.

Mailer, Norman. 'The Faith of Graffiti' [1974] in *Pieces and Pontifications*. Sevenoaks: New English Library, 1983.

Mapanje, Jack. *Of Chameleons and Gods*. Oxford: Heinemann, 1981.

Marcus, Greil. *Lipstick Traces*. London: Faber and Faber, 2001.

Marcus, Jane. 'Britannia Rules The Waves' in *Decolonizing Tradition*, ed Karen R. Lawrence. Urbana and Chicago: University of Illinois Press, 1992.

Marrinetti, F.T. *Selected Writings*, ed. R.W. Flint. London: Secker and Warburg, 1972.

Marx, Karl. *Capital*, trans. Samuel Moore and Edward Aveling. London: George Allen and Unwin, 1971.

Marx, Karl. *Grundisse: Foundations of the Critique of Political Economy (Rough Draft)*, trans. Martin Nicolaus. London: Penguin, 1977.

Marx, Karl. *Selected Writings*, ed. David McLellan. Oxford: OUP, 2004.

Matta-Clark, Gordon. 'My Understanding of Art' [c.1975]. *Gordon Matt-Clark*, ed. C. Disrerens. London: Phaidon, 2003.

Mayhew, Henry. *The Metropolitan Railway: From "The Shops and Companies of Companies"*. London: C.P. Nicholls, 1865.

McGee, Patrick. 'The Politics of Modernist Form; or, Who Rules *The Waves*?', *Modern Fiction Studies*, Vol.38, No.3, Autumn 1992.

McKie, David. 'The Fall of a Midas'. *The Guardian*, 2 February 2004.

McLaughlin, Joseph. *Writing the Urban Jungle: Reading Empire from Doyle to Eliot*. Charlottesville: University of Virginia Press, 2000.

McTeigue, James, dir. *V for Vendetta*. UK: Warner Bros, 2006.

McTell, Ralph. 'Streets of London' [1974], *Streets of London: the Best of Ralph McTell*. London: Metro, 2006.

Melly, George, ed. *The Writing on the Wall*. London: Hamish Hamilton, 1976.

Mengham, Rod and Marc Atkins. 'End of the Line' in *London: From Punk to Blair*, eds. Joe Kerr and Andrew Gibson. London: Reaktion Books, 2003.

Mengham, Rod. 'From Georges Sorel to BLAST' in *The Violent Muse*, eds. Jana Howlett and Rod Mengham. Manchester: MUP, 1994.

Meynell, Alice and William Hyde. *London Impressions*. Westminster: Archibald, Constable and Co., 1898.
Miéville, China. *King Rat*. Basingstoke and Oxford: Macmillan, 1998.
Minney, R.J. *Puffin Asquith, The Biography of the Honourable Anthony Asquith: Aristocrat, Aesthete, Prime Minister's Son, and Brilliant Film Maker*. London: Leslie Frewin, 1973.
Mitchell, David. *Ghostwritten*. London: Sceptre, Hodder and Stoughton, 1999.
Mitchison, Naomi. *A Girl Must Live: Stories and Poems*. Glasgow: Richard Drew, 1990.
Mole, Annie. Going Underground Blog: << http://london-underground.blogspot.com>>.
Moore, Alan and David Lloyd. *V for Vendetta* [1982–1988]. New York: Vertigo, 1990.
Moore, George. *Esther Walters* [1894]. London: William Heinemann, 1952.
Moore, Henry. *Shelter Sketch Book*. London: Editions Poetry, 1945.
Moore, Henry. *Shelter Sketchbook*, facsimile of first notebook, ed. Francis Carey. London: British Museum Publications, 1988.
Morris, William. *The Collected Letters*, ed. Norman Kelvin. New York: Princeton University Press.
Morris, William. 'Untitled Article', *The Commonweal*, Vol. 2, No.17, 8 May 1886.
Morris, William. *News from Nowhere* [1890], ed. Clive Wilmer. London: Penguin, 1993.
Morrison, Herbert. *The London Traffic Fraud, London Municipal Pamphlet No.8*. London Labour Publications, 1929.
Morton, A.L. *The English Utopia*. London: Lawrence and Wishart, 1952.
Mumford, Lewis. *The City in History* [1961]. New York: MJF Books, 1989.
Murdoch, Iris. *A Word Child* [1976]. London: Triad Granada, 1982.
Naipaul, V.S. *The Enigma of Arrival*. London: Penguin, 1987.
Nead, Lynda. *Victorian Babylon: People, Streets and Images in Nineteenth-Century London*. New Haven and London: Yale University Press, 2000.
Neumann, Erich. *The Archetypal World of Henry Moore*, trans. R.F.C. Hull. London: Routledge and Kegan Paul, 1959.
Nevinson, C.R.W. *Paint and Prejudice*. London: Methuen, 1937.
Oliver, Paul, Ian Davis and Ian Bentley. *Dunroamin: The Suburban Semi and Its Enemies*. London: Pimlico, 1994,
Orczy, Emmuska. *The Old Man in the Corner: Twelve Classic Detective Stories*. Mineola, New York: Dover, 1980.
Orczy, Emmuska. 'London Mysteries', *The Royal Magazine*, 1901.
Orwell, George. *1984* [1948]. London: Penguin, 2000.

Orwell, George. *A Clergyman's Daughter* [1935] in *The Complete Novels*. London: Penguin, 2001.

Orwell, George. *Coming Up for Air* [1939]. London: Secker and Warburg, 1986.

Orwell, George. *Keep the Apidestra Flying* [1934]. London: Secker and Warburg, 1978.

Orwell, George. *The Lion and the Unicorn: Socialism and the English Genius* [1941], ed. Bernard Crick. London: Penguin, 1982.

Orwell, George. 'Wartime Diary', *My Country Right or Left, Collected Journalism and Essays, 1940–1943, Vol. II*, ed. Sonia Orwell and Ian Angus. London: Secker and Warburg, 1968.

Owen, Hugh. 'The Poison Cloud', *Pearson's Magazine*. Vol.XXVI. London: 1908.

Oxenham, John. 'A Murder of the Underground', *To-Day*, 27 February – 10 April, 1897.

Page, E.V. and Vincent Davies. *Timothy Tott or The "Metropolitan Railway"*. London: Willey and Co., 1883.

Passingham, W.J. *The Romance of London's Underground*. London: Sampson Low, Marston and Co., 1930.

Pennell, Elizabeth Robins. 'London's Underground Railway', *Harper's New Monthly Magazine*, Vol.92, No.548, January 1896.

Pennell, Elizabeth Robins. *The Life and Letters of Joseph Pennell*. London: Earnest Benn, 1930.

Perry, Roger. *The Writing on the Wall*. London: Elm Tree Books, Hamish Hamilton, 1976.

Pike, David L. 'Modernist Space and the Transformation of Underground London' in *Imagined Londons*, ed. Pamela K. Gilbert. New York: State University of New York Press, 2002.

Pike, David L. *Passage Through Hell: Modernist Descents, Medieval Underworlds*. Ithaca and London: Cornell University Press, 1997.

Pike, David L. *Subterranean Cities: The World Beneath Paris and London, 1800–1945*. Ithaca and London: Cornell University Press, 2005.

Pike, David L. 'Underground Theater: Subterranean Spaces on the London Stage', *Nineteenth Century Studies*. Ed. Patricia O'Hara. Vol. 13, 1999.

Pinks, William J. *The History of Clerkenwell* [1881], ed. Edward J. Wood. London: Frances Boutle, 2001.

Priestley, J.B. *Angel Pavement* [1930]. London: Heinemann, 1969.

Priestley, J.B. *English Journey* [1934]. London: Heinemann, 1984.

Priestley, J.B. *They Walk in the City*. London: Heinemann, 1936.

Rafferty, Gerry. *Baker Street*. London: EMI Gold, 1998.

Rainey, Lawrence. 'The Cultural Economy of Modernism' in *The Cambridge Companion to Modernism*, ed. M. Levenson. Cambridge: CUP, 1999.
Reed, Henry. *The Novel Since 1939*. London: Longmans Green and Co., 1946.
Rendall, Ruth. 'A Transport of Love in the Underworld', *The Guardian*, 17 Oct. 1991.
Reynolds, G.W.N. *The Mysteries of London* [1845]. Keele: Keele University Press, 1996.
Rhys, Jean. *After Leaving Mr Mackenzie* [1930]. London: Penguin, 1971.
Rhys, Jean. *Good Morning, Midnight* [1939]. London: Penguin, 1969.
Rhys, Jean. *Voyage in the Dark* [1934]. London: Penguin, 1969.
Richards, J.M. *The Castles On the Ground* [1946]. London: John Murray, 1973.
Richardson, Dorothy. *Pilgrimage Volume 2: The Tunnel: Interim* [1919], ed. Gill Hanscombe. London: Virago, 1979.
Richardson, Dorothy. *Pilgrimage, Volume.4, March Moonlight*. London: Virago, 1967.
Riddell, Jonathan. *Pleasure Trips by Underground*. Harrow Weald, Middlesex: Capital Transport, 1998.
Robinson, Alan. *Imagining London, 1770–1900*. Basingstoke: Palgrave, 2004.
Ross, Christopher. *Tunnel Visions: Journeys of an Underground Philosopher*. London: HarperCollins, 2001.
Rothenstein, William. *Men and Memories: Recollections 1872–1938*. London: Faber and Faber, 1931.
Royle, Nicholas. *The Director's Cut*. London: Abacus, Little Brown, 2000.
Rushdie, Salman. *The Satanic Verses* [1988]. London: Random House, 1998.
Rutter, Frank. *Art In My Time*. London: Rich and Cowan, 1933.
Ryman, Geoff. *253*. London: HarperCollins, 1998.
Sadler, Simon. *The Situationist City*. London and Cambridge, Massachusetts: The MIT Press, 1998.
Saler, Michael T. *The Avant-Garde in Interwar England: Medieval Modernism and the London Underground*. OUP, 1999.
Saler, Michael T. 'The "Medieval Modern" Underground: Terminus of the Avant-Garde'. *Modernism / Modernity*, Vol.II, No.1, January 1995.
Sandhu, Sukhdev. *London Calling: How Black and Asian Writers Imagined a City*. London: HarperCollins, 2003.
Savage, Jon. *Teenage: The Creation of Youth Culture*. New York: Viking, 2007.
Schivelbusch, Wolfgang. *The Railway Journey: The Industrialization of Time and Space in the 19th Century*. Leamington Spa: Berg Publishers, 1986.
Seaborne, Mike. *Shelters: living Underground in the London Blitz: images by Bill Brandt and other unrecorded photographers*. London: Nishen, 1988.
Selvon, Sam. *Eldorado West One*. Leeds, Yorkshire: Peepal Tree Press, 1988.

Selvon, Sam. *Foreday Morning: Selected Prose 1946–1986*, ed. Kenneth Ramchand and Susheila Nasta. London: Longman, 1994.

Selvon, Sam. *The Lonely Londoners* [1956], ed. Susheila Nasta. London: Penguin, 2006.

Selvon, Sam. *Moses Ascending* [1975]. Oxford: Heinemann, 1984.

Selvon, Sam. *Ways of Sunlight* [1957], ed. Jane Grant. Harlow, Essex: Longman, 1987.

Sherman, Gary, dir. *Death Line / Raw Meat*. United Kingdom: Rank Film, 1972.

Short, K.R.M. *The Dynamite War*. Gill and MacMillan, 1979.

Sim, Stuart. *Derrida and the End of History*. Cambridge: Icon Books, 1999.

Simmons, Jack. *The Victorian Railway*. London: Thames and Hudson, 1991/1995.

Sims, George R. *The Mysteries of Modern Life*. London: C. Arthur Pearson, 1906.

Slack, Kathleen M. *Henrietta's Dream: A Chronicle of the Garden Suburb 1905–1982*. London: Calvert's North Star Press, 1982.

Sladen, Mark and Ariella Yelger, eds. *Panic Attack: Art in the Punk Years*. London and New York: Merrell, 2007.

Smith, Christopher, dir. *Creep*. UK Film Council, 2004.

Smith, Neil. 'Homeless/global: scaling places', in *Mapping the Future: Local Cultures, Global Change*, eds. Jon Bird, Barry Curtis, Tim Putnam, George Robertson and Lisa Tuckner. London: Routledge, 1993.

Smith, Stephen. *Underground London: Travels Beneath the City Streets*. London: Little, Brown, 2004.

Softley, Iain, dir. *The Wings of the Dove*. UK: Miramax, 1998.

Stanway, L.C. *Mails Under London*. Essex: Association of Essex Philatelic Societies, 2000.

Steele-Perkins, Chris and Richard Smith. *The Teds*. London: Travelling Light, 1979.

Storr, Catherine. *The Underground Conspiracy*. London: Faber and Faber, 1987.

Swingler, Randall. 'Sheltering in London Tubes', *The Daily Worker*, 14 Sept 1940.

Taylor, Sheila, ed. *Moving Metropolis: A History of London's Transport since 1800*. Laurence King, 2002.

Terreaux, L.H. du. *Waiting on the Underground*: A New Farce. Royal Strand Theatre, 1863. Lord Chamberlain's Plays, British Library, No.53052.

Timms, Edward and David Kelley. *Unreal City: Urban Experience in Modern European Literature and Art*. Manchester: MUP, 1985.

Tindall, Gillian. *Countries of the Mind: The Meaning of Place to Writers.* London: Hogarth Press, 1991.
Thacker, Andrew. *Moving Through Modernity: Space and Geography in Modernism.* Manchester University Press, 2003.
Thompson, F.M.L. *The Rise of Suburbia.* Leicester University Press, 1982.
Topolski, Feliks. *Britain in Peace and War*, intro. James Laver. London: Methuen, 1941.
Trench, Richard and Ellis Hillman. *London Under London: A Subterranean Guide.* London: John Murray, 1992.
Trocchi, Alexander. *Invisible Insurrection of a Million Minds: A Trocchi Reader*, ed. Andrew Murray Scott. Edinburgh: Polygon, 1991.
Trocchi, Alexander, ed. *The Moving Times.* London: The Stanhope Press, 1964.
Trollope, Anthony. *The Prime Minister* [1876]. Oxford: OUP, 1863.
Trollope, Anthony. *The Way We Live Now* [1875], ed. John Sutherland. Oxford: OUP, 1982.
Trotter, David. *Circulation: Defoe, Dickens, and the Economics of the Novel.* Basingstoke, Hampshire: Macmillan, 1988.
Turner, E.S. *The Shocking History of Advertising* [1952]. Harmondsworth: Penguin, 1965.
Vadillo, Ana Parejo. *Women Poets and Urban Aestheticism: Passengers of Modernity.* New York: Palgrave MacMillan, 2005.
Vague, Tom. *King Mob Echo: From Gordon Riots To Situationists & Sex Pistols.* London: Dark Star, 2000.
Vaneigem, Raoul. *The Revolution of Everyday Life*, trans. Donald Nicholson-Smith London: Rebel Press, 1994.
Vickers, Roy. 'The Eight Lamp' [1915]. *Crime On The Lines: An Anthology of Mystery Short Stories with a Railway Setting*, ed. Bryan Morgan. London: Routledge & Kegan Paul, 1975.
Vidler, Anthony. *The Architectural Uncanny: Essays in the Modern Unhomely.* Cambridge, Massachusetts: MIT Press, 1992.
Vine, Barbara. *King Solomon's Carpet.* London: Penguin, 1992.
Viney, Charles. *Sherlock Holmes in London: A Photographic Record of Conan Doyle's Stories.* Northamptonshire: Equation, 1989.
Walsh, Jill Paton. *Fireweed.* London: MacMillan, 1969.
Warburton, Nigel, ed. *Bill Brandt: Selected Texts and Bibliography.* Oxford: Clio Press, 1993.
Waugh, Evelyn. *Brideshead Revisited* [1945]. London: Laurence King, 1990.
Waugh, Evelyn. *Vile Bodies* [1930]. London: Eyre Methuen, 1978.
Wells, H.G. 'Anticipations'. *The Fortnightly Review.* Vol.69, 1901.
Wells, H.G. *Complete Short Stories.* London: A & C Black, 1987.

Wells, H.G. 'The Time Machine' [1894] in *Early Writings in Science and Science-Fiction*. Ed. Robert M. Philmus and David Y. Hughes. Berkeley: University of California Press, 1975.

Wells, H.G. *The Time Machine* [1895], ed. John Lawton. London: J.M. Dent, 1995.

Wells, H.G. *Tono-Bungay* [1909], ed. Patrick Parrinder, intro. Edward Mendelson. London: Penguin, 2005.

Welsh, David Thomas. 'Heaven or Hell: The Cultural Construction of the London Underground in Literature, 1863–1945'. Unpublished Doctoral Thesis, Senate House Library, University of London, 2005.

White, Gabriel. *Edward Ardizzone: Artist & Illustrator*. London: The Bodley Head, 1979.

White, H.P. *A Regional History of the Railways of Great Britain*, Vol.III. London: Phoenix House, 1963.

Whyman, Matt. *So Below: Key to the City*. London: Simon and Schuster, 2005.

Wilkinson, Alan, ed. *Henry Moore: Writings and Conversations*. Aldershot, Hants: Lund Humphries, 2002.

Willats, Stephen. 'Intervention and Audience' [1986] in *Panic Attack: Art in the Punk Years*, eds. Mark Sladen and Ariella Yedgar. London and New York: Merrell, 2007.

Williams, Charles. *All Hallows Eve*. London: Faber and Faber, 1945.

Williams, Conrad. *London Revenant*. London: The Do-Not-Press, 2004.

Williams, Raymond. *Culture*. Glasgow: Fontana, 1981.

Williams, Raymond. *Culture & Society 1780–1950*. Harmondsworth: Penguin, 1963.

Williams, Raymond. *The English Novel from Dickens to Lawrence*. London: Hogarth Press, 1984.

Williams, Raymond. *The Long Revolution*. Harmondsworth: Penguin, 1965.

Williams, Rosalind H. *Notes on the Underground: An Essay on Technology, Society and the Imagination*. Cambridge, Massachusetts: MIT Press, 1990.

Wilson, Colin. *Ritual in the Dark* [1960]. London: Grafton Books, HarperCollins, 1991.

Wolfreys, Julian. *Victorian Hauntings: Spectrality, Gothic, the Uncanny and Literature*. Basingstoke, Hampshire: Palgrave, 2002.

Wolfreys, Julian. *Writing London, Volume 2: Materiality, Memory, Spectrality*. London: Palgrave MacMillan, 2004.

Wolmar, Christian. *Down the Tube: The Battle for London's Underground*. London: Aurum Press, 2002.

Wolmar, Christian. *The Subterranean Railway*. London: Atlantic Books, 2005.
Woodward, Kathleen. 'Art Descends Into the London Subway', *The New York Times Magazine*, 13 October 1929.
Woolf, Leonard. *The Journey Not The Arrival Matters, An Autobiography of the Years 1939–1969*. London: The Hogarth Press, 1969.
Woolf, Virginia. *The Crowded Dance of Modern Life: Selected Essays: Vol.II*, ed. Rachel Bowlby. London: Penguin, 1993.
Woolf, Virginia. *The Diary of Virginia Woolf*, ed. Anne Olivier Bell. London: Hogarth Press, 1978.
Woolf, Virginia. 'The Mark on the Wall' [1919]. *The Complete Shorter Fiction*, ed. Susan Dick. London: HarperCollins, 1991.
Woolf, Virginia. 'Mr. Bennett and Mrs. Brown' [1924]. *Collected Essays*, ed. Leonard Woolf. Vol.I. London: Hogarth, 1966.
Woolf, Virginia. *Jacob's Room* [1922], ed. Sue Roe. London: Penguin, 1992.
Woolf, Virginia. *Night and Day*. London: Hogarth Press, 1919.
Woolf, Virginia. *The Waves* [1931], ed. Gillian Beer. OUP, 1998.
Wright, John Buckland. *For My Own Pleasure*, intro. Christopher Buckland Wright; London: Wolseley Fine Arts, 2003.
Wright, Christopher Buckland, ed. *The Engravings of John Buckland Wright*. Aldershot, Hants: Ashgate Editions, Scholar Press, 1990.
Yeats, W.B. *John Sherman and Dhoya* [1891], ed. Richard Finneran. Detroit, Michigan: Wayne State University Press, 1969.
Zamyatin, Yevgeny. *Islanders and The Fisher of Men* [1918], trans. Sophie Fuller and Julian Sacchi. Edinburgh: The Salamander Press, 1984.
Ziegler, Philip. *London At War, 1939–1945*. London: Sinclair-Stevenson, 1995.

INDEX

Aldington, Richard, 68–69, 71
Antrobus, John, 142
Arcades, 5–6, 21–22
Ardizzone, Edward, 117, 130
Asquith, Anthony, 86–88
Auden, W.H., 83
Augé, Marc, 2, 10, 14, 25, 27, 29, 35, 37–38, 41–42, 52, 61, 168, 171, 181
Aumonier, Eric, 80

Baker Street station, 28, 52, 97, 104, 106, 138
Bakerloo Line (Baker Street and Waterloo), 52, 56, 178
Banksy, 78, 150, 161–162
Banton, Eric, 47
Barlow, Peter, 46
Barnes, Julian, 7, 93, 94, 104, 106, 109, 111
Barr, Robert, 12
Barthes, Roland, 116, 129
Bató, Joseph, 120, 130
Baudrillard, Jean, 8, 151, 177–180
Bauhaus, 81, 83
Bayes, Walter, 76
Bawden, Edward, 78
The Beatles, 111, 140, 142
Beck, Harry, 63–64, 78, 136, 197
Bedford Park, Chiswick, 96–98, 100–101, 105, 108–109, 111

Benjamin, Walter, 5, 21, 26
Bennett, Arnold, 19–21
Berger, George, 150
Berman, Marshall, 21
Betjeman, John, 7, 96, 101, 105–107, 110
Blair, Tony, 15
Bomberg, David, 67, 76
Bone, Stephen, 82
Boumphrey, Geoffrey, 102
Bowen, Elizabeth, 103, 124–125, 128
Brandt, Bill, 7, 36, 86, 115, 117–121, 123, 126–131, 201
Brangwyn, Frank, 75
Brooker, Peter, 4
Brown, Gregory, F., 75
Brunel, Marc, 46
Buchan, John, 19
Buckland-Wright, John, 117

Calder, Angus, 116, 129, 131
Calypso, 139–140, 143
Carey, John, 101–102
Carlyle, Thomas, 50
Carr, Jonathan, 96
Céline, Louis,Ferdinand, 84
Central London Railway, 48–50
Chalfont, Henry, 152
Chapman, James, 52
Chesterton, G.K, 94, 96–97, 105, 109

Circle Line (Inner Circle), 21, 24–25, 29–30, 50, 141–143, 153, 167
City and South London Line, 47–49
Clark, Timothy, 147
The Clash, 138, 150–151, 162
Coates, Wells, 102
Colomona, Beatriz, 32
Connor, Edric, 140
Cork, Richard, 65–66, 79, 144
Crass, 149–150

De Amicis, Edmondo, 24
Debord, Guy, 86, 135–137, 141, 145–147, 154
De Certeau, Michel, 4, 7, 26, 29, 35, 37, 86, 156–157, 178, 181
De Gaulle, Charles, 137
Derrida, Jacques, 8, 175
District Railway, 5, 14, 16, 18–19, 24, 50–51, 56, 96, 167
Dixon, Ella Hepworth, 34
Doré, Gustave, 28
Doyle, Sir Arthur Conan, 19, 28, 38, 50
Drax, 153–155
Dreiser, Theodore, 6, 45–46, 50, 52–59
Dudok, Willem, 81
Duffield, Mike, 149
Duncan, Johnny, 140
Du Terreaux, L.H., 30–31

Edwards, Paul, 73
Elephant and Castle, 76, 123, 129, 139, 178, 180
Eliot, George, 23
Eliot, T.S., 74, 84, 103, 121–122
Epstein, Jacon, 6, 79–81, 199
Etchells, Frederick, 72, 102

Field, Michael, 35
Flather, Henry, 18
Flint, F.S., 68–70
Freud, Sigmund, 168, 170–171
Fry, Roger, 67, 77
Forster, E.M., 1–2, 8–9, 102, 110
Forsyth, Frederick, 19
Fuel, 155
Futura-2000, 150
Futurism, 65–68, 70, 74, 76–77, 81–82

Gaiman, Neil, 169–171
Galsworthy, John, 15
Gasiorek, Andrzej, 73, 83, 86
Gill, Eric, 80
Gissing, George, 27–29, 35
Goldfinger, Ernö, 102
Graffiti, 5, 7–8, 86, 136, 147–153, 155–157, 161–162, 172
Grahame, Kenneth, 67
Gray, Christopher, 147–148
Greater London Council (GLC), 8, 152
Greathead Shield, 46
Greene, Graham, 101, 103–104, 121–124, 128
Gregg, John, 116

Hammersmith and City Line, 148, 153, 159, 175
Hampstead Tube, 49, 51–52, 101
Harrisson, Tom, 130
Hassall, John, 75
Haworth-Booth, Mark, 76–77
Hayward, John, 125
Healy, John, 8, 86, 155
Heaney, Seamus, 172
Hebdige, Dick, 138–139
Henley, W.E., 98–99, 104
Herbert, James, 146
Hill, Geoffrey, 129
Hill, Tobias, 172–174
Hobbes, Thomas, 157, 161
Hobsbawm, Eric, 63
Hobson, J., 45
Holden, Charles, 6, 79–82, 200
Hollingshead, John, 16
Household, Geoffrey, 19
Huxley, Aldous, 74, 83–84, 104
Hynes, Gladys, 85
Hynes, Samuel, 94
Ibrahim, Mecca, 15
Illustrated London News, 17–18
Ironside, Robert, 127

The Jam, 148–149
James, Henry, 31–33
Jameson, Frederic, 5
Jerome, Jerome K., 14
Johnson, Linton Kwesi, 143

Johnston, Edward, 75
Jorn Asger, 135–136, 154
Jubilee Line, 15, 160, 167
Jung, C.G., 128

Kapp, Edmond, 117, 130
Kauffer, E. McKnight, 6, 75–78, 81–82, 198
Kenner, Hugh, 84
The Kinks, 142
Kirby, Lynne, 86–87
Klein, Naomi, 149
Konody, P.G., 66
Kop, Bernard, 117
Kureishi, Hanif, 8, 137, 140, 157–160

Ladbroke Grove, 150, 152, 158
Lancaster, Osbert, 105–106, 108–109
Landis, John, 147
Le Corbusier, 65, 72–73, 81–83, 86, 102
Lee, Vernon (Violet Page), 34
Lefebvre, Henri, 3–4, 6–7, 64, 83, 86
Lester, Richard, 142
Levy, Amy, 35
Lewis, Adrian, 130–131, 133
Lewis, Wyndham, 7, 67, 70–77, 81–83, 85–86
Livingstone, Ken, 152–153
Lloyd, David, 157
Lord Beginner, 139–140
Lord Kitchener, 139–140, 143
Lots Road power-station, 45–46, 50, 54–55
Luckhurst, Roger, 168

Macaulay, Rose, 29–30
MacDonald, Nancy, 153
MacInnes, Colin, 138
MacNeice, Louis, 84, 115, 131
Maholy-Nagy, Lazslo, 78, 102
Man Ray, 78
Marcus, Jane, 85
Mailer, Norman, 151–152
Marinetti, F.T., 65–68, 71, 73–74, 81, 104, 154
Marx, Karl, 16–17, 175
Mass-Observation, 117, 130
Matta-Clark, Gordon, 147

Mayhew, Henry, 18, 22, 27–28
McLaren, Malcolm, 148
McTell, Ralph, 138
Mengham, Rod, 70, 167–169, 180
Metroland, 7, 86, 93–95, 101–111
Metropolitan Railway, 5, 7, 12, 16, 20, 22–27, 31, 50, 56, 93, 101, 103, 106, 167
Meynell, Alice, 35–36
Miéville, China, 174–175
Milligan, Spike, 142
Milton, John, 110
Mitchison, Naomi, 115
Moore, Alan, 8, 157
Moore, Henry, 7, 79–80, 86, 115, 117–118, 120–121, 126–131, 203, 204
Morgan, J. Pierpoint, 51, 53
Morris, William, 98–100
Mumford, Lewis, 177–179

Nead, Lynda, 16–18, 23
Nevinson, C.R.W., 66–67, 76, 78, 104
Nicholson-Smith, Donald, 147
Northern Line, 52, 144, 156

Orczy, Emma, 11–12, 15, 50
Orwell, George, 84, 101, 103, 107–108, 110, 145
Oxenham, John (aka William Dunkerley), 14–15

Paolozzi, Eduardo, 65, 86, 144–145, 153
Paxton, Sir John, 18, 21
Pearson, Charles, 21–22
Pennell, Elizabeth Robins, 33, 36, 99
Piccadilly Line, 52, 158
Piccadilly Circus, 72, 82, 85, 117, 141, 143
Pick, Frank, 65, 75–79
Pike, David L., 2–4, 12, 14, 29, 31–32, 63–65, 94–95
Posters, 2, 5–6, 25, 34, 36, 66, 74–78, 81–82, 145, 147, 149, 156, 161, 171, 172
Post Office tube-railway, 22–23, 38, 169
Pound, Ezra, 70, 79
Priestley, J.B., 102, 107–108
Prigoff, James, 152
Prime, 155

Proud-2, 153
Punch, 14, 23–24, 50
Punk, 111, 138, 148–151, 162, 180

Rafferty, Gerry, 138
Ravilious, Eric, 78
Reed, Henry, 121–122, 124
Rhys, Jean, 84
Richards, J. M., 7, 108–110
Richardson, Dorothy, 36–37, 68
Rickett, Charles, 96
Riley, James, 145
Rimbaud, Penny, 149–150
Royle, Nicholas, 8, 175
Rushdie, 8, 137, 157, 160–161
Rutter, Frank, 66
Ryman, Geoff, 8, 110, 178–180

Sadler, Simon, 136
Saler, Michael T., 3–4, 65, 75
Sanders, H., 70
Sandu, Sukhdev, 138, 158–159
Schivelbusch, Wolfgang, 5, 13, 15–16, 18, 21–22, 26, 28
Selvon, Sam, 7, 137–144, 157
Sex Pistols, 111, 150
Sharland, Charles, 75
Shaw, Norman, 96
Sherman, Gary, 146
Sims, George R., 47
Situationist International, 8, 32, 136–137, 145–148, 151, 162
Smith, Neil, 4
Smith, W.H., 25
Starr, Ringo, 140
Stepniak, Sergius, 96
Stevenson, Robert Louis, 93, 98
Stravinsky, Igor, 74
Subsurface railways, 11–26, 50, 64

Taki-183, 151
Thacker, Andrew, 4–5, 27, 68
Thames Tunnel, 28, 46
Thatcher, Margaret, 8, 152–153, 158–160, 168

Thomson, Graham R., 35
Topolski, Feliks, 130
Tottenham Court Road station, 65, 144–145, 147, 152
Trocchi, Alexander, 145–146, 149
Trollope, Anthony, 18–19, 31
Trotter, David, 18
Tube-railways, 1–2, 6, 14, 22, 23, 45–59, 64–70
Turner, William, 50, 66

Underground Group 75–81

Vadillo, Ana Parejo, 4, 34–35
Vaneigem, Raoul, 32, 86, 148
Victoria Line, 146, 157–159, 161
Vidler, Anthony, 168
Vine, Barbara, 8, 157
Vorticism, 6–7, 67, 69–79, 81–83, 85–87
Voysey, Charles, 100

Wadsworth, Edward, 72, 76–78
Waterloo and City Line, 49
Waugh, Evelyn, 78, 101, 104
Wells, H.G., 7, 31–32, 48, 70, 94, 96, 98–102, 109.
Welsh, David, 2–4, 12
Whistler, James, 50, 99
Wilde, Oscar, 98–99
Willats, Stephen, 136–137
Williams, Conrad, 8, 176
Williams, Rosalind H., 2, 94
Willing, J., 27
Wise, David / Stuart, 147
Wolfreys, Julian, 171
Wolmar, Christian, 49, 51, 152,
Woolf, Leonard, 115–116
Woolf, Virginia, 22, 37–38, 63, 85, 104

Yeats, W.B., 96–97, 111
Yerkes, Charles Tyson, 45–46, 49, 50–53, 59

Zero (Hans Schleger), 78
Zamyatin, Yevgeny, 66–67

www.ingramcontent.com/pod-product-compliance
Lightning Source LLC
Chambersburg PA
CBHW041507291125
36065CB00039BB/2061